C0-AOE-742

INTERNATIONAL STUDIES

Britain and the Origins of the
New Europe 1914–1918

INTERNATIONAL STUDIES

PUBLISHED FOR THE CENTRE FOR
INTERNATIONAL STUDIES, LONDON SCHOOL
OF ECONOMICS AND POLITICAL SCIENCE

Editorial Board

Professor G. L. Goodwin
Professor J. B. Joll
Professor J. P. de la Wiles
Professor L. B. Schapiro

Professor D. C. Watt
Mr P. Windsor
Dr M. Leifer
Dr I. Nish

The Centre for International Studies at the London
School of Economics was established in 1967 with
the aid of a grant from the Ford Foundation. Its
aim is to promote research and advanced training
on a multi-disciplinary basis in the general field
of International Studies, particular emphasis
being given to contemporary China, the
Soviet Union and Eastern Europe and their
relationship with the outside work, and also
to European Studies. To this end the Centre,
in collaboration with other bodies (such as
the Social Science Research Council), sponsors
research projects and seminars.

The Centre is undertaking a series of
publications in International Studies, of which
this volume is the sixth.

*Whilst the Editorial Board accepts responsibility for recom-
mending the inclusion of a volume in the series, the author
is alone responsible for the views and opinions expressed.*

ALSO IN THIS SERIES

BLIT: The Origins of Polish Socialism
STEINER: The Slovak Dilemma
VAN CREVELD: Hitler's Strategy 1940–1941: The Balkan Clue
OGUNSANWO: China's Policy in Africa 1958–71
UNGER: The Totalitarian Party: Party and People
   in Nazi Germany and Soviet Russia

BRITAIN AND THE ORIGINS OF THE NEW EUROPE

1914–1918

KENNETH J. CALDER

CAMBRIDGE UNIVERSITY PRESS

CAMBRIDGE

LONDON · NEW YORK · MELBOURNE

0429327

Published by the Syndics of the Cambridge University Press
The Pitt Building, Trumpington Street, Cambridge CB2 1RP
Bentley House, 200 Euston Road, London NW1 2DB
32 East 57th Street, New York, NY 10022, USA
296 Beaconsfield Parade, Middle Park, Melbourne 3206, Australia

© Cambridge University Press 1976

Library of Congress catalogue card number: 75–12161

ISBN: 0 521 20897 1

First published 1976

Printed in Great Britain by
Western Printing Services Ltd
Bristol

CONTENTS

0429327

To Mother and Ernie

ACKNOWLEDGEMENTS

During the research and writing of this book I was fortunate in receiving the assistance of many people to whom I would like to express my appreciation. Foremost among these was Professor James Joll of the London School of Economics and Political Science without whose encouragement, advice and assistance this book might never have been completed. To him I owe a debt of gratitude which cannot be adequately expressed. Professor Hugh Seton-Watson supplied me with invaluable information about his father and was kind enough to share with me his thoughts on the subject of this book. From Lady Namier I received insights into the youth as well as the wartime activities of Sir Lewis Namier. Professor H. N. Fieldhouse and Mr Martin Gilbert were kind enough to answer my queries thus enabling me to benefit from their research. Mr A. J. P. Taylor discussed the topic with me when I began my research and after reading an earlier draft of the book pointed out a number of flaws in it. I was privileged to have the opportunity to discuss with the late August Zaleski, then President of the Polish Republic-in-Exile, his role in the movement for Polish independence. I also benefited from discussions with Professor A. Headlam-Morley, Professor M. G. Fry, Dr F. R. Bridge, and Dr M. Ekstein Frankl. I am particularly grateful to Sir Steven Runciman not only for permitting me to examine his father's papers but also for being a most gracious host.

I would like to express my appreciation to the Commonwealth Scholarship and Fellowship Commission and the Canada Council for the financial assistance that made this project possible.

I am grateful to the officials and staffs of the Public Record Office; the British Museum; the Bodleian Library; the Beaverbrook Library; the Cambridge University Library; the Institute of Historical Research; the School of Slavonic and East European Studies; *The Times* Archives; the Yale University Library; New College, Oxford; the Douglas Library, Queen's University, Kingston, Ontario, and the Imperial War Museum for permission to examine their collections and for their kind assistance during the course of my research.

For permission to quote from copyright material I am indebted to; Mary, Duchess of Roxburghe, the Earl of Balfour, Mrs M. Moorman, Mrs John Bennett, Mr L. P. Scott, Mr F. Noel-Baker, Professor A. K. S. Lambton, the Beaverbrook Library, the Yale University Library, *The Times* Archives and the University of Newcastle upon Tyne. Quotations from Crown-copyright records in the Public Record Office appear by permission of the Controller of H.M. Stationery Office, London.

I would also like to thank Professor G. L. Goodwin, the Editorial Board of the Centre for International Studies, and the staff of Cambridge University Press for their advice and assistance in the process of preparing the book for publication.

To the Controller and Staff of London House, I would like to express my appreciation for making my stay in London both pleasant and rewarding.

To my brother, Dr Robert Lorin Calder and my sister-in-law, Barbara, I am indebted for unfailing hospitality on many memorable weekends, and for being a constant source of encouragement and support.

For her patience, assistance and encouragement I would like to express my gratitude to my wife, Odile.

K.J.C.

Legend:

- Germans
- Italians
- Rumanians
- Byelorussians
- Poles
- Ukrainians
- Czechs and Slovaks
- Slovenes
- Croats and Serbs
- Bulgars
- Letts and Lithuanians
- Turks
- Magyars
- Greeks
- Albanians

Memel
LITHUANIA
Vilna
Danzig
E. PRUSSIA
W. PRUSSIA
Tannenburg
GERMANY
Posen
RUSSIA
Warsaw
Brest - Litovsk
Nuremburg
Prague
BOHEMIA
SILESIA
MORAVIA
Teschen
GALICIA
UKRAINE
R. Danube
Vienna
CARPATHO-UKRAINE
(RUTHENIA)
TYROL
BUKOVINA
BESSARABIA
TRENTINO
Budapest
AUSTRIA-HUNGARY
Gorizia
Trieste
R. Save
ISTRIA
Fiume
TRANSYLVANIA
CROATIA-SLAVONIA
BANAT
BOSNIA
RUMANIA
Zara
DALMATIA
HERZEGOVINA
Belgrade
Bucharest
ITALY
SERBIA
R. Danube
DOBRUDJA
ADRIATIC SEA
MONTENEGRO
BULGARIA
MACEDONIA
THRACE
ALBANIA
Salonika
Constantinople
GREECE
TURKEY

0   100   200   300
Scale in miles

The nationalities of eastern Europe, *c.* 1918.

INTRODUCTION

Studies of British foreign policy during the First World War usually refer, often only in passing, to the problem of national self-determination. Behind these references lies a complex and intriguing history hitherto concealed by the inaccessibility of official records.

In 1914 the British government was not interested in national self-determination in eastern Europe. By November 1918 it was deeply involved with various eastern European subject nationalities and was committed by implication to their independence. The government was not formally committed to national self-determination, but it could not have abandoned the subject nationalities without being subjected to accusations of bad faith against which it would have had the greatest difficulty defending itself. This study attempts to explain that evolution in policy by analysing the British reaction to nationality problems in eastern Europe and to the desire of the subject nationalities for self-determination. It concentrates on policy during the war, not on the origins of any future policy. It is based primarily on the official records of the British government which have been supplemented with correspondence from private collections. Most of this evidence has never been used in a thorough analysis of this subject. It concentrates on the evolution of the government's relations with the Poles, Czechoslovaks and Yugoslavs because they were the only eastern European nationalities to conduct, throughout the war, an extensive campaign in Britain for national self-determination. Among the émigrés they alone had meaningful relations with the government.

The available evidence obliges us to believe, and therefore this study argues, that British policy on national self-determination developed not as a result of theoretical speculation but as a result of the wartime relations between the government and the nationality organizations. These relations were based on the government's desire to use the nationalities as weapons of war rather than on any interest in the principle of national self-determination. Considering it as an area of secondary importance, the government sought to use the political problems of eastern Europe to improve the Entente's strategic position. In November 1918 the government's stance on the issue of national self-determination was, therefore, not the product of calculations of the long-term political advantages for Britain of the reorganization of eastern Europe but instead the product of numerous decisions made to solve immediate problems in the conduct of the war.

Nationalism began to emerge as a significant political force during the French revolution contributing both to the strength and, ultimately, the destruction of the Napoleonic empire. Yet, when the statesmen of Europe met in Vienna in 1814, they rejected nationalism in an attempt to create a stable and, hence, peaceful European system based on the balance of power. This balance of power was restored after the upheavals of the Napoleonic era by the redrawing of international frontiers without regard for national claims. Thus the territorial settlement that emerged bore little resemblance to the distribution of nationalities in Europe and left national aspirations unsatisfied. In nineteenth-century Europe these unsatisfied aspirations were a constant threat to the status quo and a frequent cause of international instability because of attempts of subject nationalities to achieve unity and independence. The Congress of Vienna could restore governments and redraw frontiers, but it was powerless to prevent the national awakening that, inspired by the German example, was taking place particularly in eastern and southern Europe. In this national awakening lay the seeds of destruction of the work of the Congress because it was accompanied by a political programme, national self-determination, which challenged the legitimacy of many of the states and most of the frontiers of Europe by claiming that each nation had the right to form an independent state and determine its own form of government.

Nationalism did not destroy in one stroke the system established in Vienna, but instead eroded it over the ensuing century by a series of national revolts and wars of liberation which led to the creation of national states like Greece, Belgium, Rumania, Bulgaria, Serbia, Norway, Italy and Germany. This process confronted nineteenth-century statesmen with an unending series of problems as each national disturbance presented some of the Great powers with an opportunity to further their own interests at the expense of others. Each nationality that succeeded in its struggle for independence did so with at least the tacit support if not open assistance of one of the Great powers. Those like the Poles and Hungarians, who lacked a powerful patron were unsuccessful. Thus almost every national struggle leading to the establishment of a new state, through the not disinterested involvement of at least one Great power, became a complex problem involving the interests of the particular nationality and those of Europe as a whole, necessitating action by all of the Great powers to adjust the European system so as to incorporate the newly emergent state in a manner which would not unduly favour one Great power and thus upset the balance of power.

Despite later claims by those interested in national self-determination, the diplomatic history of nineteenth-century Europe does not show that the British government traditionally supported peoples struggling to be free. Perhaps following Castlereagh's principle of non-intervention in the internal affairs of sovereign states and certainly looking to its own interests as a Great power, the British government generally tended to prefer the status quo, often despite the sentiments of its people, during the initial stages of any nationalist revolt. Only when that position became untenable, usually because the nationality in question had achieved *de facto* independence, would it support the establishment of a new state and then only to avoid the aggrandisement of another Great power. While this was not the case in the struggle for Italian unification, it was a pattern particularly evident in the Balkans where the British government traditionally identified its interests with those of the Sublime Porte rather than with its rebellious subjects, but would ultimately support the establishment of a new state if the alternative threatened to work to the advantage of Russia.

By 1914 European diplomats could look back on a century of experience in dealing with problems arising out of movements for national liberation and might have been justified in thinking that the most active period of such struggles was over. Yet in eastern Europe there were significant subject nationalities who remained within the grip of the German, Russian and Austro-Hungarian empires.

Poland had been partitioned by Russia, Austria and Prussia at the end of the eighteenth century, and despite a strong nationalist movement that led revolts in 1830 and 1863, had failed to regain its independence. The suppression of Polish nationalism was a common interest uniting the three empires, and as long as they remained at peace with one another they could exclude outside interference in Polish affairs, leaving little chance for a Polish state to re-emerge. The three empires, working together, could effectively thwart Polish national aspirations but they could not destroy Polish national consciousness which found a romantic expression in the poetry of Adam Mickiewicz and the novels of Henryk Sienkiewicz. Despite adversity, and perhaps because of it, the Polish national movement, although fragmented, continued to thrive after the unsuccessful revolt in 1863, and it was apparent that if an opportunity should arise to re-establish a Polish state the nationalists would take advantage of it.

In 1914 Czechoslovakia was not even a geographic expression, it existed only in the imagination of a few intellectuals. Although the Czechs and Slovaks formed a northern Slavic tier in the Habsburg monarchy they had never been united into a state unto themselves. Bohemia and Moravia, Habsburg dominions since 1527, had lost any semblance of independence after the Czech defeat at the battle of White Mountain in 1620, while Slovakia had been part of Hungary for a thousand years. By the eighteenth century both the Czechs and Slovaks had almost entirely lost any separate identity. The first symptoms of the national revival which was to halt the trend towards assimilation within Austria-Hungary can be detected at the end of the eighteenth century in the reaction to the centralist policies of Joseph II. This national revival gathered momentum during the following century as exemplified in the work of a number of intellectuals, the more notable being Joseph Dobrovský, famous for his work on Czech grammar, Joseph Jungmann, for his studies on the history of Czech literature, Jan Kollar, for his poetry glorifying the Slavic past and Paul Šafařik, for his studies on early Slavic history. The most famous figure of the Czech revival was, however, František Palacký, a historian as well as a politician, who was, if not the first, at least the first outstanding advocate of a Czechoslovak political entity. Through the study of history and philology these men gave an intellectual expression to Czech and Slovak national consciousness. The revival was accompanied throughout the century by increasing Slovak and particularly Czech political activity in the pursuit of a more equitable position within the Habsburg monarchy. Before 1914 the Czech and Slovak nationalists did not seek independence, that could not be achieved without the destruction of Austria-Hungary, a seemingly unattainable and not entirely desirable goal, but only autonomy within a federal empire which would give them equality with the Germans and Magyars. But complete independence was not unthinkable and, given sufficient frustration with their continuing failure to achieve their aims within the structure of the Habsburg monarchy and an opportunity to seek independence, they might well opt for it.

The southern tier of the Habsburg monarchy was inhabited by South Slavs, more precisely the Croats, Slovenes and Serbs, who comprised the largest and most dissatisfied Slavic element in the Empire. Like the Poles and the Czechoslovaks, the South Slavs underwent a national revival during the nineteenth century which began during their partial union in the Illyrian provinces of the Napoleonic empire. This national revival was given intellectual expression by men like Ljudevit Gaj, leader of the Croat literary revival, Valentin Vodnik, famous for his study of the history and language of the Slovenes and Vuk Karadžić, reformer of the Serbian language. Perhaps the leading figure of this cultural renaissance was Bishop Strossmayer of Djakovo, a champion of the idea of South Slav union, whose work in the establishment of educational institutions helped to promote the study of South Slav history and philology.

Although united by race and, to some extent, language, these nationalities were divided in almost every other respect. The Serbs were Orthodox and used the Cyrillic alphabet, while the Croats and Slovenes were Catholic and used the Latin alphabet. Some of the South Slavs lived in Hungary, primarily in the semi-autonomous region of Croatia-Slavonia, while others lived in various Austrian provinces like Dalmatia and Carniola or in Bosnia-Herzegovina. These historical, religious and administrative differences among the South Slavs gave rise to serious political divisions and conflicts which were often encouraged by the Imperial authorities. In 1914 many of the Serbs, particularly in Bosnia-Herzegovina, worked for the creation of a 'Greater Serbia', a union of all Serbs with the kingdom of Serbia to the exclusion of other South Slavs. This work involved anti-Austrian terrorism in which they were actively supported by the dominant party in Serbia, the Radicals, and its leader Nikola Pašić. Many of the Croats aspired to a 'Greater Croatia' either in association with Hungary or independent. Other South Slavs espoused 'Trialism', the creation of a South Slav unit within the Empire equal to Austria and Hungary. Despite such divisions there were those who, inspired by the example of the Illyrian provinces and following in the footsteps of Gaj and Strossmayer, advocated the formation of a Yugoslavia, the union of all South Slavs including those in the kingdom of Serbia. This position was supported by many of the Slavs in Austria who did not believe that the Austrians and Hungarians would ever accept the South Slavs as a third equal partner in the Empire and by many Slavs in Croatia–Slavonia alienated from the Empire by the policy of Magyarization. Many of the leading figures of the Yugoslav movement came from Dalmatia where, being exposed to Italian influence and reflecting on the history of Italian unification, they began to see in Serbia, particularly after its success in the Balkan wars, the potential Piedmont of Yugoslavia. This parallel was obvious in 1913 during the second Balkan war to Ivan Mestrović, a sculptor, Frano Supilo, the editor of the Rjeka *Novi List* and Ante Trumbić, the leader of the Croat National party, all of whom later became leading figures of the Yugoslav émigré movement. At the outbreak of war in 1914 they were prepared to act against the Austro-Hungarian empire to achieve their political aims.

On 28 June 1914 in the Bosnian capital of Sarajevo a South Slav terrorist assassinated the Habsburg heir Archduke Franz Ferdinand thus setting in motion the chain of events leading to the outbreak of the First World War. The fact that the assassin was an Austrian South Slav inspired by the Yugoslav programme and that his act was a protest against the Habsburg failure to satisfy Yugoslav national aspirations makes it impossible to consider the question of the origin of the war without some reference to the problem of national self-determination. Indeed, after the outbreak of war the supporters of national self-determination in Britain claimed that the failure of the European system to satisfy national aspirations was the real cause of the conflict. For them, it followed that the application of national self-determination would create a more peaceful Europe. In contrast, their opponents, the pacifist liberals and left-wing radicals centred around the Union of Democratic Control, attributed the European conflict not to unsatisfied national aspirations but to secret diplomacy, the balance of power, the armaments race and imperial rivalry. All of these factors contributed to a tense international climate in which recurring crises were inevitable. But that was the normal state of international relations. None of them explain why this specific crisis, arising from the assassination in Sarajevo, led to war.

In 1905 the European balance of power was tilted in favour of the Triple Alliance by the temporary eclipse of Russia as a Great power following her defeat in the Russo-Japanese war. Russian weakness gave German statesmen much greater freedom of action in international affairs but it was only a temporary advantage, as the Germans themselves realized, because military reforms in Russia would enable her, by 1917, to resume her former position in the balance of power. The threat to Germany's future position in Europe posed by the anticipated re-emergence of Russian power was increased by the danger that Germany's only reliable ally, Austria-Hungary, would be seriously weakened, if not destroyed, by internal problems created by the subject nationalities. The major threat to Austria-Hungary appeared to be South Slav nationalism fostered by Russia's protégé, Serbia. The long-term trends in European relations, as perceived by the statesmen of the Triple Alliance, tended to create the feeling that if the Serbian problem was to be solved it had to be done before 1917.

The German government saw the assassination of Archduke Franz Ferdinand as an opportunity for a permanent solution to the South Slav problem. It advocated the use of force against Serbia on the pretext offered by the assassination on the assumption that an Austro-Serbian war could be localized. By the time the German government realized that it had seriously miscalculated, the crisis was out of control and war unavoidable. The essential factor in this crisis, which distinguished it from previous crises and which made a peaceful solution impossible, was the calculated risk taken by the German government at the very beginning of the crisis that Russia was not in a position, as she would be after 1917, to intervene. In essence, Germany and Austria-Hungary adopted a position from which they could not retreat but which was unacceptable to Russia and her allies. The willingness of the German government to risk war can be explained by its estimation of Russian weakness which gave it some reason to think that Russia would not intervene. The willingness to use force to solve a problem in international relations can be explained by the fact that previous German history, particularly the events of 1848 and 1870, seemed to teach the necessity of force. When the British government attributed the war to Prussian militarism, an enormous over-simplification, it was more accurate than either the exponents of national self-determination or the Union of Democratic Control. But, even if the problem of unsatisfied national aspirations was not the primary cause of the war, it was an irritant in the European system and a significant factor in the complex relationship of causes which led to the war. As such it could become a factor influencing the course of the war and, if the conflict lasted long enough to give rise to questions about the fundamental nature of the European system, national self-determination could itself become an issue.

In August 1914 the British government entered the war in order to prevent developments in Europe detrimental to its fundamental interests. Although discussions in the cabinet during the crisis centred on the preservation of the Great power status of France and the neutrality of Belgium, these issues were only adjuncts to the essential reason for war, the need to maintain the existing balance of power in western Europe. Neither the South Slav problem, which precipitated the original crisis, nor the general condition of eastern Europe, had any influence on the British decision to declare war.

On entering the conflict the government assumed no specific aims and showed no interest in a general territorial redistribution in eastern Europe. It seemed reasonably satisfied with the eastern European status quo and showed no desire to change it. Nevertheless it was possible in 1914 to speculate that as a result of the war there might be territorial changes in eastern Europe. If such changes involved the aggrandizement of Russia or the Central powers they could not, because of their effect on the balance of power, be viewed with indifference by the British government. But in the same respect changes in the structure of eastern Europe which did not substantially increase German or Russian power and which tended to promote stability did not appear inconsistent with British interests.

Before the July crisis the British government knew little about the subject nationalities of eastern Europe and even less about the complexity of their politics; it was not and had no reason to be interested in them. Shortly after the outbreak of hostilities, however, the government was approached by various eastern European politicians and journalists claiming to represent the subject nationalities. These émigrés were introduced into official circles and their cause actively promoted in Britain by a group of scholars and journalists, usually of liberal persuasion, who believed in national self-determination and who might be called liberal nationalists in order to distinguish them from those liberals, like H. A. L. Fisher and Viscount Bryce, who were sympathetic towards subject nationalities but also suspicious of nationalism because of its potential illiberal tendencies. These émigrés offered their services to the government and in return sought support for a policy of national self-determination, a policy which if thoroughly applied involved the complete restructuring of eastern Europe. Since the government was not interested in plans for a fundamental reorganization of eastern Europe, British officials reacted cautiously and non-commitally to these approaches. Nevertheless they did recognize from the very beginning that the émigrés might prove useful and for that reason maintained contact with them.

Despite their initial failure to elicit any support for their political aspirations, the émigrés were able, after establishing contact with the government, to enlighten British officials on the conditions in eastern Europe and the political complexities of the national movements. Through contacts with the émigrés and their British supporters the officials began to realize that national self-determination was an alternative to the status quo in eastern Europe which might not involve the aggrandizement of another Great power. The retention of the status quo or the thorough application of the principle of national self-determination were in a sense two extremes which encompassed a range of alternatives in that self-determination could be given to some but not others or some frontiers could be altered to make them more consistent with the distribution of nationalities while others could be left untouched. None of these alternatives appeared to be in conflict with essential British interests. The alternative which would produce the most stable system in eastern Europe was to be preferred, but even if the government had been interested in making a choice there was no way to determine which alternative it was. The exponents of various programmes could dispute endlessly the merits of their cases, but they could not prove them.

During the war the government preferred not to make a choice and thus did not support the status quo, national self-determination or any compromise between the two. While supporting none of the alternatives, it appeared prepared to accept any of them. Until a decision on eastern Europe was absolutely necessary it would await events. By avoiding a decision which might never have to be made, the government was able to avoid unnecessary commitments and to retain the maximum number of options. The inherent flexibility of this position enabled it to meet effectively events as they arose. The future would either make a decision unnecessary or would provide more information upon which to base government policy.

Events intervened to make it impossible for the government to follow this policy consistently. Situations arose in which the successful conduct of the war necessitated the adoption of commitments. In each case acceptance of a commitment was not based on any programme for the future of eastern Europe, but was the product of the immediate situation and was designed to facilitate military success. There were also instances in which the methods used to wage war, while not involving obligations, had unanticipated repercussions which, in a subtle and complex manner, tended to close off some of the government's options. In other words, the government at times acted according to a necessity created by its own previous action. To some degree the methods of war, not political considerations, determined the results.

Some of these patterns are evident in the government's relations with the nationality organizations and help to explain how the government found itself in November 1918 in a position of being uncommitted in any legal sense on the future of eastern Europe but so deeply involved with the nationality organizations that it could hardly deny some obligations to them. As the war progressed and as the needs of the Entente grew desperate, the services offered by the émigrés, which had been confidently rejected at the beginning of the war, began to appear more enticing and were accepted. Use of the émigrés and the organizations they controlled was part of a policy which emerged gradually during the war and which involved supporting any group opposed to the Central powers and willing to translate that opposition into action. This policy did not involve any acceptance of émigré political aspirations, but the co-operation which resulted from this policy led to complex relations between the government and the nationality organizations which created the context in which British policy on national self-determination developed.

While the government did not adopt a specific policy on the future of eastern Europe, many individuals in the cabinet and foreign office tended to have their own personal preferences. Many sympathized with the émigrés and preferred national self-determination. Such preferences were important in the development of British policy, but they were just some of a great number of factors in the determination of policy. They were certainly not synonymous with policy.

The essential factor in the development of British foreign policy on national self-determination was not political theory but strategic necessity. In the interest of strategy, the government was able to overlook ideology, war aims, political considerations, and the inevitable peace settlement because national self-determination in eastern Europe was a problem of secondary importance. At the end of the war government policy on this issue was the result, not of any preconceived plan, but of a host of minor decisions often made without reference to the concept of national self-determination. By sacrificing political considerations for military flexibility, the government increased the odds of victory at the cost of losing control of the political consequences.

1 : THE INITIAL CONTACT

During the autumn of 1914 the prime minister, Herbert Henry Asquith, and his foreign secretary, Sir Edward Grey, attempted in a series of public statements to explain the government's role in the July crisis and its reasons for entering the conflict. These statements were designed to ensure public support for the uncomfortable position in which the government now found itself and contained in general terms the aims it intended to pursue. These were the first official war aims and the only ones to be defined publicly before 1917.

On 18 September 1914 Asquith, reflecting a Gladstonian approach to Continental affairs, said that the war was being fought:

In the first place, to vindicate the sanctity of treaty
obligations and of what is properly called the public law of
Europe; in the second place, to assert and to enforce the
independence of free States, relatively small and weak,
against the encroachments and violence of the strong; and in
the third place, to withstand, as we believe is in our best
interests not only of our own Empire, but of civilization at
large, the arrogant claim of a single Power to dominate the
development of the destinies of Europe.[1]

According to the official interpretation, that single power, Germany, under the inspiration of Prussian militarism, had attempted to upset the balance of power in its own favour. Grey had already made this clear on 5 September when he wrote to a public meeting:

It is against German militarism that we must fight. The whole
of Western Europe would fall under it if Germany were to be
successful in this war; but if as a result of the war the
independence and integrity of the smaller European States
can be secured and Western Europe liberated from the

menace of German militarism, for it is not the German people,
but Prussian militarism which has driven Germany and
Europe into this war – if that militarism can be overcome,
then indeed there will be a brighter and freer day for Europe
which will compensate us for the awful sacrifices that war
entails.[2]

Since Germany had caused the war, peace would be re-
established when it was defeated and its attempts to upset the
status quo thwarted. Perhaps such a defeat would so weaken the
props of militarism that it would collapse under its own weight.
Beyond doubt, the defeat of Germany would ensure the basic
requirements of British foreign policy such as the preservation
of France and the restoration of Belgium. Neither the cause nor
the cure for the war could be found in the territorial structure of
Europe. Dissatisfied nationalism had contributed to European
instability, and therefore territorial modifications might be considered, but such measures were of secondary importance and
were not to obscure the essential aim, the defeat of Germany.

The government was reluctant to discuss, define or even contemplate any other aim. Discussion of territorial modifications so
early in the war would be useless and even dangerous.

The Marquess of Crewe, lord privy seal and government leader
in the house of lords, reflected this attitude when he wrote to
Viscount Bryce in reference to the speech from the throne:

I do not think it is possible now to lay down any principle, or
even to express any opinion, on the terms upon which peace
may ultimately be made. For one thing the issue still hangs
too much in the balance for such discussion to be profitable,
and for another too many parties are involved to make any
present conclusion practicable.[3]

The foreign office wholeheartedly supported that view. The
permanent under-secretary of state, Sir Arthur Nicolson, never
ceased to emphasize the futility of such hypothetical discussions.[4]
To the ambassador in St Petersburg, Sir George Buchanan, Grey
wrote: 'Discussion of terms of peace is academic till war has
progressed sufficiently to make Germany contemplate the most
obvious terms of peace such as the restoration of two lost provinces to France and evacuation of Belgium.'[5]

Even if the moratorium on the discussion of war aims had not
existed, it is unlikely that the future of eastern Europe or Austria-

Hungary would have been seriously considered at the beginning of the war. With attention focused on Germany, the primary enemy, war was only reluctantly declared on Austria-Hungary as late as 12 August 1914. Britain had no conflicts with the Empire and no specific aims in eastern Europe. The Habsburg monarchy might collapse, but this was not desired by the British government. In fact, the idea of a separate peace with Austria-Hungary was considered from the very beginning. Sir Francis Bertie, the ambassador in Paris, recorded in December 1914:

> Grey then told me that seemingly well founded reports have
> reached him that Austria is inclined to separate herself from
> Germany and make peace with Russia. He does not think that
> there can be any objection either from a French or British
> point of view provided that terms can be arranged. We have
> no animus against Austria.[6]

Since it was not an issue, there is very little evidence from this period of the official attitudes to the future of Austria-Hungary. The possibility that the monarchy would collapse had been a matter of speculation for years, and its continued survival was a surprise to some. Sir Maurice de Bunsen, the ambassador in Vienna, wrote to Nicolson in March 1914: 'It is a standing marvel that the country still holds together.'[7] Survive it did, aided by inertia and fear of the consequences of its collapse. Alternatives to the monarchy, such as national self-determination, were not considered by the British, few of whom had ever heard of Yugoslavs or Czechoslovaks.

There was, however, a willingness to accept the destruction of Austria-Hungary if it became either necessary or inevitable. Indeed, many accepted the possibility with equanimity. In August 1914 Winston Churchill, the first lord of the admiralty, wrote to Noel Buxton, a member of parliament: 'Sooner or later, Germany will be starved and beaten. Austria will be resolved into its component parts.'[8] The British minister in Berne, E. M. Grant Duff, wrote in February 1915: 'But the Austro-Hungarian Court and Bureaucracy are past praying for and signs are not wanting that the rocks are already in sight on which the Habsburg ship with its motley crew will finally go to pieces.'[9] A collapse was clearly recognized as possible and, if necessary, acceptable. It seems that during this period British policy was not designed either to maintain or destroy the Empire; the government would await events and accept either development.

If the Austro-Hungarian empire was to survive, it would have to do so without British assistance. But if it could, there was no reason to destroy it.

In each of his speeches Asquith emphasized the sanctity of treaties, the public law of Europe, the opposition to force and, above all, the rights of small states. These vague statements of outraged morality and liberal idealism are evidence of the ideological interpretation given to the war by the Liberals, but without corroborative evidence they cannot be used as evidence of intent on specific issues. The rights of small states were emphasized because the original crisis involved two small states, Belgium and Serbia. Their treatment by the Central powers made good propaganda by appealing to the desire to defend the underdog. Thus, in every speech, Asquith spoke of small states, and, probably tiring of the same phrase, substituted for it small nations and small nationalities. On 25 September 1914, he said:

> room must be found and kept for the independent existence
> and the free development of the smaller nationalities each
> with a corporate consciousness of its own. Belgium, Holland,
> and Switzerland, and Scandinavian countries, Greece and the
> Balkan States – they must be recognized as having exactly as
> good a title as their more powerful neighbours; more power
> in strength and wealth, to a place in the sun.[10]

Each small nationality mentioned was a small state. On 9 November he again referred to nationalities:

> We shall never sheath the sword which we have not lightly
> drawn until Belgium recovers in full measure all and more
> than all that she has sacrificed; until France is adequately
> secured against the menace of aggression, until the rights of
> the small nationalities of Europe are placed on an unassailable
> foundation, and until the military domination of Prussia is
> wholly and finally destroyed.[11]

Asquith's usage of the term 'nationality' is vague, and there is no other evidence to elucidate the meaning of his remarks. In the propaganda for national self-determination the term denoted national groups denied separate statehood, but it could also refer to an existing nation state. From the context of the speeches it appears as if he used the term in the latter sense. It is possible that later propaganda modified the usage of the term making these speeches appear more ambiguous now than they did then.

Or possibly Asquith was careless in his choice of words. Although these remarks caused some confusion on the subject of war aims, it was never to the advantage of the government to clarify its position. Without further evidence, it is necessary to assume from the context of his speeches that he was not referring to the subject nationalities. In *The Truth About the Treaties* David Lloyd George, the chancellor of the exchequer, in reference to Asquith's speech quoted above, stated that:

> In effect that declaration merely assured the security of small independent countries like Belgium and Serbia against aggression of powerful neighbours. But there was nothing in the way of emancipating the oppressed races of Europe and the Turkish Empire from the bondage imposed upon them by alien conquerors. It was a war of protection for weak nations against arrogant and aggressive militarism and not a war of liberation for oppressed races.[12]

Churchill, in some public statements, seemed to go much further than Asquith on the subject of nationality. On 31 August 1914, he was quoted in *The Times* as saying:

> If we succeed, and if, as a result of our victory, Europe is re-arranged, as far as possible with regard to the principle of nationality and in accordance with the wishes of the people who dwell in the various disputed areas, we may look forward to a great relaxation and easement.[13]

These remarks were obviously inspired by the Balkan negotiations in which he was particularly interested at this time. Like Asquith, Churchill was not referring to national self-determination. Instead, he was stating the common belief that the nationality principle, the drawing of political frontiers consistent with the distribution of nationalities, was a convenient guide in territorial disputes in which there were no particular British interests. On the basis of previous experience in territorial disputes, particularly in the Balkans, it was commonly assumed that the application of the nationality principle would be the best solution as it would satisfy the aspirations of those involved. The satisfaction of those aspirations would contribute to the peace and stability of Europe. Grey himself wrote to Bertie in June 1915 that: 'the Allied Powers hope that, as a result of the war, the political balance in the Balkans will be established on a broader and more national basis, and thereby acquire greater stability.'[14]

The nationality principle, if carried to its logical extreme, would become national self-determination: the right of each nationality to constitute a state and choose its own form of government. The two terms, often used interchangeably, might have been theoretically consistent, but were certainly different in practice. The nationality principle could be used to solve crises and to maintain the essential status quo by allowing for minor adjustments in political frontiers. The application of national self-determination would involve, however, a complete revolution in the structure of Europe. British officials tended to look upon the nationality principle not as an end but as a means. Dealing in compromise instead of theoretical absolutes, the foreign office might use the nationality principle when it was expedient, but it could not accept national self-determination. Nevertheless, the acceptance of the nationality principle was a limited and pragmatic step towards the acceptance of national self-determination.

In 1914 national self-determination was not an issue, and, if the cabinet had views on this subject, there is almost no evidence of them. Nevertheless, the Liberals, imbued with the traditions of Gladstone, were sympathetic to nationalities struggling to be free. Many agreed with John Stuart Mill that:

When the sentiment of nationality exists in any force, there is a *prima facie* case of uniting all members of the nationality under the same government, and a government to themselves apart. This is merely saying that the question of government ought to be decided by the governed.[15]

Asquith had admired Garibaldi and had sympathized with the struggle for Italian unity.[16] Churchill, Grey and Lloyd George all professed sympathy for nationalism. If they had addressed the problem in 1914, they might have accepted the theoretical desirability of dividing Europe according to nationality. But even if they were prepared to go that far, it does not follow that they would have considered such an approach practical. They could not but have recognized that circumstances in 1914 made support of national self-determination completely impossible. Thus all the nationalities could initially expect was sympathy. That is a poor substitute for support, but, nevertheless, liberal philosophy did make the government potentially susceptible to the doctrine of national self-determination. The response of the government might be quite different if it ever had the opportunity to support national self-determination.

The adherents of liberal nationalism disagreed with the official interpretation of the war in believing that it was caused, not by Prussian militarism, but by the failure of the European system to satisfy national aspirations. Unlike the officials, whose views were tempered by practice, they believed that national self-determination ought to be applied to Europe. The disagreement was not on basic principles, but in degree and emphasis – between the practical and the theoretical.

In 1914 the liberal nationalists set out to convert the government to the doctrine of national self-determination. Their case was initially presented in a collection of essays entitled *The War and Democracy* published shortly after the outbreak of war. In the introduction Alfred Zimmern, formerly a fellow of New College, Oxford, stated:

> The political causes of the present war, then, and of the half century of Armed Peace which preceded it are to be found, not in the particular schemes and ambitions of any of the governments of Europe, nor in their secret diplomacy, nor in the machinations of the great armament interests allied to them, sinister though all these may have been, but in the nature of some of those governments themselves, and in their relations to the peoples over whom they rule.[17]

In one of the essays entitled 'The Issues of the War' Robert W. Seton-Watson, the author of a number of works on Hungary, wrote: 'The Europe which we have known has gone beyond recall; the new Europe which is coming to birth will be scarcely recognisable to those who have known its predecessor.' He went on to suggest that Austria-Hungary should be broken up by the application of national self-determination. On nationality he wrote:

> The principle of Nationality is not a talisman which will open all gates, for in some parts of Europe the different races are so inextricably intermingled as to defy all efforts to create ethnographic boundaries. This does not, however, affect the central fact that Nationality is the best salve for existing wounds, and that its application will enormously reduce the infected area.[18]

While disagreeing with the government on the origins of the war, the liberal nationalists supported its continuance to a decisive conclusion as this would contribute to the achievement of their own aims. Such support was eventually to become necessary on the part of anyone who wanted access to the government as can be seen by the fate of pacifists and other dissenters on foreign policy who, by their opposition to the war, lost all influence in official circles. The decline in these other and often opposing influences worked to the advantage of the liberal nationalists who were able to enhance their own position particularly as their basic attitude made them useful to the government in its propaganda campaign in support of the war effort. When the émigrés began to work in Britain for national self-determination, they found amongst the liberal nationalists, some of whom they had known before the war, valuable allies who, because of their official contacts and knowledge of British politics, could act as advisers and as links between them and the officials.

While the government did not ponder the problem of the future of eastern Europe, developments were taking place at the lower echelons of the bureaucracy which would eventually bring this question to its attention. Before 1914 the committee of imperial defence had decided, because of anticipated administrative and logistics problems, that in the event of war it would intern only those enemy aliens considered dangerous. In 1914 this plan was set aside because of a spy scare and because of the nervousness of the war office at the thought of enemy aliens being at large. The authorities began to intern all enemy aliens fit for military service, but quickly found the task to be almost impossible because of the number of aliens and the lack of facilities. Among the enemy aliens were Poles, Czechs, Slovenes, Croats and Serbs who were citizens of enemy countries but were, in fact, sympathetic to the cause of the Entente.

In September 1914 two Polish organizations, the Polish Information Committee and the Polish Society of London, separately approached the home office and offered their assistance in determining which Poles could be trusted and therefore need not be interned. They asked the home office to recognize Polish nationality, to exempt those Poles considered trustworthy from internment, and to give their organizations the authority to issue certificates of nationality to those exempted. The representatives of these organizations did not make a good impression on the home office and their unorthodox proposals were not well received. Polish nationality could not be legally recognized and the government could not authorize the use of certificates of nationality which would constitute *de facto* recognition. Nevertheless some concessions were made to these organizations despite doubts as to their authority to speak for resident Poles. In reply to a question in the house of commons on 10 September 1914, the home secretary, Reginald McKenna, announced:

> It is not at present possible in law to recognize 'Polish nationality' as distinct from the nationality of the Sovereign State of which residents in the various parts of Poland are subjects. But in the administration of the Aliens Restriction Order, all possible consideration will be shown to those persons of Polish race who, though technically 'alien enemies' are in fact friendly to this country.[19]

The foreign office agreed with McKenna's pronouncement but emphasized, in a letter to the home office, that it was undesirable to give any further recognition to Polish nationality or to self-appointed organizations like the Polish Information Committee.[20] The 'all possible consideration' mentioned by McKenna was left to the discretion of the commissioner of the Metropolitan police, Sir Edward Henry. A police memorandum written a year later on the Polish Information Committee recounted his action as follows:

> It was then necessary for the Commissioner to obtain some assistance in dealing with the Poles under the A.R.O. [Aliens Restriction Order] and he consulted Mr. Wickham Steed [foreign editor] of the Times. He also consulted the Russian Embassy and the opinion of both was that the Polish Information Committee was the best body to deal with.[21]

It was an interesting coincidence that Steed, an associate of R. W. Seton-Watson and an ardent campaigner for national self-determination, was consulted by the police. It is not surprising that the advice he gave was very favourable to the émigrés.

It appears, from what happened later, that the Serbian ministry and the London Czech Committee also approached the police on behalf of the Austrian Serbs and Czechs. Or it is possible that Wickham Steed, who had closer relations with the Czechs than the Poles, when consulted by the police, also recommended special treatment for the Czechs. In any case, by 30

October 1914, the Metropolitan police had formulated a comprehensive policy for the treatment of those enemy aliens in these three groups who were considered friendly to the Entente. Those aliens approved by authorized organizations would be exempt from internment but not from the other regulations in the Aliens Restriction Order. The Serbian ministry, the Polish Information Committee, and the London Czech Committee were selected as the agencies to vouch for the Austrian Serbs, the Poles, and the Czechs respectively. While the Polish Information Committee had been approved by the Russian embassy, the London Czech Committee had no such sponsor. According to the commissioner:

> There are strong reasons why this group should be treated
> with consideration. Unfortunately no Diplomatic guarantee is
> possible in this case, but Mr. Wickham Steed vouches
> implicitly for the honour and good faith of Mr. Kopecky [of
> the London Czech Committee] who is competent to answer
> for the names put forward.[22]

On 3 November 1914, the home office approved the police policy. Similar provisions were not made at this time for the Yugoslavs, possibly because they were not as quick as the others in approaching the government.[23] On the recommendation of the foreign office, however, exemption from police detention was given to one Yugoslav, a Croat from Dalmatia, Frano Supilo. George Clerk, a senior clerk in the war department of the foreign office, explained this request to Sir Basil Thomson of Scotland Yard by saying that Supilo might be valuable to the Allied cause.[24] Measures for the protection of other Yugoslavs were not, however, initiated at this time.

In December 1914, the home office and the war office expanded this policy by giving permission to the representatives of the London Czech Committee to visit internment camps to arrange for the release of friendly Czechs who had been interned before the policy of exemption had been implemented.[25] A similar request by the Polish Information Committee in January 1915 was refused by the war office.[26] The evidence, although meagre, suggests a pro-Czech, anti-Polish bias.

The home office and the police acted almost entirely alone in making these decisions. Foreign office approval was necessary because of the danger of international complications, but it had been given in a general sense on 9 October 1914, before the detailed policy had been formulated.[27] During November and

December the foreign office seems to have known the general trend of home office policy without knowing the details. It was as late as 12 January 1915 that the home office, in response to a query, informed the foreign office of the exact policy on the treatment of friendly enemy aliens.[28]

The home office and the police had no interest in foreign policy and their leniency was not based on humanitarian considerations. They were concerned with the magnitude of the alien problem and wanted to reduce the numbers interned. It was a problem of administration and security, not foreign policy. In the context of the whole war, the problem was trivial, but the solution was to have important repercussions.

The decision not to intern all enemy aliens enabled the émigrés to move freely and work with a minimum of inconvenience. The campaign for national self-determination could not have been fought from an internment camp. The future relations between the government and the nationality organizations all rested on this initially unimportant policy adopted in October 1914 by men who had no connection with foreign policy. Their decisions made the campaign for national self-determination possible.

The foreign office had good reason to approve the home office policy on the treatment of aliens. While the home office was considering the problems of internment, the foreign office was being approached by émigrés representing the subject nationalities of eastern Europe, each with a programme for national liberation. The officials were well aware that these émigrés might be too useful to be interned.

The partition of Poland had tended to unite Germany, Russia and Austria-Hungary on the basis of their common desire to maintain the existing Polish settlement. In war, however, Poland could become a problem because each empire would be tempted to use the Poles against the others. The Russian government made the first attempt to win Polish support when Grand Duke Nikolai Nikolaievich, the commander-in-chief of the Russian army, issued a proclamation to the Poles on 7 August 1914, promising unity and autonomy as a result of the war. The proclamation had only limited effect in Poland because many of the Poles would never be satisfied with autonomy and could never trust the Russian government.

The foreign office received word of the proclamation with approval because of the prospect of Polish support and the possible long-term advantages of a more satisfactory settlement of the Polish problem. According to Sir Eyre Crowe, an assistant under-secretary of state: 'There would however be real attraction to Poles in any scheme under which all the Polish nation was united and I consider the Russian proclamation a statesman-like move in the right direction.'[29] The proclamation was also welcomed because of its propaganda value; on 13 August 1914, Grey approved a suggestion that it be cabled in full to the American newspapers.[30]

It was dangerous for the foreign office to give more than silent approval of the actions of the Russian government on a question which, regardless of other interpretations of international law, the Russians considered to be a matter of internal policy. The sensitivity of the Russian government on all matters related to Poland made the Polish problem one of the most dangerous political issues to confront the Entente during the war. If Poland was not an issue, the three empires might, as in 1914, come into conflict regardless of their mutual desire to maintain the Polish settlement. But, if their interests in Poland were threatened from the outside, there would be good reason for the three empires to sink their other differences and unite in defence of the status quo in Poland. It could thus be the germ of a separate peace between Russia and the Central powers if France or Britain even appeared to consider a solution to the Polish problem not entirely consistent with Russian interests. Since defeat of the Central powers without Russian support was impossible, nothing could be done for the Poles which would in any way upset the Russian government. The British had good reason, therefore, to adopt a policy consistent with and in support of Russian policy in Poland. Since the Russians considered it a matter of internal policy, however, it was even dangerous for the British government to acknowledge the existence of a Polish problem.

When Dr Józef Retinger, on behalf of the Supreme National Committee, an organization representing various Polish parties in Galicia, asked the British government on 31 August 1914, to guarantee the Russian promises on Poland embodied in the grand duke's proclamation, the foreign office quite naturally refused. Retinger was not important in Polish politics but had the advantage, because of numerous social contacts in Britain, of being the first credible Polish politician to approach the foreign office.[31]

Clerk, who interviewed him, replied to his request: 'that a guarantee to Poland from France and Great Britain of Russian sincerity was out of the question and that it was impossible for the two former countries to imply any doubt of the good faith of their ally'. But Clerk did not believe in discouraging the Poles as is shown by his minute on the file:

> I would however submit with all deference that it is well worth while to get Polish feeling wholeheartedly with us and that if an occasion offers itself of welcoming the measure announced by the Grand Duke Nicholas in a way which can be made known in Poland it would have an encouraging effect there and would make it morally difficult for Russia to evade her pledge.[32]

Obviously thinking of the dangers of involvement with the Poles, Crowe rejected Clerk's suggestion, while Arthur Nicolson stated emphatically: 'We should leave this matter alone. I was asked to see this gentleman but declined to have anything to do with so foolish a matter.' They were overruled, however, by Grey who wrote: 'I do not think he should be snubbed. Mr. Clerk might tell him that H.M. Govt. were in thorough sympathy with the Russian manifesto and that it was welcomed cordially by public feeling here.' Grey's instructions were embodied in a letter to Retinger which he was later given permission to publish.[33]

Not every Pole was as well received. When the Polish Society of London and a group of Poles in the United States offered to form a legion to fight for the Entente, the war office, with approval of the foreign office, rejected the idea.[34] The time had not yet come for the adoption of unorthodox methods of warfare. Even if the war office had been more daring, the Russian government would have never tolerated the formation of Polish units in the British army.

The foreign office quickly learned that the Polish émigrés were by no means a united group. The first indication came in relation to the Polish Information Committee, the organization co-operating with the Metropolitan police. In September, M. G. Rosco-Bogdanowicz, on behalf of the Committee, presented a number of memoranda to the foreign office arguing in favour of independence for Poland.[35] Although he apparently failed to make a good impression, perhaps because he was a socialist, he might have been treated more sympathetically if the foreign office had not been warned at the same time that he was unreliable and not to be taken seriously.[36] These warnings came from Miss Laurence Alma-Tadema, an authoress and daughter of the painter Sir Lawrence Alma-Tadema, who was known to be well-acquainted with the Polish community in London and, therefore, spoke with some authority. The foreign office seemed to consider her reliable, probably because she was well-known and possibly because she appeared more respectable than Bogdanowicz, and, acting on her warning, it gave him no encouragement. The variety of Poles to approach the foreign office and the political disputes which split the Polish community caused Harold Nicolson, a member of the war department, to write:

It is characteristic of Polish politics that several self-styled representatives of Polish feeling have all produced different schemes as to the future of Poland. In this connection I heard yesterday that M. Filipowicz who had been in correspondence with the F.O. has gone off his head and had to be placed in an asylum.[37]

The foreign office maintained contact with Poles like Retinger who appeared to merit serious consideration, while discouraging others like Bogdanowicz. The feuding among the Poles created a bad impression and doubts remained as to the right of any of the émigrés to represent the Polish community. Nevertheless contact had been established which could serve as the basis for more complex relations. In deciding not to snub Retinger, Grey was making a decision to maintain and foster contacts with the Poles. Thus, in spite of Russia, Britain was to have a Polish policy. In public, it would always act with the greatest care not to upset the Russians by making statements on Poland inconsistent with Russian policy. In private, it would act independently in fostering contacts with Polish émigrés. Since the Poles might be useful, the government was maximizing its alternatives by supporting Russian policy in appearance but not in reality. The future value of the Poles was not immediately obvious, but the transmitting of the grand duke's proclamation to the American newspapers does indicate that the foreign office was aware of their potential propaganda value.

Contact between British exponents of national self-determination and the foreign office began in September 1914 when Wickham Steed introduced Seton-Watson to Clerk. Since the foreign office was involved in negotiations in the Balkans and interested in the potential conflict in the Adriatic between Serbia and Italy, Clerk asked Seton-Watson to write a memorandum on the South Slavs.[38] There is no official record of this request which suggests that Clerk may have been acting on his own initiative. At about the same time G. M. Trevelyan, an authority on Italy and a supporter of national self-determination, recommended Seton-Watson as an expert on the South Slavs to Harold Nicolson.[39]

In his memorandum, submitted 2 October 1914, Seton-Watson attacked both Austro-Hungarian rule over the South Slavs and Italian claims in Dalmatia. He stated that the best solution to the problems of this area of the Balkans would be the creation of a federal Yugoslav state consisting of Serbia, Montenegro, Bosnia, Herzegovina, Croatia, Slavonia, Dalmatia and the Slovene territories. According to his own interpretation, this programme would be consistent with British policy:

> The abstract principle already laid down by Sir Edward Grey, Mr. Asquith and Mr. Churchill in their speeches since the outbreak of war – that in any settlement due regard must be shown for the principle of nationality – only requires to be translating [sic] into concrete facts.[40]

This memorandum struck a responsive chord in Arthur Nicolson who noted on the file: 'Mr. Seton-Watson is one of the very few who comprehends the Southern Slav question, and his views should be treated with sound respect.' He added that on the basis of his own experience he agreed with Seton-Watson and concluded: 'When the terms of peace come to be discussed and the rearrangement of the Dual Monarchy's possessions has to be considered we should keep these remarks of Mr. Seton-Watson in mind!'

On the outbreak of war a number of Yugoslav politicians, realizing that this was the opportunity for which they had been waiting, left the Habsburg monarchy to campaign for Yugoslav independence in neutral and Allied countries. Some, including Supilo, went to Italy where they attracted the attention of the ambassador in Rome, Sir Rennell Rodd, who kept the foreign office informed of their activities.[41] When Supilo arrived in Britain in October, Seton-Watson and Wickham Steed presented him to the foreign office which immediately arranged for his exemption from police detention as an enemy alien.[42] In December Clerk asked Supilo to submit his views on the South Slav problem and later, in his report, said of Supilo: 'He speaks with great and real authority for the Yugo-Slavs, and the views he expressed call for serious consideration by H.M.G. . . .'[43]

In the memorandum, submitted in January 1916, Supilo gave

a detailed account of conditions in the South Slav areas of Austria-Hungary and, rejecting Italian claims in Dalmatia as well as any form of Habsburg rule, proposed the creation of a Yugoslav state. Judging his audience carefully, he claimed that the value of such a state would be in its ability to act as a barrier to German expansion towards the East.[44] This theory, which obviously appealed to the British, was to become a major theme in Yugoslav propaganda, especially after the publication in Germany of Friedrick Naumann's *Mitteleuropa*. The foreign office found the memorandum significant enough to have it printed for the cabinet. Unfortunately, the only evidence of the reactions to the idea of a Yugoslav state comes from the foreign office. Arthur Nicolson, who assumed that Austria-Hungary would not survive the war, undoubtedly agreed with Supilo as he had agreed with Seton-Watson.[45] Clerk pointed out the immediate value of the Yugoslavs when he wrote on the file:

> The time is not yet come for a detailed consideration of these questions, – we have still to beat Germany – but their importance, particularly as regards Italian pretensions, is great, for here lies Serbia's real avenue to progress and the justification for the cession to Bulgaria which can alone secure for us united Balkan support.

The idea of a Yugoslav state had some appeal because of its own intrinsic merits. That appeal was strongly reinforced, as Clerk pointed out, by the fact that the Yugoslav programme might help to promote the negotiations in progress in the Balkans, particularly those to bring Bulgaria into the war on the Allied side. Yugoslav areas could be used to compensate Serbia for concessions to Bulgaria. Thus both Clerk and Nicolson, for different reasons, accepted the Yugoslav programme although that acceptance was personal and in no way reflected government policy. Nevertheless, for the Yugoslavs, it was a beginning.

On 5 November 1914, Seton-Watson submitted to the foreign office a memorandum entitled 'The Future of Bohemia' which was based on conversations in Rotterdam with Thomas Masaryk, the leader of the Czech Realist party and soon to be the leader of the Czechoslovak émigré movement. In it he proposed the creation of a new state in central Europe consisting of Bohemia, Moravia, Silesia, and the Slovak districts of Hungary.[46] The idea was so incredible in 1914 that Clerk was prompted to reassure the foreign office by noting on the file: 'Masaryk is a man of

0429327

great weight among the Czechs, and the ideas here advanced are serious and worth bearing in mind.' It was too early even to comment on the subject, but at least Masaryk gave the foreign office something to ponder.

From the very beginning of its contact with the émigrés the foreign office, like the home office, seemed to prefer the Yugoslavs and Czechoslovaks to the Poles. The explanation may be that the former were strongly supported by Wickham Steed, Seton-Watson and Trevelyan, while the latter had to act alone without the support of those respected by the officials. The Poles also made a bad impression by their attacks on each other. In contrast, the Czechoslovaks and Yugoslavs worked together as they had done before 1914 within the Habsburg monarchy.[47] These preferences were to become more pronounced and more significant later.

By the end of 1914 contact had been established between the émigrés, their supporters in Britain, and a number of officials in various government departments. The émigrés, being the first to realize the possibilities presented by the war, seized the initiative in establishing this contact and began a process of educating the government on the opportunities presented by the war for the reorganization of eastern Europe. The government, realizing that the émigrés might be useful, responded with cautious interest and some encouragement.

2 : YUGOSLAVIA IN THE BALKAN NEGOTIATIONS, 1914–15

When approached by émigrés, the British government accepted no commitments to national self-determination as there was no immediate advantage in adopting utopian programmes for the future of Europe. Commitments were to be avoided as they would only restrict the government's freedom of action. With no specific war aims in eastern Europe, the government was not compelled to adopt strategy to produce specific results, but could use political issues to support military policy. During the Balkan negotiations, from August 1914 to December 1915, strategic necessity and the nationality principle influenced the formation of British policy. Since nationalism appeared to be the root of Balkan problems, the nationality principle represented a long-term political consideration. Yet when the nationality principle came into conflict with strategic necessity, the latter determined policy.

Strategic considerations played a decisive role in the formation of foreign policy in part because of their own intrinsic importance and in part because of the attitude of the foreign office. It was generally assumed, particularly by Grey and Arthur Nicolson, that diplomacy in war would achieve nothing unless it was supported by favourable military action. In practice, this assumption led to the adjustment of diplomacy to strategy. Foreign policy was determined not by long-term political considerations, but by immediate strategic necessity. According to Lord Eustace Percy, a member of the war department: 'Sir Edward Grey tended to make a virtue of this necessity by his dictum that, in war, a Foreign Secretary could have no policy but to do what the soldiers wanted.'[1]

Grey's policy had merit particularly when victory was uncertain, but its rationale is insufficient to explain its adoption. During the first year of the war, the foreign office began to disintegrate. In December 1914 Eyre Crowe was transferred to the contraband department because he supposedly lost his head and was insubordinate to Grey.[2] In the spring of 1915 Sir William Tyrrell, Grey's private secretary, suffered a serious breakdown as a result of the death of his son and was replaced by Eric Drummond.[3] Arthur Nicolson, never a very capable administrator, appears to have been unable to adjust to the war and its effects on the conduct of foreign policy. Although still capable of excellent advice, he seems to have suffered a loss of faith.[4] Grey was going through the same process as Nicolson, made worse by his growing blindness and feelings of guilt over the outbreak of war. Walter Runciman, the president of the board of trade, wrote in February 1915: 'Grey nearly broke under the strain [August 1914] but is now well again, although greatly aged.'[5] By October 1915 Bertie was convinced that Grey was no longer capable of making any virile decision.[6] Grey's willingness to tailor policy to strategy possibly resulted from a disillusionment with diplomacy because of its failure to prevent war. Such a reaction would be reasonable in a period when the major issues were being settled by force. The disintegration of the foreign office probably explains, in part, its unwillingness to accept a dominant role in the making of policy and its willingness to submerge political considerations for the sake of strategy. This tendency is evident in its conduct of the Balkan negotiations and in large measure explains the policy it followed.

The relations between the government and the Yugoslav émigrés developed within the context of the Balkan negotiations which temporarily gave the Yugoslavs a position of importance. Those officials who were aware of the Yugoslavs showed a distinct preference for the creation of a Yugoslav state. Yet such a preference, while influencing policy, by itself was not enough to determine policy. When it was advantageous, the government did not hesitate to sacrifice Yugoslav aspirations. When the Yugoslav programme was consistent with British Balkan policy, and when it presented valuable opportunities in the negotiations, it was supported by the government. The future of Austria-Hungary was never a serious consideration.

In August 1914, all of the Balkan states, except Serbia and Montenegro, remained neutral awaiting a suitable opportunity to take advantage of the hostilities. The overweening territorial ambitions of these states and their mutual hatred made the recently established status quo highly unstable. Serbia, Greece, and Rumania were on good terms because they shared the desire to retain the territories they had taken from Bulgaria in the second Balkan war. Bulgaria wanted revenge and the return of the lost territory. Serbia and Montenegro supported the Entente, Greece favoured the Entente, Rumania was neutral and Bulgaria was pro-Austrian. The belligerents saw in the Balkan neutrals potential allies and were willing to pay for their support. The neutrals were willing to be bought by the highest bidder.

The Entente hoped to create a Balkan league of Greece, Serbia, Bulgaria and Rumania directed against the Central powers. If the Balkan powers fought one another, there would be no advantage in their participation in the war. If, however, they formed a league, as they had against Turkey in 1912, their combined military strength might be enough to tip the balance in favour of the Entente. In order to facilitate the formation of a league, the Allies were willing to offer enemy territory to the Balkan states.[7] According to Churchill:

> It is only by reclaiming from Austria territories which belong naturally to the Balkan races that the means can be provided to satisfy the legitimate needs and aspirations of all the Balkan states. Without taking Austrian territory, there is no way by which any Balkan state can expand except by internecine war.[8]

If a league was to be formed, Serbia, Greece, and possibly Rumania would have to make concessions to Bulgaria to compensate for its losses in the second Balkan war. The Entente offered enemy territory to Serbia and Greece as an inducement to make such concessions to Bulgaria but, in the first months of the war, this policy met with no success.[9] A possible alternative was to exert pressure on Greece and Serbia, but Grey refused to adopt such methods for fear of alienating them.[10]

By February 1915, the Entente had made no progress in its attempts to create a Balkan league. Arthur Nicolson had the best explanation for the failure: 'these wavering Balkan states will not be influenced by promises or assurances but will be guided simply by the events of the war and by their estimate as to which combination is likely to be the winning one . . .'[11] Despite the lack of progress in the negotiations, however, the belief persisted that a Balkan league could be created. It was assumed by the British that if Balkan territory could be redistributed along national lines, the disputes between the Balkan states could be eliminated. It was this assumption which prompted Grey to tell the Bulgarian minister: 'that I was as favourable to Bulgaria getting districts which were Bulgarian as I was to Serbia getting districts that were Serbian. I was in sympathy with the national aspirations of Bulgaria on national lines.'[12] The foreign office saw in the Yugoslav programme a possible solution to Balkan problems because, if Serbia were offered the Yugoslav territories of Austria-Hungary, the Serbian government might be willing to give Macedonia to Bulgaria.[13] Macedonia was a necessary part of either a Greater Serbia or a Greater Bulgaria but not of a Yugoslavia. Therefore, a Greater Bulgaria could not coexist with a Greater Serbia, but could with a Yugoslavia. If the Serbian government would abandon the Greater Serbian programme in favour of the Yugoslav programme, the aspirations of both Serbia and Bulgaria could be satisfied and a league could be formed. During the negotiations, the British government, under the influence of the Yugoslavs, overestimated the strength in Serbia of the exponents of Yugoslavism. The flaw in the British approach to the Serbo-Bulgarian problem was that the Serbian government was never willing to abandon the Greater Serbian programme and therefore never willing to cede Macedonia to Bulgaria.[14]

On 19 February 1915, the British navy began the campaign against the Dardanelles. Following Nicolson's theory that diplomacy would be influenced by the course of the war, the campaign was undertaken, among other reasons, in the hope that a serious military defeat of Turkey would induce Bulgaria to join the Entente.[15] On 13 February 1915, Grey had written optimistically to Buchanan:

> To reinforce my point that diplomacy in the Balkans must be co-ordinated with strategy: you might point out to M.F.A. [Minister of Foreign Affairs] that if our attack on Dardanelles opens well and makes progress next week it will much improve the opportunity for diplomatic steps at Sophia and elsewhere.[16]

Although the campaign seemed to have little influence on Bulgaria, it had an effect on the Italian government which, on 4 March 1915, expressed its willingness to join the Entente in exchange for promises of rather large areas of the Habsburg monarchy.

The Italians wanted, among other things, Dalmatia, a province inhabited predominantly by South Slavs and coveted by the Serbians and the Yugoslavs. As a result of the work of Seton-Watson and Supilo, however, the foreign office knew that Italian possession of Dalmatia would be a violation of the principle of nationality. It was for that reason considered the most objectionable of the Italian claims. An earlier report from Buchanan that the Russian government would bitterly oppose Italian designs in Dalmatia had prompted Arthur Nicolson to write:

> Mr. Sasonov [Russian foreign minister] is quite right. Dalmatia is Slav and anxious to unite with Croatia–Slavonia and she would bitterly resent Italy attempting to incorporate her and we should have a South Slav question with Italy instead of with Austria.[17]

To agree to Italian claims and, thereby, to violate blatantly the principle of nationality in dealing with a people as nationalistic as the South Slavs could only be considered a most short-sighted policy because, as Nicolson pointed out, it would inevitably create problems. But the foreign office had even more immediate reasons for opposing the Italian demands. The Russian government would certainly oppose the Italian claim to Dalmatia, and the solidarity of the Entente necessitated at least some support for the Russian position. If a Balkan league was to be created by the application of the nationality principle and the transformation of a Serbian state into a Yugoslav state, the nationality principle could not be so openly violated by giving Yugoslav territory such as Dalmatia to Italy. It would hardly induce the Serbian government to make concessions to Bulgaria. It might even alienate the Yugoslavs and drive them to support Austria-Hungary against Italy. The Habsburg monarchy would thus be strengthened, and the Entente would lose potentially valuable allies. The foreign office was well aware of this danger, for Rodd had written that when he asked Supilo how the Southern Slavs would react to the war: 'Supilo replied if you come in the character of liberator the Slavs will fire in the air as they have been doing in action against the Russians, but if you come with annexationalist views they will fight you.'[18]

When the terms were first received by the foreign office, Clerk wrote: 'This, to my mind, is quite inadmissible. On the basis of nationality and local sentiment, there is no foundation for the Italian claim.'[19] Arthur Nicolson agreed and warned Grey of the dangers involved in submitting to the Italian demands.[20] At first both Clerk and Nicolson, as Yugoslav sympathizers, hoped that the Italians might be kept out of Dalmatia by being promised all of Istria.[21] When this possibility failed, both tended to support the Russian opposition to the Italian demands. Grey agreed that these demands were excessive, and on 17 March 1915, he wrote that the claim to Dalmatia:

leaves to Serbia very restricted opportunities and conditions
for her outlet to the sea and it shuts in the Jugo-Slav provinces
who have with reason looked to this war to secure for them
the legitimate possibilities of expansion and development of
which they have hitherto been deprived.[22]

A few days later he wrote to Buchanan that: 'The Prime
Minister and some of my colleagues had discussed the Italian
conditions yesterday and we had all felt that the Italian conditions left no real outlet for Serbia or the Jugo-Slavs.'[23] Supilo
seems to have influenced Grey, for he wrote of the Yugoslavs:
'National unity and commercial liberty and opportunity was what
I would claim for them.'[24] But, regardless of such sentiments,
which may or may not have been sincere, Grey had absolutely
no intention of opposing the Italian demands for the sake of the
Yugoslavs or the Serbians. In October 1914, he had been informed
that if Italy joined the Entente, Rumania would follow suit; the
Rumanian intention was confirmed again on 18 March 1915.[25] On
4 March 1915, he had written to Bertie that Italian participation
might end the war. Grey was faced with a choice between two
courses of action, both of which might create a Balkan league.
He could continue the policy of using Dalmatia as an inducement
to the Serbians in an attempt to create a Serbo-Bulgarian agreement which would lead to a Balkan league. Or, he could accept
the Italian position, while risking the alienation of Serbia, in
the hope that it would create a chain reaction in the Balkans in
which Rumania, then Greece and finally Bulgaria would join the
Entente.[26] Serbo-Bulgarian relations gave little reason to think
that the first course of action would be successful. On 22 March
1915, Grey clearly stated his position to Buchanan:

> We must therefore decide either to admit the Italian claim or
> forgo the prospect of Italian co-operation. Italian co-operation
> will decide that of Rumania and probably some other neutral
> states. It will be the turning point of the war and will very
> greatly hasten a successful conclusion.[27]

Two days later Asquith wrote to the king: 'The importance of
bringing in Italy without delay appeared to be so great that it
was agreed to give a general consent to what she asks and to
press on Russia to do the same . . .'[28] During the negotiations
Grey did not oppose the Russian government so openly as to
damage the Entente, but neither would he support the Russian

opposition to the Italian claims.[29] He sought a compromise and applied pressure on either whenever it seemed necessary. Although the negotiations were protracted, a compromise was finally reached largely because of the efforts of the British government. The Italian claim to Dalmatia was accepted although, due to Russian opposition, slightly reduced. The treaty of London, signed on 26 April 1915, promised Italy northern Dalmatia, many of the Dalmatian islands, and other Habsburg territories like Cisalpine Tyrol, the Trentino and most of Istria. The British government played an important role in the negotiations and shared the responsibility for the final agreement. There can be no doubt that the policy of the government was based on immediate strategic considerations, while the future political repercussions of the treaty, although anticipated, were disregarded. Grey himself admitted: 'The Allies have, in order to meet Italy, allowed serious inroad upon the principle of nationalities, for which they hope this war will secure general recognition.'[30]

The negotiations were supposed to be secret, but on 3 April 1915, Sasonov disclosed the terms to Supilo. According to one account Supilo tricked Sasonov, but it is equally possible that Sasonov leaked the terms intentionally.[31] Since the negotiations were still in progress, he might have thought a leak would strengthen his position. His action, however, only served to embarrass the Entente and to produce unfortunate reactions among the Serbians and the Yugoslavs who were justifiably outraged by the Italian terms. Supilo informed Wickham Steed who, on 14 April 1915, wrote: 'My informant adds that the demands are being vigorously supported by our F.O. This I rather doubt, though I have not at the moment any definite information.'[32] The foreign office had been so receptive to Yugoslav ideas that the news seemed incredible.

Steed, Seton-Watson, Arthur Evans and the other supporters of the Yugoslavs immediately attempted to put pressure on the government to modify its policy. On 23 April 1915, Seton-Watson wrote to *The Times* vigorously attacking the Italian claim to Dalmatia as a violation of the principle of nationality. If Italy annexed Dalmatia:

> In that event the entire population will offer a desperate resistance to the Italian invader, and Austria-Hungary, by representing the Entente Powers as the inspirers of an anti-Slav conspiracy will have one last chance of rallying her

disaffected Southern Slav population. For Britain and France
to yield on this question would not merely destroy for ever
their prestige and influence in the Balkans, but it would also
go a long way towards weakening the Entente.[33]

Both Nicolson and Clerk are supposed to have seen and
approved of the letter before publication.[34] On 24 April 1915,
Wickham Steed wrote: 'It may interest you to know that Seton-
Watson's letter has the complete approval of some very high
people in the F.O.'[35] Again, on 29 April 1915, he wrote: 'I begin
to understand George Clerk's remark to Seton-Watson on Monday
that unless Italy comes in at once and turns the scale seriously
against Austria and Germany, Grey, Delcasse and Sazonof will
deserve to be hanged.'[36]

While there is not enough evidence to clarify Nicolson's role
in the incident, or even to identify the Nicolson involved, Harold
or Arthur, the information on Clerk is undoubtedly correct.
Although Clerk favoured the nationalities, there is reason to
believe that he was not entirely straightforward in his relations
with Seton-Watson. On 9 April 1915 he wrote of the Yugoslav
reaction to the negotiations: 'We wish the war to be ended as
far as possible, on the basis of nationalities, certainly, but we did
not set out on a Nationality Crusade.'[37] Seton-Watson wanted a
Yugoslav state because of its own intrinsic merits. Clerk may
have shared Seton-Watson's attitude, or he may have only supported the idea because it would assist the creation of a Balkan
league. He may have exaggerated his support for the Yugoslavs
when speaking to Seton-Watson in order to maintain contact with
him regardless of the nature of government policy.

The Yugoslav supporters also appealed to those who might be
able to influence the negotiations, like Count Benckendorff, the
Russian ambassador, Runciman, Asquith and Grey.[38] It was, however, too late to affect the negotiations with Italy. But the government could not entirely overlook the dissatisfaction manifested
in the campaign because, if alienated, the Yugoslavs could be a
great nuisance. The foreign office was warned by Rodd that
attacks in the British press on Italian policy could seriously affect
Anglo-Italian relations.[39] The Yugoslavs were useful as a source
of information on the Balkans and, as Percy pointed out in a
memorandum on 2 May 1915, their allies, particularly Seton-
Watson, were doing valuable work in combating the anti-war
propaganda of the Independent Labour party and the Union of

Democratic Control. Percy warned that it would be not only unfortunate but also dangerous to lose this support because the campaign against Italy might assume far greater proportions. He recommended that Seton-Watson should be taken into the confidence of the government on the assumption that he could be reconciled to government policy.[40] Possibly as a result of this memorandum, Grey wrote to Seton-Watson on 3 May 1915, and saw him on the following day.

Grey's reaction to the criticism from the supporters of the Yugoslavs might have been influenced by a guilty conscience for agreeing to accept terms which he knew would create future problems and for giving Italy Yugoslav territories while professing sympathy for their aspirations. No doubt he wanted to salvage as much as possible from the situation created by Sasonov's disclosure of the terms. He informed Seton-Watson that as a result of an Allied victory Serbia would receive the adjoining Slav territory under Austrian rule and wide access to the Adriatic in southern Dalmatia; the terms were not defined precisely but he added:

> The greater part, at any rate, of the Slav districts will become free and enabled to settle their own destiny. Whether, for instance, Croatia remains an independent state or wishes to unite with other Slavs, we presume to be for her to decide.[41]

He then pointed out that since the Slavs were going to gain so much, it was hardly fair of them to deny the Entente the means to achieve victory or to expect the complete satisfaction of their aspirations. As a result of Grey's efforts, Seton-Watson and his associates reluctantly accepted the need for Italian support. The attacks on the treaty diminished although, to the discomfort of the foreign office, they never entirely ceased. Grey's action enabled the relations between the government and the Yugoslavs to continue without impairment, but the price of reconciliation had been the recognition by Grey of the right of self-determination for the most important Yugoslav area, Croatia.

Following the treaty of London the prevention of friction between the Italians and the Yugoslavs became a permanent function of the foreign office. One of the ways in which it attempted to do this was by sending G. M. Trevelyan, the most pro-Italian of Seton-Watson's colleagues, to Italy to work for an understanding between the two groups.[42] In July 1915, he wrote to Hubert Montgomery, an assistant clerk in the foreign office: 'I have therefore written to Seton-Watson (with whose *views* I entirely agree) that as a matter of *tactics* I think that he and Evans had better now let the subject rest awhile, in the interest of the object they have in view.'[43] Drummond also attempted to stop attacks on Seton-Watson by A. Cippicio, an Italian lecturer at University College, London.

The closeness of the relations between the government and the Yugoslavs was indicated by the decision of the home office, with the approval of the foreign office, to give the Yugoslavs similar rights of exemption from internment as those enjoyed by the Czechs and the Poles.[44] The Yugoslav Committee was not given quite the same status as the London Czech Committee and the Polish Information Committee because instead of operating independently it was expected to work through the Serbian ministry. While it can be shown that the Yugoslavs were in constant contact with the foreign office throughout this period, it is difficult to determine the degree of their influence.

It was not enough to placate the Yugoslavs, for the Serbian minister also protested against the rumoured terms of the treaty of London and there were reports that there was so much dissatisfaction in Serbia that in some circles, particularly the army, a separate peace with Austria-Hungary was being considered.[45] To counter this difficulty, Grey sent a letter to Charles Des Graz, the minister in Belgrade, who on 7 May 1915, with the support of his French and Russian colleagues, delivered it to Nikola Pašić, the Serbian prime minister. After indicating that as a result of the successful conclusion of the war Serbia would receive Bosnia, Herzegovina, and wide access to the Adriatic, the letter went on to state: 'Whether the Federation of Croatia will follow will naturally be a matter to be decided by the Croats themselves.'[46] The letter seemed to have some pacifying effect on the Serbian government although no mention was made of the fact that it did not represent any binding obligation on the part of the British government. Grey had acted on his own initiative without consulting the cabinet so that the letter represented, according to his own interpretation, only a personal, not official, obligation. It is doubtful whether anyone in the government outside of the foreign office ever knew of the letter which, overshadowed by later negotiations, was eventually forgotten. The letter was never considered by the government as representing an official commitment, but it did eventually have some embarrassing repercussions. Grey was not to escape the consequences of the deception or stupidity involved in confusing his official and private roles.

As Grey had hoped, the treaty of London led to negotiations with Rumania. But these negotiations showed that a chain-reaction among the Balkan states was not a simple process by which a Balkan league could be formed. On 25 April 1915, the Rumanian government signified its willingness to join the Entente in exchange for southern Bukovina, Transylvania and the Banat. If the Italians had large appetites, they were surpassed by the Rumanians whose claims, if accepted, would almost double the size of their country. The possible effect of these claims on Austria-Hungary prompted Arthur Nicolson to write:

> We cannot blot Austria and Hungary out of the map and convert them into large Switzerlands with no access to the sea. Promises hastily made now for an immediate object will be most embarrassing to realize when peace terms come to be discussed.[47]

The most annoying of the Rumanian claims was for the whole of the Banat, the south-west corner of which was inhabited by South Slavs and bordered on the Danube just across the river from Belgrade. The Serbians naturally aspired to some of the Banat so that their capital would not be adjacent to the territory of a foreign power. The situation was almost exactly identical to the Italian negotiations with almost the same reasons for and against the acceptance of the proposed terms. But this time the foreign office was more aware of the possible Serbian reaction and more unwilling to face it.

The negotiations were conducted directly between St Petersburg and Bucharest with the British government playing only a secondary role. Grey gave the Russians a free hand except for the stipulation that Serbian interests in the Banat must be safeguarded. He wrote concerning Serbia to Buchanan: 'I could not urge that she should agree to the handing over to someone else of people of Serbian nationality who were living at the very doors of her capital.'[48] Since the Rumanians would not compromise, no progress was made in the negotiations through May and June. Grey continued to maintain his position:

> I am of opinion that Allies must adhere to their attitude about the Banat. Serbian feeling is very excited and resentful over offer of Macedonia to Bulgaria, and very suspicious of what

has been arranged as regards Adriatic coast with Italy. I
think that it would be neither fair nor prudent to sacrifice
Serbian interests in the Banat.[49]

But the Entente had gone so far in attempting to create a chain
reaction in the Balkans that it could hardly stop now. On 28 June
1915, Clerk pointed out that 'if the advent of Rumania and Bulgaria really means the beginning of the end of the war, and still
more if it means the difference between success and failure in
the Dardanelles, then arguments in favour of sacrificing Greece
and Serbia are very strong'.[50] In the first week of July 1915 the
Russian government, faced by Rumania's complete refusal to
compromise, accepted the Rumanian terms with the approval of
the British government.[51] Although the treaty was not signed
until 1916, and Rumania did not enter the war until then, the
terms had been settled in July 1915. The Rumanian negotiations
were an exact parallel with the Italian negotiations in that politically regrettable terms were accepted for strategic reasons.
Fortunately the negotiations remained secret.

The Rumanian refusal to join the Entente in 1915 ended the
possibility, which had inspired the negotiations, that a Balkan
league could be formed by a chain reaction among the Balkan
states precipitated by the Italian declaration of war. The Entente
therefore reverted to the earlier policy of seeking a Serbo-
Bulgarian agreement in which Serbia would cede to Bulgaria, in
exchange for support, that part of Macedonia termed the uncontested zone in the Serbo-Bulgarian treaty of 1912. In August
1915, in an attempt to open negotiations, the four powers of the
Entente offered to guarantee in precise terms the territories the
Serbians could expect as a result of the war on condition that
the proper concessions were made to Bulgaria. The negotiations
which preceded the offer to Serbia were long and protracted
because it was almost impossible to find a formula both appealing to the Serbians and acceptable to the four powers of the
Entente. The conflict centred on Croatia and Slavonia which the
Russians wanted to promise to Serbia. The Italians objected
because they were reluctant to see a large Slav state created on
the Adriatic.[52]

The British government, primarily concerned to achieve agreement on a note which would be a real incentive to the Serbians
to abandon their intransigence towards Bulgaria, as usual acted
as a mediator between Italy and Russia. In the negotiations the

foreign office tended to favour a solution equivalent to the creation of a Yugoslav state because the only possible compensation for the Serbian loss of Macedonia was in the Yugoslav areas of the Habsburg monarchy. In the negotiations Grey suggested that Serbia should be promised Slavonia and a guarantee to facilitate a union with Croatia, subject to the wishes of the Croatians.[53] The refusal of the Italian foreign minister to accept these proposals created some embarrassment, for as Percy pointed out: 'We have already pledged ourselves to the "freedom of Croatia" – at least by inference.'[54] Grey was forced to waive his proposals because of the Italian objections, but since the note had to mention Croatia and Slavonia in some form, the following clauses were adopted: 'If the future of Slavonia is in the hands of the Allies at the end of the war, it shall be assigned to Serbia . . . The future of Croatia . . . is reserved without prejudice to be decided at the final peace.'[55] The note, as it was finally presented to the Serbian government, also promised to Serbia, Bosnia, Herzegovina, and wide access to the Adriatic in southern Dalmatia in precise geographical terms.[56]

In May, Russia, France and Britain had promised that in the event of victory Serbia would receive Bosnia, Herzegovina and wide access to the Adriatic, while Croatia would have self-determination. The four-power note of August might appeal to the Serbians because, for the first time, the areas were defined in precise geographical terms and because Slavonia was mentioned. But the reference to Croatia in the later note constituted less than had been said in May. The note of August also stated that these guarantees were subject to Serbian concessions to Bulgaria in Macedonia; a condition never previously mentioned. The Serbian government would, therefore, have been quite justified in thinking that the Entente was now offering less at a far higher price. By making unofficial promises Grey had manoeuvred himself into a ridiculous position. The note failed to convince the Serbian government to make the desired concessions to Bulgaria.

These negotiations show that Italy was beginning to assume in Anglo-Yugoslav relations the position of Russia in Anglo-Polish relations. It was a role that the Italians were to play for the rest of the war. The Italian opposition to the creation of a Yugoslav state made it impossible for Britain to openly espouse the Yugoslav cause. It even made Anglo-Yugoslav relations difficult because the foreign office had to discourage the public activities of the Yugoslavs to avoid annoying the Italians. Austria-Hungary was never as great an obstacle to Anglo-Yugoslav relations.

The Italian attitude was a source of great annoyance to the foreign office which obviously preferred the Yugoslavs, if only because the Italians were a much greater nuisance. No sooner had Italy joined the Entente than it began to make negotiations in the Balkans impossible. Drummond echoed foreign office opinion when he wrote to Grey:

> I do not think that the Italian policy as regards Croatia and Slavonia is altogether to be trusted and I feel that we ought not to identify ourselves with it. Monsieur Supilo thinks that Italy does not wish to see Croatia and Slavonia Servian or federated with Servia which I am convinced it is our interest to encourage.[57]

The foreign office might have preferred the Yugoslavs, but it considered the Italians more important in the conduct of war. Whenever there was a conflict of interests between the Italians and the Yugoslavs, the government supported the Italians. Yet regardless of the Italian government, relations between the Yugoslavs and the government continued. A report on 30 August 1915, from Sir Cecil Spring-Rice, the ambassador in Washington, that the Yugoslav organizations in the United States were assisting the Entente by working against German-inspired strikes in munitions factories supplying the Allies, substantiated the view that the Yugoslavs were too valuable to be alienated unnecessarily. The foreign office even gave facilities to a Yugoslav agent to recruit for the Serbian army in the South American Yugoslav settlements. On behalf of the Yugoslavs in London, Seton-Watson offered to supply the war office with information regularly smuggled out of the Central powers.[58] The émigrés had their own courier system which enabled them to maintain contact with their compatriots in Habsburg territory. The offer was readily accepted and the information was, in future, channelled through the British authorities in Switzerland.[59] These incidents, while not necessarily important in themselves, indicate the willingness of the Yugoslavs to work for the Entente and the confidence placed in them by the foreign office.

On 30 August 1915, Grey told Supilo that he was willing, if the Serbian government agreed, to promise self-determination to Bosnia, Herzegovina, southern Dalmatia, Slavonia and Croatia in the event of the successful conclusion of the war.[60] Grey's proposals on these areas in the previous negotiations, if carried out, would have created a Yugoslav state unappealing to many of the Yugoslavs because it would have been, in essence, merely an enlarged kingdom of Serbia. This latest proposal made to Supilo, and undoubtedly inspired by him, was a more truly Yugoslav solution since it would give the Yugoslavs the power to negotiate a union with Serbia instead of being absorbed by it. The offer, however, was vetoed by the Serbian government which was more interested in a Greater Serbia than in a Yugoslavia.[61]

Throughout the Balkan negotiations, in all of his references to Croatia, Grey insisted that its future must be determined by the Croats themselves. It was an indication of the influence of the Yugoslavs because they were the only possible source of the idea; it would never have come from Italy, Serbia or Russia. The only possible explanation for his insistence upon such an idea was either his belief in the Yugoslav programme or his desire to please the émigrés. Although the Yugoslavs were in constant contact with many of the foreign office officials, it is impossible to determine, in most cases, the degree of their influence because the necessary connections in the transference of ideas cannot be established. Grey's references to Croatia, and the general preference of the foreign office for the Yugoslavs, are at least indications that their influence was significant.

On 1 September 1915, Serbia accepted in principle the cession of the uncontested zone to Bulgaria, thus appearing to fulfil the conditions stated in the four-power note.[62] On 7 August 1915, Grey had agreed that while the uncontested zone must be ceded its borders could be modified.[63] The Serbians used this loop-hole to propose so many modifications as to make the cession unacceptable to Bulgaria. It could be argued, depending on the interpretation of the four-power note, that despite the modifications the Entente was committed to fulfil its promises to Serbia since the Serbians had agreed to cede the uncontested zone. According to the Entente, however, the Serbian response was unsatisfactory, and therefore the guarantees proposed in August did not become commitments. Grey's promises in May, overshadowed by the offer in August, had been forgotten.

In October 1915 Bulgaria finally made its choice by joining the Central powers and attacking Serbia in the east in conjunction with the Austro-German offensive in the north. Since without immediate Allied assistance Serbia could not hope to withstand such a two-pronged offensive, Seton-Watson and his colleagues tried to convince the government to deploy large military forces in the Balkans.[64] They failed and Serbia collapsed. Seton-Watson could accept the treaty of London, but not the failure of the government to help Serbia. At the cost of losing some of his influence in the foreign office he responded by attacking Grey's Balkan policy in an article entitled 'The Failure of Sir Edward Grey' published in February 1916.[65] The collapse of Serbia ended the Balkan negotiations the failure of which was blamed on Serbia for its unwillingness to negotiate an agreement with Bulgaria. On 29 November 1915 Drummond wrote:

> Sir Edward asks me however to point out that it was not Russia but Serbia who was so slow in responding to our proposals. We feel here that if Serbia had been really willing to assent to the cessions of territory which we urged, Bulgaria would certainly have not gone to war and would probably have come out on our side.[66]

Serbia was the scapegoat because the government would not recognize its own miscalculations. It had believed that an equitable division of the Balkans on national lines would lead to the creation of a Balkan league. Bulgaria was not interested in an equitable division but rather in the highest price, and the Central powers could always outbid the Entente. If the Central powers had been losing the war or if Turkey had been defeated at the Dardanelles, Bulgaria might have settled for a lower price and joined the Entente. But, as it was, Bulgaria accepted the highest bid, and the expectation that she might have acted otherwise was merely wishful thinking. When the French government suggested, in December 1915, a guarantee to Serbia of its territorial integrity and of its expected gains from the war, the British government refused.[67] As Percy, a sympathizer with the nationalities, noted on the file: 'we all know perfectly well that we cannot and will not continue this war until Jugo-Slavia is constituted'.[68] Since a Balkan league was no longer possible, such promises were unnecessary.

During 1915 the government had promised, or had been willing to promise, vast areas of Austria-Hungary to Italy, Serbia and Rumania. Although it might well be assumed that at some time a decision had been made to destroy the Habsburg monarchy, in fact the issue was never seriously considered and the decision was never made. While Habsburg territory was promised because it was necessary in order to create a Balkan league, little thought was given to the repercussions of these promises. In December 1914 the government expressed interest in a separate peace with Austria-Hungary. But when the possibility actually arose and it became a choice between a separate peace and a Balkan league, the government chose the latter.[69] The decision was not to destroy the Habsburg monarchy but just to give it no special consideration.

In March 1915 Drummond, in reference to public comments on the breakup of the Habsburg monarchy made by J. D. Gregory, an assistant clerk, expressed the official indifference or indecision on the future of Austria-Hungary when he wrote:

> I will send Gregory a warning that he must be extremely
> careful about discussing these very big questions, all the
> more so as I believe Sir Edward is of opinion that things are
> not sufficiently advanced to enable him to take any definite line
> as regards Austrian eventuality.[70]

There was never any consideration given to the idea of making sacrifices in order to preserve the Empire. Indeed, there seemed to exist a willingness, although not a desire, to destroy the monarchy. Few seemed to be aware of the ultimate effect of the war on Austria-Hungary, and it is possible that many assumed that the Empire would continue to exist regardless of territorial losses. Arthur Nicolson was alone in expressing the significance of the promises of Habsburg territory. In July 1915, he wrote: 'At the same time I cannot disguise the fact that the concessions which we offered to her, and which comprise practically one half of Hungary, cannot be realized until we have actually pulverized Hungary and Austria.'[71] To fulfil the promises, even to Italy alone, the Empire indeed had to be 'pulverized'. It was extremely doubtful that the monarchy could survive such losses or the defeat necessary before such losses would be accepted. The treaty of London was eventually to prove an insurmountable barrier to a separate peace with the Empire because the Habsburgs would never accept the treaty, Italy would never accept less than the treaty, and the Entente would fulfil its obligations. The monarchy was, in a sense, doomed by the treaty of London. It is ironic that to the Yugoslavs and their supporters the treaty of London was one of the most iniquitous acts of the British government. Yet beyond any doubt, the acceptance of the treaty did more than any other single act of the government to destroy the monarchy and to ensure the creation of a Yugoslav state. In essence, the British were indifferent to the future of the Habsburg monarchy. They might not desire its destruction, but they would not alter strategy to preserve it.

The Balkan negotiations gave the Yugoslavs a position of far greater importance in British policy than that possessed by the Poles or the Czechoslovaks. The official preference for the Yugoslavs was strengthened by the possibility that the Yugoslav programme might facilitate the creation of a Balkan league. After 1915 the Balkans ceased to be an area of primary importance and, therefore, while the relations with the Yugoslavs continued, they lost much of their significance. The preference for the Yugoslavs continued, but when it was no longer allied to the self-interest involved in the creation of a Balkan league, promises to the Yugoslavs were no longer considered.

3 : ESPIONAGE AND PROPAGANDA, 1914–16

Since the initial relations between the government and the nationality organizations were established by the émigrés, the government responded on the merits of each particular case without reference to any clearly defined comprehensive policy for the treatment of the enemies' subject nationalities. The officials were quick, however, to realize that the disgruntled émigrés were potential weapons of war. But the Entente also possessed subject nationalities, and the Central powers came to the same conclusion. Since the use of subject nationalities as weapons of war began gradually, almost imperceptibly, it is difficult to determine which belligerent acted first. The British may have begun the process, but throughout the war they acted as if they were merely responding to German initiatives. The British government was at liberty to accept or reject the use of the émigrés in unorthodox warfare against the Central powers, but once it was clear that the enemy intended to use subject nationalities against the Entente, the government had little choice but to retaliate in a similar fashion or accept the unfortunate consequences of enemy policy. Circumstances seemed to compel the government to use the nationalities. This unorthodox type of warfare was not new; nevertheless, it was a symptom of the development of total war.

The Germans used the Indian and Irish nationalists while the British used the Yugoslavs and the Czechoslovaks. The Poles, however, were unique in that their national cause was not necessarily committed to either the Entente or the Central powers. The belligerents were able to use the Poles but, in contrast to their relations with the other nationalities, also had to compete for Polish support. During 1915 and 1916 the use of the subject nationalities by the belligerents and the competition for Polish support was concentrated in the United States as part of the Anglo-German rivalry for American support. But, before discussing this rivalry in the context of Anglo-American relations, it is necessary to examine the type of assistance offered by the émigrés and its relationship to the administration of the British government.

Co-operation between the government and some of the nationality organizations developed shortly after the outbreak of war. While no agreement existed on ultimate aims, the desire for the defeat of the Central powers constituted a common basis for co-operation. Agreement on this one aim was reinforced by the immediate advantages of co-operation for both the officials and the émigrés. It has already been pointed out that the nationality organizations assisted the government on the question of the treatment of enemy aliens and that the Yugoslavs supplied the government with information on conditions in the Balkans and the Habsburg empire during 1915. These specific examples represent only a small and relatively unimportant part of the co-operation, primarily in espionage and propaganda, which developed between 1914 and 1916. The role of the government in this co-operation was purely opportunistic and unrelated to the question of war aims. The officials were perfectly willing to accept assistance from nationalities for which the government planned to do nothing at the peace conference. The assistance accepted by the government was offered unconditionally and promises about the future of eastern Europe were not given in exchange.

The government was able to avoid commitments but not, ultimately, the consequences of its own action. As the émigrés had anticipated, the assistance tended to create among British officials a feeling of indebtedness to the nationalities. Those émigrés who assisted the government were able to prove both their political ability and their dedication to the Entente, thereby winning the respect and even the admiration of the officials. While numerous representations were made to the foreign office during this period on behalf of national self-determination in eastern Europe, relations between the government and the nationalities were dominated by the experience of practical co-operation which had far more effect on official attitudes than any number of memoranda. The co-operation tended to convert those officials involved into supporters of national self-determination and they, in turn, were in a position to influence policy. Official assistance to the nationality organizations also contributed to their campaign for national liberation. The use of the subject nationalities against the enemy and the competition for their support focused public attention on national self-determination. Eventually the campaign began to have some effect and it produced results which could not be overlooked in the formulation of British policy. Thus the government contributed to the creation of conditions which were to limit future British alternatives.

An analysis of the degree of co-operation which developed is severely limited by the lack of evidence. The co-operation existed primarily in propaganda and espionage – two fields of government activity in which little documentation survives. After the war the records of the propaganda agency of the British government were destroyed.[1] Some relevant documents survived in the records of other ministries, but they represent only a fraction of the original material and, because they relate only to incidents involving other ministries, do not accurately represent the activities of the propaganda agency. The destroyed records presumably related to the daily operations and detailed activities of that agency which can now only be reconstructed with great difficulty. There are, therefore, many unanswerable questions about British propaganda. While it is possible to show that the agency had close relations with certain nationality organizations, the details of those relations can never be adequately determined. The study of espionage is even more difficult. No documents on the subject should exist because the intelligence agencies commit little to paper and destroy as much documentation of their activities as possible. During the war the foreign office sought to keep all reference to the secret service out of its records, and when such references appear, they are often so circumspect as to be almost meaningless. Fortunately some documents have survived, and on that basis some discussion of the role of the nationalities in British espionage is possible. Due to the scarcity of documents on both propaganda and espionage, all that is possible is a minimum estimate of the degree of co-operation. It may only be the tip of the iceberg.

The most obvious type of assistance given by the émigrés was in the supply of information. From the very beginning of their relationship with the government the Yugoslavs and Czechoslovaks followed a policy of passing on any useful information collected by their organizations. In order to maintain contact with their compatriots in Austria-Hungary, these émigrés established, early in the war, a courier system through Switzerland.[2] The system supplied a flow of information on internal conditions within the Central powers until the Austrians, late in 1915, established tighter security along the Swiss frontier. During the spring of 1915 the émigrés sent this information, which was not easily accessible to British intelligence, directly to the foreign office.[3] In August 1915, as a result of a suggestion by Seton-Watson, a regular system was established by which information could be passed directly to the British intelligence authorities in Switzerland.[4]

The émigrés were also a source of information on developments in the United States. While the British had no difficulty in acquiring information about developments in the mainstream of American politics, the collection of information about the activities of the various national minorities was much more difficult because they tended to form closed communities. Through their compatriots in the United States the émigrés had access to this type of information which they supplied to the officials.[5] Such information often related to propaganda or censorship as, for example, a list forwarded by Seton-Watson in August 1915 on behalf of the Yugoslavs containing the names of a number of American Slavic language newspapers which opposed the Entente. The list enabled the government to ban the circulation of these newspapers in British territory and to warn British firms to cease advertising in them.[6]

Once the émigrés had proven their reliability, the officials began to seek their assistance. On one occasion Clerk asked Seton-Watson to arrange for the translation from Czech of letters intercepted by the government.[7] When approached by hitherto unknown émigrés, the foreign office often checked their *bona fides* with the known and reliable émigrés, like those on the London Czech Committee. Since the foreign office tended to follow their recommendations, the established émigrés acquired the power to eliminate competition by merely advising the foreign office to have no relations with their political opponents.[8] Such incidents were of little importance in themselves, but they were symptoms of the growing confidence of the officials in the émigrés. If the total of all the information supplied by the émigrés during the war could be calculated, it might prove to be of considerable importance.

In August 1914, a number of Czechs in New York, unconnected with Masaryk but with similar aims, formed an organization entitled as the Bohemian National Alliance.[9] This organization, which was to become a major source of funds for the Czechoslovak movement, contacted Masaryk and accepted his political leadership through Emmanuel Voska, Masaryk's agent in America. Voska became the head of the section of the Bohemian National Alliance for propaganda in the eastern United States.[10] Through Michael Pupin, a professor at Columbia University and the Serbian consul general in the United States, and Madame Slavko Grouić, the wife of the Serbian *chargé d'affaires* in London, Voska met Captain Sir Guy Gaunt, the naval attaché in Washington and the head of British naval intelligence in the United States.[11] The date of this meeting is uncertain, but from Voska's account it appears to have been not later than June 1915. Since Gaunt was trying to establish an intelligence organization in the United States, he readily accepted Voska's offer of the services of his organization to British naval intelligence. Voska was inspired by the thought that: 'we must make ourselves so useful that when Britain and France dictated peace they could not deny our claim to an independent republic'.[12] Czech agents could be of inestimable value to Gaunt because as American or Austrian citizens they could work in the United States, particularly against the Austrians, with greater effectiveness than a British agent.[13] If their activities were exposed, it would be difficult to prove that they were working for the British government.

These agents cannot be considered merely 'reliable sources' who occasionally contributed information to Gaunt. They were, in effect, agents working for the British government. Documentary evidence on this subject is rare, but the files of the British embassy in Washington for February 1917 show that like other British agents they had code numbers for identification.[14] According to Voska, his organization initially worked without financial support from the British government because his agents worked without salary. In 1916, however, arrangements were made to supply his operating expenses from secret service funds.[15] Masaryk later claimed that he made these arrangements in London because the Bohemian National Alliance lacked the funds to support Voska's work.[16] This testimony is to some degree substantiated by a letter Gaunt wrote to Spring Rice on 20 December 1915:

Would it be possible for me to be allowed a small sum not exceeding Five Hundred Pounds to be placed at my disposal for use in connection for the information that is supplied to me. As I told you before, I have an office and a stenographer

here [New York] in connection with the Czech movement –
though of course the girl does not know of my existence and
recently I have had to do the same thing in Chicago on
account of German activities being shifted to that city . . .

In addition to these small items occasional expenses, such
as for instance, secret mission which left hurriedly for
Philadelphia and other Austro-German Consulates. It was
most important to know what their object was and I allowed
the expenses of a patriotic man to keep in touch with them.
Personally he gets no pay, his travelling expenses alone are
allowed.

I have kept careful account of the sum that was allowed
me before, a considerable portion of which has been used in
keeping one or two men on the road who have influence
among the Slav races with a view to counteracting the
German propaganda.[17]

It was obviously not the first such request. Although the letter
contains that element of circumspection always found in official
correspondence on espionage, there can be little doubt that
Gaunt was referring to his Czech agents. On the basis of a strong
recommendation from Spring Rice the request was approved by
Arthur Nicolson who controlled the secret service fund.[18]

Working for Gaunt, Voska's agents were active in espionage,
counter-intelligence and propaganda aimed at thwarting Austrian
and German plots against the Entente in the United States. It
seems that the Czechs achieved notable success in this work, contributing to a number of well-known Allied espionage coups by
infiltrating the Austrian embassy as well as a number of German
organizations.[19] In exchange the British authorities assisted the
Czechs and thereby indirectly furthered the campaign for
national self-determination. For example, when the Bohemian
National Alliance wanted to transfer funds to Masaryk, it was
arranged.[20] When members of the organization wanted to travel
to Europe, the British embassy in Washington supplied the passports.[21] When the courier system through Switzerland broke down
late in 1915, the British authorities helped Voska establish a new
system for American-Czech couriers through Holland.[22] On at
least one occasion when Masaryk wanted to send messages to
Prague, the courier, en route from the United States to Holland,
was detained by British authorities so that a meeting could be
arranged with Masaryk without arousing suspicion.[23]

In December 1915, Sir William Wiseman became the head of the British secret service (M.I.1c) in the United States. Before leaving London Wiseman met Masaryk through Seton-Watson, and it was arranged that Voska should henceforth work for Wiseman's organization.[24] According to Wiseman, securing the services of Voska was 'the luckiest thing that happened to me on that side of my work'.[25] Arthur Willert, a member of Wiseman's staff, claimed that by December 1915 Voska had eighty agents working for him. Many years later he wrote: 'Voska, whose code name was "Victor", must have been one of the most outstanding of the "secret agents" of the first war.'[26] The relationship between the Bohemian National Alliance and the British intelligence agencies was a good example of mutually advantageous co-operation because each needed the other. As in all such relationships the government gained more because the émigrés were satisfied to wait for a future reward. The work done by the Czech agents in the United States, which will be more thoroughly discussed later in the context of Anglo-American relations, was the most valuable assistance given to the Entente by any nationality organization before 1917.

Another émigré who worked as a British agent was Count Jean Marie de Horodyski, a Galician Pole. In the spring of 1915 Horodyski, through contact with Gregory, began to work for the foreign office under Drummond's direction.[27] In the foreign office documents Horodyski is always referred to in such vague terms that little is revealed about his status. J. H. Priestley of M.I.1, however, not accustomed to the subtlety of the foreign office, stated in a report: 'Count de Horodyski arrived on Sunday 13/8/16 en route for London to see the Foreign Office, for whom he is now working . . . He . . . has been engaged in obtaining political information for the British Foreign Office.'[28] Although Horodyski began working in Europe, he was sent in 1916 to work among the Polish organizations in the United States. Unlike Voska, he appears to have had no organization of his own, but by working directly for the foreign office, as will be explained in greater detail later, he was in a better position to influence policy.[29]

In August 1914, the government created at Wellington House, London S.W., a propaganda agency under the direction of Charles Francis Masterman, the chancellor of the duchy of Lancaster. The creation of such an agency to influence opinion in neutral countries showed that the government was aware of the importance of neutral opinion in influencing the policies of neutral states and their relations with the Entente. The staff of Wellington House consisted of authors, journalists and academics who had some knowledge of public opinion and the ability to produce propaganda. Most of the propaganda was in the form of pamphlets dealing with the issues of the war which were either selected from those already on the market or commissioned by Wellington House. They were published commercially without any official markings so that their true origin remained secret. Great effort was always taken to surround Wellington House with a shroud of secrecy so that its propaganda would be more effective.[30]

The pamphlets were distributed in the United States, the most important target, by mail. The section for propaganda in America, under the direction of Gilbert Parker, the Canadian novelist, compiled a list of prominent Americans – academics, journalists, politicians, lawyers, clergy and civil servants – to whom they sent selected pamphlets. Each package contained a letter from Parker giving the impression that he was a private individual sending the pamphlets on his own initiative. The theory was that if these individuals could be influenced they would, in turn, influence the general public. By June 1915, the list consisted of at least 14,000 prominent Americans.[31]

Any issue which reflected unfavourably on the enemy, such as the treatment of subject nationalities, was used for propaganda. The Germans followed the same policy by using the Irish problem to discredit Britain. One of the first pamphlets produced by Wellington House was *The Submerged Nationalities of the German Empire* and similar ones followed.[32] Regardless of the intentions of Wellington House, propaganda which dealt with subject nationalities helped the émigrés by focusing attention on their plight and on the issue of national self-determination. Even if national self-determination was never openly discussed, it was the obvious conclusion of any pamphlet which dealt with the suffering of subject nationalities under German, Austrian or Hungarian rule.

Besides focusing attention implicitly on national self-determination, some of the pamphlets came very close to actually promoting the idea. Ernest Barker, for example, stated in *Great Britain's Reason for Going to War*: 'England stands for the right of each national group to enjoy the form of government to which it aspires.'[33] G. M. Trevelyan in *The Serbians and Austria* wrote:

'When Eastern Europe is directed as far as possible on racial and national lines, there may at least be peace and content in those unhappy regions.'[34] In *Germany and Eastern Europe* Lewis Namier recommended independence for Czechoslovakia and wrote: 'Europe has to be rearranged in accordance with nationality.'[35] These are only a few examples of the type of comment relevant to national self-determination found in the pamphlets produced between 1914 and the end of 1916.[36]

While these pamphlets were being distributed, neither national self-determination nor the promotion of that idea were part of British foreign policy. If this material went slightly beyond the limits of approved policy, the explanation can be found in the refusal of the government to define its war aims. With no direction from the foreign office on the nature of war aims and what might be published on that subject, and with no foreign office scrutiny of the propaganda, the officials of Wellington House had only Asquith's early speeches as a guide. Those speeches had been so vague that they could easily lead to a divergence between policy and propaganda. Many of the writers, like Trevelyan and Namier, were supporters of national self-determination, and it was quite natural for their pamphlets to reflect such sympathies. Regardless of the interpretation of the exact meaning of these vague references to the nationalities, there can be no doubt that the distribution of these pamphlets substantially contributed to the émigrés campaign for national self-determination. It is almost impossible to evaluate the effect of propaganda, but it may well be that Wellington House did more to win public support for national self-determination particularly in the United States than the émigrés who lacked the resources of the British government.

The use of the nationalities as a weapon of propaganda undoubtedly stimulated in Wellington House an interest in the nationality organizations. Early in 1915, on the recommendation of his good friend Lord Eustace Percy, Lewis Namier was employed by Wellington House to write summaries of the Polish press and to advise on propaganda. Namier was uniquely suited for this work because he came from an eastern Galician Jewish family which had converted to Catholicism and which had brought him up as a member of the Polish gentry. Before the war he had studied at the London School of Economics and Political Science and at Balliol College, Oxford, and had worked in the United States for the American Association of Foreign Language Newspapers. He undoubtedly knew more about Poland than anyone else in the British government – British officials were abysmally ignorant of the subject – but he was particularly valuable to Wellington House because of his knowledge of the eastern European minorities in the United States. While his enemies were correct in saying that his advice on Polish affairs was distorted by his own personal bias, it must be remembered that informed, unbiased advice on Polish affairs did not exist. Namier was responsible for bringing the importance of the Polish-Americans to the attention of British officials and for establishing contact between Wellington House and the Polish émigrés.[37]

Aware of the dangers from Russia of any British action on the Polish issue and holding the lowest opinion of Polish émigrés, Namier opposed government involvement with them. In a report on his relations with the émigrés he wrote:

> I don't, however, for a moment defend the policy of the
> Polish Information Committee – nothing could be worse advised
> than to give *that* any official encouragement. They try to make
> the Polish Question, which Russia considers an internal problem
> of her own, into an international question, and they advocate
> Polish independence. But for the same reason, in my belief, no
> support or encouragement should be given to *any Polish
> politicians or organizations whatever* because all of them agree
> on these two points, which are diametrically opposed to the
> programme of Russia and therefore of the Entente. The
> differences between Polish politicians are merely in the degree
> of personal honesty or dishonesty in the direction of their
> intrigues: usually they intrigue against the Power by which
> they profess to stand.[38]

When Namier began to compile a list of prominent American Poles for Gilbert Parker's system of distribution, he found that he had to overcome his aversion to working with the Polish émigrés and seek their support. He made an arrangement with the Polish Information Committee whereby they were supplied with pamphlets which they addressed to prominent American Poles and then returned to Wellington House. The officials sealed and mailed the packages, thus having total control over the contents. As Namier pointed out, the real advantage of the arrangement was that the divergence of policy between the government and the committee would make it difficult for anyone to trace the pamphlets back to the British government.[39] The recipients would be under the impression that they came from their own compatriots. Wellington House also produced and distributed pamphlets like *Poland Under the Germans* and *Germany's Economic Policy in Poland* which originated with the Polish Information Committee.[40] The Committee was therefore distributing its own propaganda at the expense of the government. By the end of 1916 Wellington House distributed propaganda relevant to Poland on a large scale. Pamphlets were being produced in Polish and were distributed to over six hundred prominent Poles in the United States as well as through other Polish organizations like the *Agence Polonaise Centrale* and the Polish National Alliance.[41] The latter organization was based in Chicago and was associated with Horodyski's work in the United States on behalf of the Entente.

The Yugoslavs may have assisted Wellington House but, other than a few comments, there is little evidence of it in the documents. After the treaty of London, the anti-Italian flavour of Yugoslav propaganda made such co-operation difficult. The Czechs, not suffering from such inconveniences, probably established contact with Wellington House through Namier or Trevelyan. During 1915 and 1916 Wellington House produced and distributed Masaryk's two pamphlets: *The Slavs Among Nations* and *Austrian Terrorism in Bohemia*, as well as *Memorial to the International from the Bohemian Branch of the Socialist Party in America*, originating from the London Czech Committee.[42] Distribution of British propaganda in the United States was carried out by Voska's section of the Bohemian National Alliance which, unlike the Polish Information Committee, was allowed to work without the constant surveillance of Wellington House.[43] These differences in the relations between Wellington House and the various nationality organizations seemed to be determined largely by Namier's own preferences. On 31 May 1916, he wrote: 'None of the American Poles seem to be an element on which one could rely, or with whom one could work as one can with Tchechs or Jugoslavs ...'[44] By October 1916, about 20,000 pamphlets had been distributed by the Bohemian National Alliance, and by early 1917 it had expanded its distribution to include South America.[45] Information from the Czech agents also helped Wellington House assess the type of propaganda needed in the United States.[46]

There can be no doubt that the Poles and particularly the Czechs gave valuable assistance to Wellington House in the production and distribution of propaganda. The émigrés could be more effective in the distribution of pamphlets because of their contacts in the United States and because they had no apparent connection with the government. The émigrés benefited because much of the propaganda of Wellington House promoted their own cause. They also received, in effect, an indirect subsidy when Wellington House produced their own propaganda and supplied them with it. Although the effectiveness of British propaganda cannot be evaluated, it undoubtedly contributed to the campaign in the United States for national self-determination.

The nationality organizations also assisted the Entente by recruiting their compatriots for military service. Although some émigrés had expressed a willingness to serve at the very beginning of the war, such offers were not initially accepted because there was no shortage of manpower and therefore no compelling need to adopt the complex and somewhat unorthodox methods for the recruitment of enemy aliens. Only when the shortage of manpower became evident did the war office abandon its original reluctance to recruit aliens and begin, despite considerable misgivings in the foreign office, to press for the enlistment of Poles, Czechoslovaks and Yugoslavs.

During 1915, South Slavs in Britain were released from internment for service in the Serbian army, and efforts to recruit South Slavs in neutral countries were given limited and secret government support.[47] Since the British army accepted only British subjects, those Czechs and Poles who wished to serve were sent to the French Foreign Legion.[48] During the summer of 1916, Yugoslav recruitment became a serious issue because of the difficulty in finding replacements for the Serbian army. Since the only source of replacements were the Yugoslav communities in neutral countries, a plan for recruiting there was supported by the Yugoslav organizations, the Serbian government and the French government. The foreign office was reluctant to become involved in any recruiting scheme which would involve the United States, but the plan was supported by the war office and the cabinet.[49] Under pressure Grey agreed, with the greatest reluctance, to a plan whereby recruiting in the United States would be done by Yugoslav or Serbian agents who would send their recruits to Canada for training before being sent to the Serbian army. The costs involved in recruiting, training and shipment would be borne equally by the British and French governments. Grey stipulated, however, that no British official in the United States was to be involved in any way with this programme. If the recruiting agents needed assistance, they would have to look to the French authorities who, Grey believed, could act with greater impunity in the United States.[50] Grey's sensitivity on this issue stemmed from difficulties in Anglo-American relations caused by British consular officials in California who had recruited for the British army. He was not as particular about the South American states, for he instructed British officials there to give all possible assistance to Serbian and Yugoslav agents.[51]

Unlike the Yugoslavs, the Czechoslovaks and the Poles had no army to join other than the French Foreign Legion – an unappetizing prospect even for the most ardent patriot. The situation began to change in June 1916 when the war office decided to permit the enlistment of friendly aliens, which included Russian, but not German or Austrian, Poles. In August the war office went even a step further by permitting the enlistment of enemy alien 'friendlies' (Poles and Czechoslovaks) not in the army but in labour units.[52] An exception was made, however, for the Czechs who were allowed to join the army as if they were British subjects. On 10 November 1916, an instruction from the Army Council stated: 'Czechs who are in possession of a green registration certificate, duly authenticated by the Czech Committee, . . . may be accepted in any category of service in which British subjects are now accepted'.[53] As a result of this decision, the London Czech Committee began to recruit in the Czech colony, and it has been estimated that ninety per cent of the able-bodied Czechs in Britain volunteered for the British army.[54]

The decision of the war office to recruit the citizens of an enemy power was quite remarkable, but it never gave any explanation of its obvious favouritism towards the Czechs and its discrimination against the Poles. If the German and Austrian Poles were accepted into the British army, there would be little to distinguish the British treatment of them from the treatment of the Russian Poles. It may well be that fear of the possible Russian reaction to the failure of the British government to distinguish between Russian Poles and Austrian or German Poles, which might be interpreted as a tacit recognition of the indivisibility of the Polish nation, inhibited the war office. Or this favouritism might be explained by the fact that the Poles were not entirely trusted in any branch of the government while the Czechs had already proven their ability and loyalty to the Entente by services in espionage and propaganda.

While the Poles in Britain were not accepted into the British army, arrangements were made for the recruitment of American

Poles. In October 1916, Horodyski was sent to the United States to recruit Poles to be sent to Canada for the Canadian army. Although his mission was jointly sponsored by the war office and the foreign office, and his expenses were supplied by the government, he was instructed by Drummond before he left that while in the United States he was not a representative of the British government.[55]

The enlistment of the nationalities, which began in 1916, was to become far more important later in the war. It was inspired by the war office and only reluctantly accepted by the foreign office. As in all cases of co-operation with the nationality organizations, it was based on immediate needs resulting from the war regardless of future peace terms.

It is important to note that, while the foreign office was involved in the various aspects of co-operation discussed above, the action tended to come from other branches of the government, such as Wellington House and the war office, more specifically orientated to the conduct of the war. The foreign office co-ordinated the co-operation but seldom initiated it. It is also significant that the Czechoslovaks were pre-eminent among the nationalities for their willingness and capability to contribute to the war effort.

Between 1914 and 1916 the relations between the government and the nationalities were most significant in relation to the United States. While the foreign office in a general sense conducted Anglo-American relations, the war office, the admiralty and Wellington House used the nationalities in the United States for their own specific purposes. To some extent the foreign office oversaw and co-ordinated these activities if only to ensure that they were not carried to such an extreme as to rebound unfavourably on the government. While often unrelated to the daily conduct of Anglo-American relations, the co-operation and the reasons for it were an integral part of the British foreign policy, particularly on Anglo-American relations. Only on occasion were the examples of co-operation significant enough to appear on the surface of Anglo-American relations, but, however unseen, they were always present.

The position of the United States in relation to the war was of the greatest importance to the Entente because, even if America remained neutral, the character of that neutrality could determine the course of the war. The success of the blockade depended upon a favourable reaction on the part of the American government. If the Americans decided to disregard or break the blockade because of the disruption of their commerce and the irritation of commercial restrictions, it could have fatal consequences for the Entente. Or if the American government decided to retaliate by restrictions on trade with the Entente, it might cripple the Allied war effort. As the most powerful neutral and a major source of raw materials, munitions and loans, the United States was in a position to affect substantially the course of the war. Anglo-American relations were, therefore, the most important problem handled by the British foreign office during the period of American neutrality.

The Central powers were equally aware of the importance of the United States and, like the Entente, sought to win American support. An intense rivalry developed in which both sides tried to influence the American government. Since that government would be influenced by public opinion, both sides attempted to win public approval, if not public support. The recognition of the importance of American public opinion had contributed to the British decision to establish Wellington House. The British authorities were also aware that the population of the United States was not homogeneous in that it contained large and politically significant ethnic minorities whose support or opposition could be decisive. Grey's decision in August 1914 to cable to the American press the full text of Grand Duke Nikolai Nikolaievich's proclamation to the Poles suggests an awareness of the importance of Polish-American opinion.[56] On 29 September 1914, Parker wrote: 'The importance of influencing the public opinion of Chicago and the State of Illinois cannot be overestimated . . . It is apparent that the foreign population of Chicago is very powerful and needs very careful handling.'[57]

The initial contacts between the émigrés and the British embassy in Washington were established within a few months of the outbreak of war.[58] Most of these contacts were insignificant except in the case of the Bohemian National Alliance which appealed to Spring Rice for the release of interned Czechs. Spring Rice was able to reassure them about the Czechs in England and able to arrange for Czech and even Croat agents to visit internment camps in Canada to arrange for the release of their compatriots.[59] He sought to satisfy them; for as he wrote to Grey: 'It is desirable to conciliate Bohemian opinion in U.S. as far as possible as it is strongly on the side of the Allies.'[60] He was undoubtedly motivated by the growing opposition to the Entente which was becoming evident among other minorities in the United States. In addition to fears about the Irish, Jewish and Catholic Americans, he was becoming increasingly alarmed, as his reports for January and February 1915 show, by the activities of the German-Americans. In these reports he claimed that the German-Americans, with considerable financial backing, were organizing politically in order to put pressure on Congress, influence elections and conduct German propaganda. Their immediate aim was the imposition of an embargo on the sale of arms to the Entente. If they gained the support of the Irish-Americans, whose leaders Spring Rice believed were in German pay, they might even succeed.[61] On 5 January 1915, he wrote:

> American opinion has on the whole been favourable to the Allies. A considerable section of it, however, that is the opinion of the German-Americans has been furiously on the side of Germany, and the average politician has much more to fear from this active, violent and interested position of the minority than from the rather tepidly taken position of the majority.[62]

The dangers, while possibly exaggerated, were very real. The German and Irish Americans were unalterably opposed to the Entente and because of their size, organization and political awareness were the two most powerful ethnic groups in the United States. Their combined opposition was a threat of considerable proportions.[63] Spring Rice did not recommend any measure to counteract the activities of the German-Americans, but he did warn that the creation of a counter-balancing foreign movement was not the solution. Yet this idea was implicit in his reports. On 12 February 1915, he wrote that one American politician had said:

> The Allies should refrain from following the example of the Germans and undertaking race propaganda. It was evident however that if one race organized in its own interest all the others would follow suit and as the Germans were not in the majority among the foreign element, their organization would in the end cost them dear.[64]

Unfortunately those ethnic minorities in the United States which were potentially anti-German – the Czechs, Slovaks, Serbs, Croats, Slovenes, and Poles – were disorganized and politically inactive. These minorities were not as numerous as the Germans or Irish and did not have their tradition of political involvement in the United States. They were not as yet factors in American politics and did not constitute a counter-balancing force to the German-Americans.[65] But the formation of the Bohemian National Alliance in 1914 showed that the situation was changing.

Late in February 1915, Namier wrote an analysis of Polish-American opinion for Wellington House. He pointed out that the Poles were roughly divided into pro-Austrian and neutral factions with Austrian agents working vigorously to win the support of all of the American Poles. The neutral faction, led by Jan Smulski of the *Chicago Journal*, while anti-Russian, was not opposed to Britain or France. If some effort was made, possibly through Slav émigrés like Masaryk, their support might be secured. He continued:

> *There is an interesting practical point in Smulski's political programme.* He is in favour of a closer understanding between all the Slav nationalities in the United States . . . Whatever we may think of that idea, one thing appears clearly from it, namely that *the only way of approaching 'the neutrals' among the American Poles and of gaining their support for our side is through the intermediary of the other American Slavs.* However impracticable a Slav Union may be in Europe it is by no means impracticable in the United States and it might give excellent results.[66]

This memorandum, which might never have been seen outside of Wellington House, was brought to the attention of the foreign office by Namier's close friend, Eustace Percy, who in a separate note added his own views. After emphasizing the threat posed by the Austrian agents in the United States, Percy wrote:

> the Allies want Polish opinion in America as a makeweight to the German vote . . . It is very possible that on the whole Polish-American opinion is with us, but the annexed appeal shows clearly that it is not with us in any *positive* way . . . There is, I believe, some idea at present of starting a campaign to form Slav opinion in America. Mr. Seton-Watson has, I believe, some idea of this kind.[67]

Percy emphasized that the work among the American Poles had to be done by the Russians working through prominent Poles like Smulski. In addition, the greatest secrecy was necessary so as not to offend the American government which was naturally sensitive to intervention in its own internal affairs. Since the Russian government claimed priority on the Polish issue, the Polish-American problem was its responsibility. It was obvious that Russia would be more effective in dealing with the Poles because it, unlike Britain, had something to offer them. It would also be preferable if Russia not Britain took the risks involved in meddling in American internal affairs. If the Russians could be induced to tackle the problem themselves, the foreign office could also avoid the danger of offending the Russian government by working for Polish-American support.

As a result of these memoranda, the foreign office requested the views of Spring Rice, and instructed Buchanan, if he thought it prudent, to draw Sazonov's attention to the problem.[68] Grey was so sensitive about mentioning the Poles to the Russians that he did not go so far as to make any positive proposals. The despatch, however, contained a memorandum that Buchanan, at his own discretion, could show to Sazonov. It dealt with the dangers to the Entente of Austrian attempts to win Polish support in the United States and stated:

> it might be of great use to the Allies, as the war proceeds, to have in Polish American feeling, a counter-balancing influence to the German vote in the United States, though of course no action must be taken which would arouse the suspicion that we are interfering in American politics by organizing a pro-Allies vote. It is obvious that no influence can be brought to bear on the American Poles except through Russia and equally obvious that H.M.G. must do nothing which would be distasteful to the Russian government in this connection.[69]

The memorandum ended with a statement to which both the British and the Russians could agree: 'The whole question seems to be one which must be treated from the point of view of relations with the U.S. and not from the point of view of the Polish question in Europe.'

On 1 April 1915, Spring Rice replied to the query that a counter-weight to the German vote would be most useful but that his embassy could not become involved in its formation.[70] Before Buchanan could reply, an incident in the United States added a sense of urgency to the Polish-American problem. On 5 April 1915, almost four hundred American foreign language newspapers published an appeal for an embargo on the sale of arms to the Entente. The appeal had been engineered by Louis

Hammerling, the head of the American Association of Foreign Language Newspapers. Control over the advertising accounts, which were a major source of income for these small newspapers, gave Hammerling some power over their editorial policy which enabled him to arrange for the publication and endorsement of the appeal. Of those newspapers involved, forty-eight were Polish and twenty-seven were Austrian Slav.[71] The possibility of an arms embargo resulting from such a campaign was an immediate and direct threat to the interests of the Entente. Hammerling's control over the foreign language press was a serious threat because, although most of the American Slavs were not opposed to the Entente, they could, over a period of time, be alienated from it because of the influence of their own press. If the Entente was ever to win their support, Hammerling's influence had to be destroyed.

With greater urgency, Grey addressed another despatch to Buchanan in which he emphasized that the threat of an arms embargo now made action on the Polish-American problem a military necessity. An accompanying memorandum stated:

> In general it may be said that the agitation against the export of arms is the one form of German agitation in the United States which is, on the whole, making distinct headway. The possibility that agitation will have some measure of success . . . is the one distinct danger to the relations between the Allies and the United States.[72]

The British foreign office did not want the Russians to organize the American Poles; that was neither possible nor prudent. Organization of the Poles had to be done by their own leaders. The foreign office wanted the Russians to produce propaganda on the Polish issue and to attempt to win the support of the Polish organizations by working through Polish leaders favourable to the Entente. But the appeals to Sazonov had little effect because neither he nor the Russian ambassador in Washington showed any enthusiasm for working with the American Poles.[73] Sazonov did not reject the idea, but he took no action. By 15 June 1915, the foreign office realized that further appeals to Sazonov were useless and abandoned them. It had raised the issue with some trepidation and would not continue to risk offending the Russians.

While these negotiations were in progress, the British officials were working among the other Austrian Slavs in the United States as they hoped the Russians would work among the Poles. But while the support of the Poles had yet to be won, the other Slavic minorities were already potential supporters of the Entente. The problem was how that support could be used most effectively. The British authorities wanted the various Slavic minorities to state publicly their support for the Entente and to be seen to organize for political purposes so as to offset the potential German-American influence on the American politicians.

On 11 April 1915, G. M. Trevelyan arrived in the United States on the invitation of Harvard University to speak on Serbian Relief.[74] He appeared to be merely a private citizen, although he carried with him five hundred Wellington House pamphlets on eastern Europe.[75] The original suggestion of the visit was made sometime before 9 March 1915, about the same time that Percy brought the Polish-American issue to the attention of the foreign office.[76] On 14 March 1915, Trevelyan wrote to Runciman:

> It has been settled that I am to go to America, but only if and when I am invited to lecture on Serbia etc. by Harvard or some other University. Steps are being taken to see if such an invitation can be got. Meanwhile the affair is private and I am not telling those whom it does not concern.[77]

Like Namier, Trevelyan worked for Wellington House which had, in conjunction with the foreign office, arranged the trip.[78] The invitation, arranged after it was decided to send him, was merely a cover. Reasons of security dictated that the real purpose of Trevelyan's mission was never clearly stated in any official document. Spring Rice was, for example, always concerned about the security of his reports and was therefore always circumspect in dealing with sensitive issues. He once wrote to Drummond: 'It is dangerous to give intimate personal details in writing.'[79] Since the greatest mistake of German agents in the United States during the war was to keep thorough written records, this concern for security was justified. Trevelyan's official status was secret, he was a friend of Seton-Watson, and he was a supporter of national self-determination; if the government wanted someone with great influence among the nationalities to act as a liaison between the British authorities in Washington and the various American Slavic leaders, it could not have made a better choice than G. M. Trevelyan. Despite government secrecy, a number of official references to Trevelyan's work, along with what is known of his movements in the United States, give an indication of the nature of his mission. On 1 April 1915, Spring Rice, who always claimed

that his officials could have nothing to do with the organization
of the American Slavs, wrote:

> The organization of the American Slavs here is a matter which
> they must arrange themselves. I have no doubt however that
> the advent of a gentleman like Mr. Trevelyan who can present
> the Slav cause before the American public will be of immense
> service in bringing home to them [the Slavs] the duties they
> have to the interests of their races in this continent, . . . [in
> organizing against the German-Americans].[80]

Trevelyan arrived in the United States a week after the publication of the appeal for an arms embargo. In discussing possible
measures to counteract Hammerling's campaign, such as organization of the American Slavs, Percy showed that Trevelyan was
expected to do more than discuss Serbian Relief: 'The nourish-
ment of a pan-Slav feeling of this kind cannot be much helped
on by the F.O. and it may be left in the hands of those people
who are already doing a good deal to foster it – especially Mr.
Seton-Watson and Mr. Trevelyan.'[81] It is difficult to believe that
the government was so concerned about Serbian Relief as to send
Trevelyan, particularly since the sending of lecturers to the
United States was contrary to the policy of Wellington House.
In his own report, written after his return on 22 May 1915, and
submitted to the cabinet, Trevelyan wrote: 'My only *public*
activity was lecturing on Serbia and the Austrian and Balkan
questions.' He also stated:

> . . . Croats, Serbs, Slovaks and Czechs are all strongly pro-Ally.
> I saw their leaders at Chicago and New York. These various
> branches of the Slav race are drawing together and being
> organized politically to counteract the German vote and
> influence.[82]

If Trevelyan's sole interest had been Serbian Relief and Balkan
questions, why did he contact the Czech and Slovak leaders in
Chicago and New York? According to James Stepina, the
treasurer of the Bohemian National Alliance, in their meetings
Trevelyan urged the various Slav leaders to oppose Hammerling
and those newspapers which had supported the appeal for an
arms embargo.[83] It is also probable that Trevelyan urged the
leaders of the Czechs, Slovaks, Croats and Serbs to organize their
supporters for political purposes, to co-ordinate their activities
and to work towards that union of Slavs which Namier thought

possible and the foreign office desirable. The true reason for the Trevelyan mission was probably to promote, in his own words, political consciousness among the Slavs. According to Spring Rice, his work was 'extraordinarily useful'.[84]

The work of Spring Rice on this issue is difficult to determine because his own reports cannot be accepted at face value. He always disclaimed any involvement in the organization of the various Slavic minorities because it was not diplomatically correct for official representatives of the British government to advise American citizens on the subject of American politics. Yet he never opposed Gaunt's use of the Czechs for naval intelligence. On 20 March 1915, he even recommended that Supilo should be sent, at the expense of the government, to the United States to work on the organization of the American Slavs.[85] His remarks on protocol obviously referred only to known representatives of the government and not to agents like Trevelyan who were secretly employed. He was not opposed to involvement but merely the appearance of involvement.

Possible action by Spring Rice on this problem was limited; he could not himself organize the Slavs. He was, however, in contact with the various Austrian Slavic leaders and from them learned the prevailing mood among the ethnic minorities. Much of the information he used in his reports probably came from such sources. While he might not have given them advice on American politics, he undoubtedly expressed his opinion that political organization and co-ordination among the various Slavic minorities was in their own interest in view of the political influence of the German-Americans. He may have even encouraged them.[86] By 17 April 1915, he was able to write optimistically: 'The Slavs are at last beginning to organize and are setting to work in earnest to defend themselves against the constant and virulent German attacks to which they have been exposed and which they deeply resent.'[87]

The efforts of Trevelyan and Spring Rice to use the Austrian Slavs in America against the German-Americans were supported by the propaganda campaign of Wellington House on eastern European questions which was now gaining momentum and which was to be a continuing influence throughout 1915 and 1916. Some of the political organization was done by Voska who informed Masaryk in March 1915 that contact had been established between the Czechs and Slovenes.[88] Czech agents were also active in counteracting German intrigues among the Slovaks who had been slower than the Czechs to organize.[89] By June 1915, the various Slavic minorities; Serbs, Croats, Slovaks, Czechs and Slovenes; seem to have achieved some degree of co-ordination with one another. Concerted action had been initiated to offset the influence of the German-Americans.[90] The desired Slav union now seemed possible although much still needed to be done.

Hammerling's campaign for an arms embargo was a more immediate and tangible threat to the Entente than the German-American vote. The danger could be eliminated by weakening Hammerling's hold over the foreign language press. Both Trevelyan and Spring Rice urged the leaders of the nationality organizations to repudiate Hammerling and to establish political control over their own press. On 7 April 1915, Spring Rice, who was not above veiled threats, wrote to Pupin, the most important South Slav organizer in the United States:

> I fear that friends in Europe will not fully understand how it happens that anyone however influential has been able to obtain the assent of the leaders of Slav public opinion, as represented by the newspapers, to such a declaration as we have seen printed. It would be very regrettable if this policy were to be continued.[91]

On the same day he urged the foreign office to act: 'Please draw attention of Slav and Jewish leaders in England to the disastrous result to their interests among the allied countries of allowing their national press to be misused for such purposes. Steps are being taken here.'[92] While the government had never promised national self-determination in exchange for support, it was quite clear that any group which opposed the Entente could expect nothing. The émigrés were left to draw their own conclusions. Seton-Watson was asked to bring the matter to the attention of all Czechoslovak agents going to the United States. In May 1915, apparently as a result of the efforts of Spring Rice and the foreign office, the Bohemian National Alliance and the Slovak League of America publicly repudiated any support for an arms embargo. The Bohemian National Alliance, undoubtedly under Voska's guidance, also convinced many of the Slavic newspapers to repudiate the appeal for an arms embargo they had originally endorsed.[93] This action contributed to the ultimately successful British campaign to eliminate Hammerling as a serious threat.

It was not enough, however, to stop the campaign for an arms embargo because German agents were also sabotaging the sale of arms to the Entente by promoting strikes in munitions factories. One hundred and three such strikes in a three-month period of 1915 were not pure coincidence.[94] On 10 June 1915, Spring Rice wrote to Grey: 'Violent efforts are being made by the Germans to induce the labourers employed in the arms factories to strike. The leaders of the Italians and the Slavs are doing everything to prevent it.'[95] The assistance given by the émigrés to the government in confronting this threat can be seen by a report by Arthur Nicolson which stated:

> The Foreign Office have had several rumours about strikes in the United States engineered by German agents . . . Efforts were being made some time ago among the Czech and Slovak workmen, but a good deal has been done lately by European Czech emissaries to counteract these intrigues, and the workmen of these two races are probably safe now.[96]

The nationality organizations counteracted the attempts to promote unrest in the munitions industry by warning their compatriots not to strike; much of the work being done by Voska and his agents.[97] An unsigned report in the embassy files dated 28 June 1915, probably from Gaunt, gives an indication of the type of work done by Voska:

> About two months ago at a General Meeting of the Federation of Labour at New York it was decided to have a big strike in the Ammunition Works turning out goods for the Allies. That resolution was referred to the Executive Committee in Chicago with Gompers sitting as Chairman. The result was an equal ballot . . . About ten days ago Congressman Buchanan of Illinois brought the matter up again and . . . it had been arranged to carry the resolution in favour of a strike by one vote. Fortunately Mr. Vaska [sic] (a Bohemian gentleman) got wind of it, and the vote went against them by a majority of one, though I regret to state that the two votes cost Mr. Vaska [sic] two thousand dollars apiece.[98]

The original source of the four thousand dollars was never disclosed. The document gives a sample of Voska's work for naval intelligence and substantiates, to some degree, the published accounts. Space does not permit a thorough discussion of his work on propaganda, espionage and counter-intelligence, in which he achieved a reasonable degree of success, but there can be no doubt that it was a contribution to the Entente. Until the United States entered the war, Voska continued this work which was a major aspect of the British use of the nationalities in America.

By July 1915, when it was obvious that the Russians would do nothing about the American Poles, the British authorities had achieved some success in promoting political consciousness among the Yugoslavs and Czechoslovaks in the United States. These nationalities were organizing and working in their own interests, and those of the Entente, against the German-Americans. They publicly supported the Entente and privately continued to assist the government in espionage and propaganda.[99] Although their relations continued with the admiralty, war office and Wellington House, the fact that their support had been secured and channelled into desired directions meant that they ceased to be an important issue for the foreign office. Attention was now directed towards the American Poles who were as yet uncommitted.

The American Poles were important to the Entente, because their numerical strength was greater than all of the other Slavic minorities combined.[100] The Czechs, though few in number, might be important because of their work for the government, but the Poles were a necessary part of any effective counter-balancing force to the German-American vote. More than any other Slavic minority in the United States, the Poles could become a real and important factor in American politics. During 1915 the government confined its activities on the Polish-American problem to propaganda and it does not appear as if any significant contact was established with the Polish-American organizations.[101] The government could not deal with the Poles as it had dealt with the others. Diplomatic protocol gave the initiative to the Poles who, unlike the others, did not appear willing to donate their services to the Entente.

The American Poles were disorganized and politically divided. While their leaders often favoured Austria or the Entente but were never entirely committed to either, the bulk of the Poles were neutral. Unlike the other nationalities, the Poles had a choice, albeit between the lesser of evils, because they could expect little from either the Entente or the Central powers. The American Polish community would ultimately favour whatever side offered Poland the most and therefore the leading Poles could hardly afford to commit themselves to one side as the Czechoslovaks and Yugoslavs had done.[102] If the Poles were to be used as a counter-weight to the German vote, their support had yet to be won and similar efforts by Austrian agents had to be thwarted. In competition with the Austrians, however, the British were placed in an almost impossible position by the Russian government because nothing could be offered in exchange for support. Possibly the most the British could achieve would be to neutralize Polish opinion so that it would not support the Central powers.

The competition for Polish support began in earnest over the issue of Polish relief. The idea had been discussed early in 1915, but it did not become an important issue until September, after the German occupation of Russian Poland.[103] The foreign office disliked the idea of Polish relief, assuming that it was promoted by the Germans to embarrass the Entente and win the support of the American Poles. While the British government attributed food shortages in an agricultural country like Poland to German requisitions, it could, as the blockading power, be made to appear responsible for the failure of assistance to reach Poland. Although allowing relief appeared equivalent to aiding the Central powers by making food requisitioning easier, the idea could not be entirely rejected without appearing responsible, especially to the Poles, for any ensuing starvation in Poland.

Serious negotiations on Polish relief began in January 1916 on the instigation of the Commission for Relief in Belgium and the American government, both of which attempted to mediate between the belligerents. The active role of the American government in these negotiations was an unmistakable sign of President Wilson's developing interest in the Polish problem.[104] Now the British government could not avoid the issue without risking the alienation of the American government, the Poles, and neutral opinion.[105] Throughout the negotiations, the knowledge that German agents were active in the United States trying to win Polish support and that they would use this issue for that purpose inspired the foreign office to handle the negotiations with the greatest care so as to throw the blame for the failure of any relief programme on the Central powers.[106] With that in mind the Entente accepted, on 10 May 1916, a programme for relief suggested by the American government on condition that the Central powers cease requisitioning food in occupied Poland. To this offer the German government never replied, and although the mediators continued to work for Polish relief, the stalemate between the belligerents was never overcome. By conditionally accepting the American programme, the British government was able to prevent Polish relief on unacceptable terms while avoiding the appearance of responsibility for its failure. Through the careful handling of these negotiations, it avoided alienating the Poles, but it is doubtful whether it won any additional Polish support.

During the negotiations, the propaganda of Wellington House on issues related to Poland increased. It was probably during this period that Namier began, on behalf of Wellington House, to use the Polish Information Committee for the distribution of pamphlets in the United States. After the negotiations, the production of Polish propaganda became intensive and continued well into 1917.[107] It was accompanied by an equally intensive German propaganda campaign and, while each campaign might have neutralized the effect of the other on the Polish Americans, the combined effect of all of the propaganda strengthened the Poles in the United States by bringing their cause to the attention of the general public. The issue of Polish relief marked the real beginning of American sympathy for the Polish cause.[108]

The negotiations also led to contacts between the British embassy and Polish leaders like Jan Smulski and Ignacy Paderewski.[109] In May 1916, Spring Rice arranged for one of Paderewski's supporters to visit internment camps in Canada to arrange for the release of interned Poles; a step which usually signified the development of close relations between the government and the nationality organizations.[110] But, although contact was established, close relations did not develop as they did with the other nationalities. The others offered concrete assistance unconditionally whereas the Poles offered nominal support in exchange for concessions on Polish relief. Since the government did not want any programme for Polish relief to succeed, it merely wanted to cast the blame for failure on the Germans, vague promises of Polish support were not worth such concessions.[111] Until at least September 1916, there is no evidence of any Polish organization in the United States co-operating with or assisting the British authorities as the Czechoslovaks and Yugoslavs had been doing for over a year. Paderewski and Smulski warned Spring Rice that unless concessions were made on Polish relief the mass of the Poles might turn against the Entente.[112] These warnings made the officials careful but did not endear them to the Poles. Along with the reports of the pro-Austrian activities of many Poles, they gave the British officials the impression that the

Poles were politically unstable and, unlike the others, not entirely trustworthy.[113]

If British policy on Polish relief and the accompanying propaganda had any effect on Polish-American opinion, it was not obvious to the British authorities. The activities of enemy agents may have been thwarted and the status quo of Polish opinion maintained, but it did not appear as if Polish support had been won. On 1 July 1916, Spring Rice wrote of the Polish vote:

> The result is rather uncertain – they drift one way or the other. But they are not *solidaire* with either one side or the other and though Catholic are Slav. But the general result is vague; you cannot say for certain which way a Pole will go.[114]

Throughout 1916 the American presidential election, due in November, was a major preoccupation of Spring Rice. Wilson, a Democrat, was running for his second term against the Republican candidate Charles E. Hughes, a former member of the supreme court. Had the candidates favoured different sides in the war, the election would have had a great significance for the belligerents who might have been inspired to interfere in American politics. But on 21 July 1916, Spring Rice wrote to Grey:

> As I have frequently had occasion to observe the British Government has no interest in the success of either party. The platforms do not differ in any essential point . . . Neither one candidate nor the other can be said to have strong leanings towards either one party or the other in the European conflict. They both publicly profess absolute neutrality.[115]

The interests of the Entente were not bound to either candidate although some officials might have preferred Wilson. The government, regardless of such preferences, took pains to appear completely disinterested in the election. In October 1916, the foreign office warned members of the cabinet not to give any interviews to American newspapers and warned the British press to make no comment on the American election.[116]

There is, indeed, no evidence of any involvement in the promotion of either of the candidates. On 2 June 1916, Gaunt wrote to Spring Rice that he had been asked, probably by the Czechoslovaks and Yugoslavs, which candidate was to be supported.[117] Spring Rice replied: 'Say they are better judges than we are and we must not give any advice as principle we go on is non-

interference as against German interference. Please destroy draft
of your tel. No. 79 at once by fire.'[118]

Although the outcome of the election was a matter of indifference, Spring Rice was deeply concerned about the election campaign. From January until November he sent countless despatches
to the foreign office concerning the growing strength of the
German-American vote and its effect on the campaign.[119] To the
parliamentary under-secretary of state and minister of blockade,
Lord Robert Cecil, he wrote on 12 February 1916: 'The govern-
ing fact in the situation is that the German-American voters are
organized and the foreigners are not. This gives a large organized
mass like that of the Germans . . . a preponderating influence in
the country.'[120]

Spring Rice was concerned not about who would win, but how
they would win. He feared that one of the candidates, in order
to gain the support of the German-Americans, would secretly
agree to adopt certain pro-German policies.[121] This fear was reinforced by the apparent danger that the Irish, Jewish, Hungarian,
Catholic and Polish voters would ally with the German-Americans to form a voting bloc so large that no politician could afford
to overlook it.[122] On 14 July 1916, he wrote to Lord Hardinge,
who had replaced Nicolson as permanent under-secretary of
state: 'Somebody said that the German vote was like a Ford car
or a mistress. More people would like to have it than to be seen
with it.'[123]

The obvious way to counteract this threat was not to support
one of the candidates but to create a counterweight to the German vote so that none of the politicians would benefit by a deal
with the German-Americans. The factions would cancel out one
another, and the candidates would be able to retain their position
of neutrality. The Czechoslovaks and Yugoslavs were already a
counterweight but of insufficient size to be important. The solution to the problem lay with the Poles.

On 6 July 1916, Drummond asked Rodd to arrange a visit to
the Vatican for Count Horodyski. He explained that the visit was
important because of the Polish vote in the United States.[124] A
day later, after reading one of Spring Rice's pessimistic despatches, he wrote to Grey:

> I do not think we need at all despair of getting the Polish
> vote in the United States generally on the side of the Allies
> when the time comes for the Presidential elections . . . the

Austrians have been working hard among the Poles in the
U.S. and have had some success, but not of such a character
that when the right moment arrives for our friends to go to
work, which I am told is just before the elections, the position
cannot be completely changed in the Allies favour.[125]

On 23 August 1916, Drummond asked Spring Rice about the
possibility of Horodyski being sent to the United States to work
on the Polish vote.[126] Spring Rice replied that British officials
could not advise American citizens on how to vote and that the
outcome of the election did not matter, but he added: 'What is
required is a body of voters animated by resolve to counteract
weight of German vote which at present is prevailing factor.
Change the wind and you will change the weathercock.'[127]
Arrangements had already been made with the war office to
send Horodyski to the United States, at the expense of the
government to recruit Poles for the Canadian army. Drummond
instructed Horodyski that he was not, while recruiting in the
United States, a representative of the British government. In a
report to Grey on these instructions, he wrote:

> . . . I told him that while we would of course be very glad to
> see the Polish vote consolidated in order to counteract the
> German vote, we could not possibly offer any advice as to on
> which side it should be cast and that if he wished to do
> anything he had better go out there and judge for himself,
> but that in this case also it must be perfectly clear that he was
> not acting as our agent in any way, nor could we provide for
> any expenditure.[128]

This description of Horodyski's status, probably the result of
Drummond's desire for secrecy, cannot for a moment be taken
seriously. Recruiting of Poles in the United States for service in
the armies of the Entente was a political activity requiring
organization. The distinction between organization for enlistment and organization for the election was completely artificial.
While not a representative of the government, Horodyski was its
paid agent. Since it must have been perfectly obvious that if sent
to the United States he would become involved in political
organization for the election, officials like Drummond, who sent
him, could not entirely disclaim responsibility for his subsequent
action regardless of the conditions which they appeared to stipu-
late prior to his departure. Horodyski arrived in the United

States in October 1916 and did some political work among the Polish voters, although the details cannot be determined.[129] Gaunt acted as his official contact, and it is no coincidence that shortly after his arrival Paderewski's organization, the Polish National Alliance, began to distribute British propaganda.[130] After the election Horodyski claimed, with some accuracy, that Wilson was re-elected by the Polish vote.[131] Horodyski's mission was significant as the first important example of co-operation between the government and some of the Polish organizations in the United States.

During 1915 and 1916 the British government became deeply involved with the nationality organizations, not because it accepted their aims but because it needed them as weapons of war. This involvement was related more to the United States than to Europe because it resulted from the competition for American support. To the British the use of the nationalities seemed necessary in order to counteract German initiatives. The organization of the German-American vote, the threat of an arms embargo, and the promotion of strikes in munitions factories all demanded a response from the British government whose agents naturally turned to the other minorities in the United States as convenient weapons against the German-Americans. This Anglo-German competition in the United States in turn affected American politics.

In 1914, the Yugoslav, Czechoslovak and Polish minorities in the United States, being unorganized and politically passive, were not sufficiently important factors in American politics to influence American government policy. After the outbreak of war the situation began to change because these national minorities underwent a political awakening which led to organization for the purpose of influencing American politics. Although the potential influence of the Czechoslovaks and Yugoslavs was severely limited by their size, by the end of 1916, the Poles had become a real and important factor in American politics. The interest of the American government in Polish relief showed that it was aware of the importance of the Polish vote.

National self-determination as a specific political programme for eastern Europe was not an indigenous American idea, but one imported from Europe by the belligerents and the émigrés. The interest of the American public in national self-determination for eastern Europe was the product of the work of the émigrés as well as the propaganda which resulted from the competition between the belligerents for American support. The growth of the political power of the nationalities and the interest of the general public in their cause inspired American politicians, for the first time, to interest themselves in the question.

No single group was solely responsible for the development of these general trends in American politics. But in the distribution of propaganda and in the assistance and encouragement given to the nationality organizations the British government made a substantial contribution to the spread of the idea of national self-determination and to the growth of the nationality organizations. In doing so, the government helped to create conditions which, in future, it could not overlook in the formation of foreign policy.

4 : WAR AIMS, 1916

During 1915 the relations between the government and the Yugoslavs had centred on the Balkans, those with the Czechoslovaks and Poles on the United States. In the conduct of these relations the nationalities sought support for their war aims while the officials, avoiding the whole question of aims, saw the nationalities only as weapons of war. Throughout 1916, despite increased discussion of war aims, the policy of the government on the future of eastern Europe remained unchanged – the retention of the greatest flexibility for the future formulation of policy by avoidance of open support for any of the basic alternatives and avoidance of all commitments unnecessary to the conduct of the war. As in the Italian negotiations, commitments would be dictated only by strategic necessity. While government policy remained static, however, the situation was evolving, if not towards commitments, at least towards the reduction of Britain's future alternatives in eastern Europe. Contacts between émigrés and officials continued to develop so that while policy did not change, many of the individuals who might later influence policy began to develop, often under the influence of the émigrés and their work for the government, their own personal preferences on the question of national self-determination. More significantly, the co-operation between the government and the émigrés, by its success, began to influence the conditions under which the Entente waged war. By adjusting to the newly created conditions according to calculations of strategic necessity, the British government eventually limited to some degree those future alternatives most detrimental to the cause of national self-determination. While the émigrés had no reason, therefore, to rejoice over the nature of British policy, the course of the war seemed to be moving in their favour and forcing the government along with it.

The failure of the Balkan negotiations brought an end to serious consideration or active support of the Yugoslav programme. These negotiations had enabled the Yugoslavs, in contrast to the Poles and Czechoslovaks, to make extraordinary progress in establishing relations with and presenting their programme to the government. The foreign office had even supported the idea of the creation of some form of Yugoslav state but had been unwilling to pursue the issue in the face of opposition from Serbia and Italy. That opposition was to remain a constant obstacle preventing the British government from giving any open support to the Yugoslavs. Nevertheless, the attitude of the foreign office towards the concept of a Yugoslav state changed very little after the end of the negotiations. While no support was given to the Yugoslav programme, it remained the dominant preference of the foreign office insofar as it was consistent with the treaty of London.[1] In May 1916, following a conversation with Paul Miliukov, a leading Russian Constitutional Democrat, Grey wrote to Buchanan: 'M. Miliukof told me that M. Sazonof wished the Slav element to be retained in Austria to neutralise the German element. I said personally I had favoured the liberation of the Slav element.'[2]

The amount of contact between the Yugoslav Committee and the government declined during 1916 because there were fewer issues of mutual interest after the end of the Balkan negotiations and because the Serbian government pre-empted the committee's position. With the acquiescence of the Yugoslav Committee the Serbian government claimed a prerogative in South Slav affairs which the British government would not challenge. Contact between the committee and the government was weakened further in June 1916 when Supilo, who had hitherto conducted Anglo-Yugoslav relations, resigned in protest over the committee's subservience to the Serbian government. Throughout 1916, however, those relations which did exist between the Yugoslavs and the government were cordial although they produced no significant changes in the already pro-Yugoslav attitudes of the officials. The Italian government made relations with the Yugoslavs difficult, but it is significant that the foreign office, despite repeated requests from the Italian government, refused to place any limits on Yugoslav propaganda.[3] For the present nothing could be done, but, if changes in the Balkans made a Yugoslav state possible, it would not be opposed by the British government.

The Czechs, without an immediate issue to focus attention on their cause, had much greater difficulty than the Yugoslavs in presenting their views to the foreign office. Few had heard of the

Czechoslovaks: when J. D. Gregory suggested, in March 1915, the creation of Polish and Bohemian states, Drummond could only comment: 'The proposals put forward in the enclosure seem to me somewhat fantastic.'[4]

On 1 May 1915, Seton-Watson submitted to the foreign office an essay by Masaryk, entitled 'Independent Bohemia', designed to 'facilitate an understanding of the Bohemian Question'. The essay, a thorough exposition of the Czechoslovak case, listed the advantages of such a state and posing every possible objection countered each in turn. Masaryk proposed the union of Bohemia, Moravia, Silesia and the Slovak areas of Hungary into a democratic and constitutional Czechoslovak monarchy. For the sceptics he pointed out that this state would be larger than either Sweden or Norway and, while landlocked, would, like Switzerland, be able to survive. He argued that, since Austria-Hungary was no longer an independent Great Power but merely a German vassal, the creation of an anti-German Czechoslovak state would benefit the Entente at the expense of Germany. In his own words: 'Every weakening of Austria is a weakening of Germany.' He also maintained that an independent Czechoslovakia, in conjunction with an independent Yugoslavia, would act as an effective barrier to the German drive towards the Near East.[5]

The obvious impossibility of acting on Masaryk's programme in the foreseeable future, combined with what must have appeared in 1915 to be the sheer incredibility of his proposals, dictated a cautious but not hostile reaction from the foreign office. On the file Clerk wrote: 'The Allies have a long way to go before the points in this memo can come up for their practical consideration, but Prof. Masaryk is a recognised leader of Czech political thought and this paper should be borne in mind.' Arthur Nicolson was more sceptical, but not hostile: 'Mr. Masaryk is the leader, if I am not mistaken, of the young Czechs, and can hardly be considered an exponent of the views of the more moderate sections of the Czech party. Still he is an important man.'[6]

As might be expected, no action followed, but good relations, encouraged by the foreign office, continued with the Czechs who were already co-operating with other branches of the government. Although such co-operation might be expected to have influenced the attitude of the foreign office, and might have done so, there is little evidence of it during 1916. But, at best, time was necessary for such influence to have effect. It is also probable that during this period the full extent of Czech co-operation, related as it was to sensitive issues, was not widely known in the foreign office.

The Czech issue was not seriously discussed again until August 1916, when the Czechoslovak and Yugoslav émigrés requested a letter of support from the prime minister to be read at a public meeting on the anniversary of the outbreak of war. Since the émigrés were planning to pass a resolution proposing the destruction of the Habsburg monarchy, Grey wrote to Masaryk:

> I am afraid that the text of the proposed Resolution, . . . goes beyond any official pronouncement hitherto made in this or any Allied Country, and the Prime Minister could scarcely send an official letter on an occasion of this kind which would be tantamount to an endorsement by him of a policy which has not yet been discussed by the Allies.[7]

It is an indication of the attitude of the foreign office towards the Czechs and their cause that the idea was rejected, not because of the Czechs, or for that matter the Habsburgs, but because, the Yugoslavs being involved, such a letter might offend the Italian government.[8]

Unlike the Yugoslavs and the Czechs, the Polish nationalists were not united. Among the numerous parties in Poland there were two easily recognizable and antagonistic groups which adhered to quite different policies for the creation of a Polish state and which competed with each other for recognition abroad and support at home. The left wing, which centred around the Polish Socialist party, was led by Józef Pilsudski and was essentially anti-Russian. While neither pro-German nor pro-Austrian, Pilsudski was prepared to undertake limited co-operation with the Central powers against Russia because he believed that the defeat of Russia was necessarily the first step in the liberation of Poland. He gambled that the Central powers would collapse shortly after Russia, thus creating a momentary power vacuum in which a Polish state could be established. Pilsudski's opposition, the Polish right wing, consisted of a coalition of the Realists and the National Democrats under the leadership of Roman Dmowski. He believed Germany to be the greatest threat to the Polish nation and, dismissing Pilsudski's idea of the simultaneous defeat of Russia and the Central powers, maintained that some form of Polish independence could only be achieved in co-operation with the Russian government. He was prepared, therefore, to pursue Polish independence through co-operation with the Entente. Although sharply divided in their opinions about Russia, neither Polish faction was hostile to Britain or France. Indeed, both competed for their recognition and support. In turn, the British government had no reason to assume that Pilsudski was an enemy unless it accepted the unlikely assumption that the enemies of Russia were, by definition, the enemies of Britain.[9]

Wherever there were Poles the political split existed, although in various manifestations. In Britain, at the beginning of the war, the Polish Left had the advantage over its competitors, through control of the Polish Information Committee, of superior organization: the right-wing was represented only by Horodyski and Alma-Tadema. British officials, at this time unaware of the split and incapable of distinguishing one Polish politician from another, were willing to accept the assistance of Polish émigrés regardless of their political orientation. Horodyski worked for the foreign office while the Polish Information Committee worked with the Metropolitan Police and Wellington House.[10] Regardless of being anti-Russian, the committee was prepared to co-operate with the British government, and was initially more successful than its opponents in establishing relations. But this early success was not to go unchallenged once Dmowski's supporters were sufficiently organized.

British officials first became aware of the split in Polish politics and its significance for their own interests through developments in America where the Polish Left adopted a pro-Austrian attitude thus creating a considerable degree of uneasiness among British officials.[11] These Poles were justifiably considered as enemies of the Entente and treated as such. In contrast, the Polish Right under Smulski and Paderewski established relations with Spring Rice and began to co-operate with the Entente after Horodyski's arrival in the United States. As a result of the activities of pro-Austrian Poles in the United States British officials began to view all Polish émigrés, particularly those of the Left like Pilsudski's supporters in Britain, with a degree of suspicion never shown towards the Yugoslavs or Czechoslovaks. This suspicion was not always justified because, although the Polish Right in the United States and the countries of the Entente formed one loosely united coalition and might, therefore, be assumed to represent one policy, the left-wing Poles in Britain do not appear to have been in contact with their American counterparts and could not, therefore, be associated with their action.[12] Contact with the pro-Austrian Poles in the United States or the adoption of a pro-Austrian policy would have discredited the Polish Left in Britain and would have led to internment. But, even in the absence of such contact, the left-wing Poles in Britain were always more vulnerable than their right-wing opponents to charges of being pro-Austrian, thus giving the right-wing a natural advantage, which they did not hesitate to use, in the competition for British support.

During 1915 Alma-Tadema began to attack the established position of the Polish Information Committee in the hope of replacing it with her own organization, the Polish Exiles Protection, in dealings with the authorities on the subject of enemy aliens. Whatever organization was used by the authorities to handle Polish aliens had great power because it could arrange for the release of its supporters and the internment of its opponents. Alma-Tadema was in a strong position and had little difficulty in attacking the committee.[13]

In 1914 the home office had only reluctantly accepted the use of the Polish Information Committee and was now only too willing to reconsider the arrangements for Polish aliens. Its prejudice against the committee was never explained, but it may have resulted from the feeling that the committee and its members were not entirely respectable. In contrast, Alma-Tadema had a social position and influential friends like John Buchan, Arthur Steel-Maitland and Arthur Nicolson.[14] As a follower of Dmowski, she also had the support of the Russian embassy which alone was enough to turn the scales in her favour. When she approached the home office, she justified the replacement of the committee by accusing its members of accepting bribes and of releasing aliens dangerous to the Entente. She offered no evidence to substantiate these charges, but that did not deter the home office from the immediate resolve to replace the committee with the Polish Exiles Protection.[15]

The Metropolitan Police, who were working with the committee and who were more particular on the question of evidence, opposed the change. Since Alma-Tadema's accusations were only supported by the testimony of a former member of the committee, Rosco de Bogdanowicz, who the police considered the most disreputable, their refusal to believe these accusations was justified. The police only bowed to the decision of the home office after consulting Wickham Steed and after it was obvious that Alma-Tadema had the support of the Russian embassy.[16] By May

1916, the Polish Exiles Protection was the recognized committee for consultation on the release of interned Poles. It was the first victory for Dmowski in his struggle to eliminate his Polish opponents in Britain.

At the request of the home office, Alma-Tadema's accusations led to investigations by Scotland Yard and military intelligence (M.I.5) of the members of the Polish Information Committee.[17] Although no evidence was found, Alma-Tadema had effectively cast a pall of suspicion over the committee and its associates which never completely disappeared. Since the committee was never confronted with these accusations, it had no opportunity to defend itself.

Similar attempts seem to have been made late in 1916 to destroy the relationship between the Polish Information Committee and Wellington House.[18] Namier, who had established the connection, was able to thwart this attempt by showing that the committee was only used as an addressing agency and could not possibly be a threat to the work of Wellington House.[19] The arrangement was maintained although Wellington House also began to distribute propaganda through the Polish Relief Fund, another of Alma-Tadema's organizations.[20]

During 1915 and 1916 the foreign office strictly adhered to the position that Poland was a Russian question. The only public statement that showed any British interest in Poland came on 2 March 1915, when Grey expressed, in the house of commons, sympathy with Grand Duke Nikolai Nikolaievich's proclamation to the Poles.[21] But when the issue again arose in the House in August 1916, Cecil stated: 'It is not the intention of His Majesty's Government to make any recommendation on a matter of internal policy of another State.'[22] The government not only maintained a public stance thoroughly consistent with the wishes of the Russian government but also undertook no steps to influence Russian policy. For example, when the foreign office urged the Russians to act on the Polish-American question in the spring of 1915, it made no reference to any possible change in Russia's Polish policy. Again in March 1916, when Dmowski urged the foreign office to act on the Polish question, the suggestion was not only completely rejected but also Buchanan was specifically instructed to avoid any discussion of the Polish issue.[23] The wisdom of this decision was shown when the French ambassador approached Sazonov on the subject and only succeeded in provoking a violent outburst of temper.[24]

The British government justifiably refused to jeopardize unnecessarily its relations with an ally as important as Russia. Even if the risk had been slight, which is doubtful, the government would have been irresponsible to accept it while engaged in what appeared to be a war for survival. Grey feared that if provoked on the Polish issue Russia would make peace with the Central powers. In August 1916, he noted that the German government might use the Polish issue to obtain a separate peace with Russia.[25] Later he wrote: 'For England and France to intervene further [in the Polish question] would be to split with Russia and to destroy all chance of victory by the Allies . . .'[26]

In spite of official policy, the foreign office always hoped that the Russian government, to win Polish support, would voluntarily modify its Polish policy. In May 1915, Grey wrote to Buchanan about his conversation with Miliukov:

> I said it was hardly for us to make suggestions about Poland.
> I hoped Russia would fulfil in a liberal spirit, the proclamation of autonomy that she had issued at the beginning of the war.
> I was sure there would be disappointment here if that was not done.[27]

A more liberal Russian policy on Poland might solve the Polish-American problem which perplexed British officials throughout 1915 and 1916. It might also indirectly strengthen the Russian war effort and thwart the widely rumoured German efforts to win support in Poland.[28] According to Lord Hardinge of Penshurst, who had replaced Nicolson as permanent under-secretary of state

> It is so unfortunate that the Russians are so blind to their own interests that they are doing absolutely nothing at present to conciliate Polish opinion, which, in spite of the inborn hatred of Germany in Poland, is slowly but steadily veering round to Germany.[29]

Despite the very real and sincere desire in the foreign office for changes in Russian policy, there was nothing that could be done. But to offset the danger of losing Polish support inherent in that policy, the foreign office promoted relations with the Polish émigrés within the limits allowed by the attitude of the Russian government but without its support. From the very beginning of the war the foreign office and its diplomatic agents had been approached by numerous, often insignificant, Polish émigrés, but close relations had not been established with any particular faction. Alma-Tadema's warnings in September 1914 had created a suspicion in the foreign office about the Polish Information Committee which prevented it from establishing a pre-eminent position as it had done with the home office.[30]

In March 1915, August Zaleski, Pilsudski's representative and a member of the Polish Progressive party, arrived in Britain to assume the leadership of the left wing Poles. Zaleski was a close friend of Namier with whom he had been a student at the London School of Economics and Political Science and, through contacts with Seton-Watson and Burrows, he was, to some extent, assimilated into that group of émigrés and academics, centred around Seton-Watson and Wickham Steed, who worked for national self-determination.[31] On 23 March 1915, Zaleski explained Pilsudski's programme to Drummond and submitted to the foreign office a memorandum which explained that, while not anti-British, Pilsudski was anti-Russian and was working for the complete independence of Poland.[32] Zaleski received little attention and was denied the facilities, which he had requested, to travel to Switzerland.[33] The foreign office was not hostile to Zaleski, but there seemed to be no immediate advantage in assisting him. According to Percy: 'He is probably not entitled to more consideration than a host of other Poles.'[34] The most significant aspect of this brief encounter was that Zaleski's obvious anti-Russian bias caused neither comment nor opposition.

In November 1915 Dmowski arrived in London seeking British and French support. He had attempted through the Russian government to find a solution to the Polish problem such as autonomy within the Russian empire. Now disillusioned with Russia, he sought the internationalization of the Polish issue which he hoped would lead not to autonomy but to independence.[35] Opinion in the foreign office on Dmowski was divided. According to Percy:

> It would, I think, be well if we kept clear as far as possible of Mr. Dmowski who is hanging about London. I do not know him and I do not know what his 'game' is, but I do know that he has been informing all the Poles in London that he is in the confidence of the F.O. and has been helping us to draft our 'notes to Germany about the relief of the population of Russian Poland'.[36]

In the foreign office Percy tended to be a spokesman for Namier, who was to be Dmowski's most determined antagonist, and this minute may have reflected Namier's opinion.[37] Arthur Nicolson, who had known Dmowski in St Petersburg and probably preferred him to other Polish émigrés because he appeared pro-Russian, reacted strongly to this minute by writing a defence of Dmowski who, he claimed, was an exception among Polish politicians.[38] Percy remained unconvinced, but Nicolson's friendship ensured Dmowski access to the foreign office.[39]

Dmowski had an advantage over other Polish émigrés in that, as the leader of the Polish members of the second Duma, he was a recognized politician representing a considerable segment of Polish opinion. He could not be dismissed as Zaleski and others had been. Although he was becoming more anti-Russian, a fact probably not fully appreciated by the foreign office, he appeared to be, as the leader of the pro-Russian faction, the safest émigré with whom the British government could deal.[40] In March 1916, Dmowski submitted a memorandum to the foreign office recommending the internationalization of the Polish problem. He was careful to avoid the difficult question of the future structure of Poland but appears to have made verbal references to a Poland sufficiently independent to have its own king and army. Unlike other Polish memoranda, it was read by most of the members of the war department and even sent to Lord Lansdowne, a member of the cabinet.[41] Contrary to Dmowski's hopes, no action was taken in Petrograd, but when Grey instructed Nicolson to consult Benckendorff on the Polish problem, he was undertaking more action than had been inspired by any previous Polish memorandum.[42]

In March 1916, a conference of Polish émigrés in Lausanne, attended by Dmowski, decided unanimously to work for the internationalization of the Polish issue. As a result of Dmowski's activities during this conference, Namier stated in a press summary for Wellington House that Dmowski had become pro-Austrian and had abandoned his former principles. In these press summaries, Namier freely expressed his personal opinions both on the Polish émigrés and the attitude the government should adopt towards them. These opinions were pro-Russian and were entirely consistent with the British policy that Poland was an internal Russian problem beyond the scope of British foreign policy. By discussing matters of foreign policy in his press summaries, Namier obviously went beyond the limited prerogatives of his own rather unimportant office. But in the past his advice had been sound and had been of value to the government because he was pre-eminent among the officials for his knowledge of Poland. On this occasion, however, he went too far.

Someone in the government showed the report to Dmowski who immediately complained to Nicolson.[43] Nicolson protested in writing to Grey and added: "I hear that M. Namier is employed at Wellington House, I remember Miss Alma-Tadema warned me about him. And I believe Mr. Gregory's Austrian Polish friend [Horodyski] has no high opinion of him.'[44] Dmowski, Horodyski and Alma-Tadema had good reason to dislike Namier, who reciprocated in kind: 'Polish politicians in general incline towards being unbalanced and are easily swayed, and their politics are frequently tortuous and dangerous . . .'[45] It is incredible, however, that Nicolson accepted without question these accusations against a government official. The result was that Namier was warned to restrict himself in future to strict press summaries.[46] But if Dmowski thought that he had eliminated his 'Polish Austrian Jewish' antagonist, he was very much mistaken. Indeed, in Namier Dmowski had a particularly dangerous enemy because of his intelligence, his pugnacity and his determination.

Another incident similarly reflects the influence of Dmowski's supporters. In May 1916, Clerk was approached by Retinger, an independent, who had been the first Polish émigré to contact the foreign office in 1914 and who now proposed that Britain and France should finance a Polish resistance movement in Austria.[47] To this Nicolson replied:

> Our attitude is to consider the future of Poland chiefly a
> Russian question; and I would deprecate any encouragement
> to the numerous Polish emissaries who are wandering about
> with cut and dried schemes of their own. I understand that
> Dr. Rettinger [*sic*] is of small account among Poles.[48]

Despite Nicolson's attitude and although the proposal had little chance of success as it went far beyond anything yet considered by the government, it was not immediately rejected.[49] Clerk, who had no particular bias on the Polish question but was sympathetic to national self-determination, seemed somewhat interested. A decision on the proposal was still pending when, on 12 June 1916, Drummond wrote the following minute:

> Count Horodyski spoke to me yesterday with regard to M. M.
> Nemir [*sic*], Zaleski and Retinger. He said that he thought that
> these three gentlemen were, perhaps unwittingly, being used

for pro-Austrian purposes and he urged that their correspondence should be closely watched and that it was desirable
that they should not be allowed to travel about but should be
confined to this country.[50]

Horodyski, in supplying no evidence for this accusation, was
following Alma-Tadema's tactics of slander recently used with
considerable success on the home office. In Namier's case, as a
British subject, it was virtually an accusation of treason. Like
Nicolson in the previous incident, Drummond accepted the truth
of these accusations without question and without the slightest
consideration that Horodyski might have some ulterior motive in
slandering his opponents. On 14 June 1916, the foreign office
informed M.I.5 of the accusation against Zaleski, Retinger and
Namier, and although an investigation followed, the results were
inconclusive. Drummond also informed Cecil and added: 'I do
not like the way M. Namier is always trying to have a hit at M.
Dmowski who I believe to be entirely reliable and a strong pro-
Ally.' Cecil agreed but added: 'All the same Dmowski is rather
too clever for my taste.'[51]

Horodyski's accusation discredited Retinger and destroyed any
chance that his proposal might be accepted. To avoid alienating
Retinger, the foreign office did not actually reject the proposal but
only gave a polite, non-committal reply.[52] The same sequence was
re-enacted in December 1916 when Retinger again approached a
British official and Drummond responded by issuing instructions
that all relations with him were to cease.[53] This incident shows
the degree of influence acquired by Horodyski through his work
for the foreign office and the complete willingness of some members of the foreign office, because he had proven his loyalty, to
accept his views without any critical analysis.

Although Nicolson, Drummond and Gregory supported
Dmowski, Percy remained in opposition. On 5 July 1916, he wrote
to Clerk:

There are two opinions about Dmowski – one that with him
and the pro-Russian party lies all hope for Poland – the other
that he is a self-seeking politician surrounded by all that is
least efficient, least trustworthy and most effete in Poland.
Officially the first attitude is the only one we can adopt, but as
it isn't a very sound one, probably, it seems best that we
shouldn't adopt any attitude at all.[54]

In this dispute, although he might have been tempted to agree with Percy, Clerk remained neutral. Although continuing to defend Namier against the attacks of other officials, Percy could not, as a minor official, effectively oppose those who supported Dmowski. Power among the permanent officials obviously rested with Dmowski's supporters.

The Namier–Dmowski feud arose again in June 1916 when the Russian government, to discredit Dmowski, published a report of his activities in Lausanne containing accusations similar to those made by Namier. On 30 June 1916, the Polish Club in Russia, probably at Dmowski's instigation, published a refutation of these accusations which stated: 'The author of accusations against R. Dmowski . . . is a certain Namier, who has recently been unmasked in London by the British Government authorities.'[55] The secrecy surrounding Namier, as an employee of Wellington House, must have given Dmowski the false impression that he had actually eliminated his antagonist. On 23 August 1915, in response to this attack on Namier, Drummond wrote Buchanan:

> We naturally do not want to identify ourselves with anything hostile to Dmowski or take sides in these Polish squabbles at all but as Namier wrote what he did write with the sanction of his immediate official superior it seems fair that he should be protected as far as possible.

Drummond seems to have adopted, for no apparent reason, a more objective attitude towards the Namier–Dmowski feud. The following statements had been deleted from the final draft of the despatch:

> Long before this time Dmowski had tried to throw suspicion on Namier and he appears, for a variety of reasons, to have his knife into him . . . We have no doubts as to Namier and his information has been very useful to us in many ways. The feud between him and Dmowski is probably due to a question of 'Semiticism' . . .[56]

While Namier's attacks on Dmowski were based on reasons of foreign policy, he might have been influenced by Dmowski's open and rabid anti-semitism. When Buchanan replied that a Galician Jew was a very unsuitable person to advise on Polish policy because the Jews in that area were notoriously pro-Austrian,

Drummond merely dropped the issue. By this time Percy had convinced him that Namier's views were perfectly consistent with official British policy.[57]

These episodes, in a dispute which was to continue until the end of the war, showed the influence acquired by the National Democrats over the foreign office. Dmowski and Alma-Tadema had influence over Nicolson who, like Grey, preferred the idea of a united, autonomous Poland within Russia but would not have gone further and would certainly not favour an anti-Russian Polish policy. Horodyski, because of his services, had influence over Drummond and Gregory who were the strongest Polish advocates in the foreign office and who probably preferred complete independence. Both Drummond and Gregory were Catholic and, although in Drummond's case it is uncertain, there can be no doubt that Gregory, nicknamed the Jesuit, saw the Poles as the defenders of Catholicism against Russian Orthodoxy.[58] Namier thought that the Poles were useful for propaganda but that relations with the émigrés were inconsistent with official policy. Unlike Nicolson, who favoured Dmowski above other émigrés because he appeared pro-Russian, Namier was aware that Dmowski was moving towards a more radical independence policy which made him, in terms of British policy towards Russia, no different than the other émigrés. Because he had only the support of Percy, who could scarcely challenge Drummond and Nicolson, he could not change the dominant trend in the foreign office. His position was also weak because the secrecy of Wellington House tended to reduce his official status and his Jewish origins cast doubt on his expertise. During 1916, the National Democrats became the major Polish influence on the foreign office. At the same time, a National Democratic organization replaced the Polish Information Committee as the recognized authority on Polish aliens. Ruthless and unscrupulous tactics had proven successful. On 30 November 1916, Seton-Watson, who preferred Zaleski to Dmowski, wrote:

> the Russophil Poles here – I won't mention names – have been engaged for over a year on a whole series of extremely underhand intrigues against our people . . . they affect King's College [where Zaleski taught Polish], the F.O. and our propaganda in neutral countries.[59]

Dmowski had established influence over the foreign office while opposing the established policy of the government by proposing the internationalization of the Polish issue. Namier lost influence and was even accused of treason by consistently supporting the official British policy that Poland was an internal Russian question. Nothing shows more clearly the divergence between official policy and the personal preferences of the pro-Polish officials like Drummond, Gregory and Nicolson. While the government refused to support the internationalization of the Polish issue, the dominant preference of the foreign office varied between a united, autonomous Poland within Russia to the more radical policy of Polish independence.

During the summer of 1916, the British government for the first time, seriously considered the problem of war aims. The discussion of these aims was prompted by two aspects of the general strategic situation. During the spring of 1916, the belief was widespread in the government, based on numerous reports, that President Wilson would attempt to mediate in the European conflict. Before the government could respond to such an initiative, some formulation of aims was necessary. In addition, the military prospects of the Entente in the spring and summer of 1916, based on the Somme offensive, the Brusilov offensive and the Rumanian entry into the war, created a general but shortlived feeling of optimism conducive to the study of war aims. Under these general conditions, the impetus to discuss these aims apparently developed simultaneously but separately in various branches of the government.[60]

Since the beginning of the war, the foreign office, under the influence of Nicolson, had avoided any systematic study or discussion of war aims. Hardinge, who replaced Nicolson in June 1916, reversed this policy. He established a committee, under Sir William Tyrrell, a senior clerk, and Sir Ralph Paget, an assistant under-secretary, to undertake a thorough review of possible war aims.[61] Excluding the text of the final report, there is no evidence on the structure of the committee, the documents it used or how it reached its conclusions. In some cases, however, the original but not immediate sources of the recommendations are obvious because of their uniqueness. Unfortunately the process by which these ideas reached the committee cannot always be determined. The report was not a statement of policy but merely a series of recommendations which tended to reflect the dominant preferences within the foreign office. Its treatment of eastern Europe indicated the degree of progress achieved by the émigrés.

The report, completed by 7 August 1916, stated that the recommendations were based on the principle of nationality as enunciated by members of the government in 1914.[62] It would be applied subject to economic factors, treaty obligations, Allied war aims and, above all, British interests. These exceptions were so extensive as to allow for almost any application of the general principle; but at least in that sense the statement was consistent with Asquith's speeches at the beginning of the war. In stating elsewhere in the report that the 'Allies who went to war for the emancipation of nationalities will inevitably be called upon to deal with the Polish question', Paget and Tyrrell showed that they had adopted, through a strong bias in favour of national self-determination, an interpretation of Asquith's early speeches which went far beyond anything that he had intended.

The authors recommended, in accordance with the principle of nationality, that the Habsburg empire should be destroyed. They based this proposal on Masaryk's and Supilo's argument that Austria-Hungary was and, if it survived, would remain subject to Germany regardless of the outcome of the war. To weaken Germany, Austria-Hungary had to be eliminated. In place of the Empire, they first recommended the creation of a Yugoslav state. Since they deplored the violations of the principle of nationality in the treaty of London, they hoped that it might be voluntarily modified by the Italians. If the Italians refused, Paget and Tyrrell recognized the necessity of fulfilling the obligations of the treaty, but they maintained that a Yugoslav state could still be formed from territories not covered by the treaty. This state, which the government should support, was to be 'a free and voluntary union, not imposed from without implying subjection of any one portion to the other'. Since it was to include Serbia, Paget and Tyrrell were rejecting the concept of a Greater Serbia in favour of Supilo's concept of a federal union of South Slavs. They also opposed the resurrection of Montenegro and, in opposition to Italian policy, the leaving of Croatia to Hungary.[63] On a question in which there were almost an infinite number of variations, the authors positively rejected the Serbian, Italian and Montenegrin solutions in favour of a proposal which in all essentials was identical to Supilo's Yugoslav programme. They even used Supilo's argument:

> We consider that Great Britain should in every way encourage and promote the union of Serbia, Montenegro and the Southern

Slavs into one strong federation of states with a view to its
forming a barrier to any German advance towards the East.

It was assumed that such a state, supported by Britain, would
be pro-British. Although the proposal represented the strongest
endorsement ever given to the Yugoslav position by any British
official and, in contrast to similar proposals during the Balkan
negotiations, was made regardless of any current negotiations, the
evidence suggests that it reflected the dominant preference within
the foreign office.

The proposals in the report on the future of Czechoslovakia
bore no resemblance to any Czechoslovak programme. Paget and
Tyrrell considered the possibility of an independent Bohemia,
but in listing the various alternatives did not include Masaryk's
idea of a state consisting of Bohemia, Moravia, Silesia and the
Slovak areas of Hungary. Since this was an essential point in
Masaryk's programme, it can only be assumed that the authors
did not consult the memoranda which, like 'Independent
Bohemia', Masaryk had submitted to the foreign office. After
listing the various alternatives, which showed a slight knowledge
of Czechoslovak views, they proposed that Bohemia should be
attached to an independent Polish state: 'As far as we understand, this solution is desired both by far-seeing Czechs and
Poles . . . The Czechs fully appreciate that they would benefit by
the superior culture and civilization of the Poles.'

This astounding proposal certainly did not come from Czech
sources. It is difficult to imagine where Paget and Tyrrell found
the far-seeing Czechs they claim to have consulted; for there is
no evidence that any of the Czechs ever considered or suggested
union with Poland. The Czechs were not about to trade Austrian
for Polish rule, particularly since the Poles in Austria-Hungary
had, prior to 1914, supported the status quo in opposition to the
Czechs and South Slavs.[64] Nor would the Czechs agree with the
authors on 'the superior culture and civilization of the Poles'.
Since the proposal never appeared in any previous foreign office
document, it is impossible to determine its origin. There is also
no reason to assume that it reflected the opinion of those officials,
like Clerk, who were very close to the Czechs and their supporters. It did, however, reflect the lack of any dominant
preference in the foreign office on this issue as well as the inability
of many of the officials to conceive of a reasonable solution to the
Czechoslovak problem. While the Yugoslavs had succeeded in

convincing the foreign office, the Czechs had as yet failed, despite the fact that during this period they were, in co-operation with other branches of the government, making a greater contribution to the Entente than either of the other nationalities. Robert Cecil later claimed that he first heard of Czechoslovakia only in December 1916.[65]

On Poland, the report rejected both total absorption by Russia and autonomy within Russia. It proposed the establishment of an independent and sovereign kingdom of Poland to be ruled by a Russian Grand Duke but in no other way connected to the Russian state. The authors did not deny the difficulties involved in this proposal, but they speculated that at the end of the war Russia might need Allied assistance in freeing its territory from German occupation. In this event Britain and France would be able to intervene in the Polish question in favour of an independent kingdom. By decreasing the power of both Germany and Russia and by acting as a buffer state between these two powers, an independent Poland would be in the best interests of Britain. In March 1916, after consulting various Polish émigrés, Gregory had made the same proposal using the same justification, claiming that it was the solution most preferred by the Poles.[66] Since he was a close friend of Horodyski and a supporter of Dmowski, the émigrés he consulted were undoubtedly National Democrats. Paget and Tyrrell probably based their recommendation on this report which, in turn, was based on Dmowski's policy. While Gregory would have supported the recommendation, it was probably too radical for others, like Grey and Nicolson, who seemed to prefer Dmowski's earlier programme of a united, autonomous Poland within the Russian empire.

The sections of the Paget–Tyrrell memorandum on eastern Europe were an exposition on the practical application of national self-determination. It was based on the belief, constantly expounded by the émigrés, that national self-determination would be in the interests of Britain because the newly created states would be pro-British. The willingness of the émigrés to co-operate with the government in the conduct of the war gave substance to this belief. When the report was submitted to the foreign office in September 1916, Hardinge wrote: 'This is an interesting report requiring a good deal of digestion . . . It seems premature at present to express any decided opinion.'[67] Although he did not express his opinion on national self-determination, it seems, from other sources, that he agreed with the report.[68] Drummond, Clerk and Percy, while possibly having reservations on specific points, undoubtedly approved of the support expressed by the authors for the nationalities.

Grey's opinion is always hard to determine because of the lack of evidence. His only comment on the report – 'It seems to me to be very ably done' – gives little indication of his views. But his promises to Supilo and his conversation with Miliukov shows that the report's emphasis on national self-determination reflected his own personal preference for the future of Europe.[69] But Grey was responsible for the policy on war aims that commitments unnecessary to the conduct of the war were to be avoided in order to preserve the greatest freedom of action. It was unlikely, therefore, regardless of his own preferences and those of his officials, that he would do more than agree that such recommendations were theoretically desirable. During 1916, Grey was sufficiently interested in the possibility of a negotiated peace attained through American mediation that he would never make negotiations impossible by the adoption of extreme war aims.[70]

Most members of the foreign office would agree with Grey that these recommendations, while desirable in principle, were completely impractical in the present political context. The exception was Cecil who had absolutely no sympathy for nationalism and who could be expected to oppose such recommendations on both a theoretical and practical basis. In December 1916, he wrote: 'Nationalism whether Irish or Slav arouses all the worst passions of my nature.'[71] Many of the Paget–Tyrrell recommendations had been made before but had been rejected as unfeasible because of inter-allied relations. The situation had not changed. The preferences of the foreign office and the personal views of officials on hypothetical questions neither reflected nor as yet influenced actual policy. No one in the foreign office seriously suggested the immediate incorporation of these proposals into British foreign policy. When the memorandum was sent to the cabinet, it was sent as a suggested basis for future not immediate policy.

On 10 August 1916, the war committee discussed the possibility of formulating armistice terms in preparation for any attempt at mediation.[72] On 17 August 1916, Field Marshal Sir William Robertson, the chief of the imperial general staff, wrote to Lloyd George, the secretary of state for war, expressing his belief in the need for a discussion of war aims. Robertson feared that the French, with their war aims carefully formulated, would be able, in the event of negotiations, to seize the initiative to the detriment of British interests:

> We may be sure that M. Briand [premier of France] will have very decided views, carefully worked out for him under his general direction by the clever people who surround him and who do not appear on the surface of political life.[73]

Robertson seemed aware of the Paget–Tyrrell committee, but it is unlikely that he was aware of their report which had not yet been submitted to the foreign office. With the letter he enclosed his own memorandum on war aims which was the antithesis of the Paget–Tyrrell report in that it emphasized the balance of power instead of the nationality principle.[74] Robertson neither mentioned national self-determination nor showed the slightest concern for subject nationalities. He proposed the maintenance of a diminished Austria-Hungary including Bohemia and Moravia which, he believed, could not be independent. He recognized the necessity of accepting Russian policy in Poland and supported the Greater Serbian concept by proposing to give Serbia Bosnia, Herzegovina and Slavonia. For the émigrés, nothing could be worse than these proposals except the victory of the Central powers.

At one point in the memorandum Robertson stated: 'Of far greater import to the matter under immediate consideration is the intention to break up Austria-Hungary.' He came to this conclusion after examining the promises of Habsburg territory to Serbia, Italy and Rumania. The decision had never been made and the intention never expressed, but in view of the territorial promises it was not an unreasonable assumption. But it was an assumption which showed that confusion existed within the government on the subject of war aims.

At a meeting of the war committee on 30 August 1916, Asquith asked the members of the cabinet to submit their views on war aims. His statement that 'Everything indicated that M. Briand considered that we should be face to face with this question before the end of the autumn' creates the suspicion that the impetus for Asquith's request come from Roberston.[75] As a result of this request, the Robertson and Paget–Tyrrell memoranda were submitted to the war committee and they were followed, in October 1916, by another memorandum by Arthur James Balfour, the first lord of the admiralty. In January, he had written: 'If the map of Europe was brought by the present war into close harmony with the distribution of nationalities, one perennial cause of international disturbance would be mitigated.'[76] In his appreciation of nationalism, Balfour was an exception among his Conservative colleagues who, because of the Irish problem, abhorred nationalism in any form.[77] In a paper submitted to the cabinet in May 1899, on the South African question, Balfour had written:

> Were I a Boer ... nothing but necessity would induce me to adopt a constitution which would turn my country into an English Republic or a system of education which would reduce my language to the 'patois' of a small and helpless minority.[78]

Balfour was not a nationalist, but he had sympathy for subject nationalities which was the product of his remarkable ability for real understanding of many sides of any question. He could appreciate the feelings which motivated the émigrés, and he understood very clearly the importance of nationalism in European affairs. In his memorandum, Balfour recognized both the necessity of solving some of the European nationality problems and the possibility that the nationality principle could be used to achieve the Entente's cardinal aim of the weakening of Germany.[79] As a convenient principle upon which to base the territorial reduction of the Central powers, national self-determination was more a means than an end. Balfour opposed the creation of an independent Poland, rejecting the Paget–Tyrrell proposal, because he feared that it would succumb to the same weakness that had led to the partitions. He doubted its effectiveness as a buffer state which, in any case, would not be in the interests of Britain because it would relieve Germany of Russian pressure. Instead he favoured, as did many in the foreign office, a reunited autonomous Poland within the Russian Empire. He disliked the idea of the German sections of Austria joining Germany and therefore desired to see the continued existence of the Dual monarchy shorn of its Italian, Rumanian and South Slav possessions. In reference to the Czechs he stated:

> To Bohemia Germanic civilization is profoundly distasteful. The Czechs have been waging war against it for some generations, and waging it under grave difficulties with much success. Whether an independent Bohemia would be strong enough to hold her own, from a military as well as from a commercial point of view, against Teutonic domination ... I

do not know; but I am sure the question deserves very careful consideration. If the change is possible it should be made.

Although Balfour did not elaborate, presumably if independence were not possible, Bohemia would remain a part of the Dual monarchy. While he could offer them little, Balfour singled out the Czechs for special consideration without apparent reason. By its context, the statement indicates that he had been influenced by Czech propaganda. It may be that he was influenced by knowledge of Czech assistance to the government; for he was first lord of the admiralty while Voska was working for naval intelligence. Balfour did not refer to the Yugoslav programme but appeared to support the idea of a Greater Serbia by recommending that it should receive the South Slav areas.

The Balfour memorandum was, perhaps, unconsciously, a compromise between the previous memoranda. His recommendations were based on a synthesis of the balance of power and the nationality principle which avoided the impracticability of Paget and Tyrrell and the lack of relevance to European problems of Robertson. While Robertson's proposals most accurately reflected the stated official policy of the British government in 1916, Balfour's proposals probably reflected the dominant preference of the cabinet, if such existed, on the subject of war aims in eastern Europe. In that the émigrés could find little comfort.

The submission of these memoranda to the cabinet was not followed by any discussion of war aims. The optimism of the summer had not survived the military reverses on the Somme, in Galicia and Rumania, and there was no longer any need for haste in the discussion of war aims. The policy of the government remained, therefore, as it had been since 1914, one of flexibility through the avoidance of unnecessary commitments in areas of secondary importance. On specific issues such as the future of Austria-Hungary or the application of national self-determination, it cannot be said that the government had a policy.

Since national self-determination was not important enough to be discussed by the cabinet, there is little evidence of the personal views of its members. Asquith and Runciman probably shared the limited sympathy for the nationalities shown by Grey and Balfour but would not have gone further.[80] In contrast, there is no reason to assume that Lansdowne, Curzon, Bonar Law or Chamberlain had any sympathy whatever for the subject nationalities. Lloyd George at least appeared to be a supporter of national self-determination; for in August 1916, in a conversation on war aims, he said to H. A. L. Fisher:

It is clear to me that Germany must be strong. We have to
consider Russia . . . What would be the objection to joining
German Austria to Germany? I would cut off Hungary from
Austria. Hungary should be an independent kingdom. It is
very unwholesome for Hungary to rule the Slavs. They should
be separated. I admit that Bohemia is a difficulty.

Lloyd George was not particularly well informed about the
distribution of nationalities in eastern Europe. When Fisher suggested that the Slovaks might also be a difficulty, he replied:

Who are the Slovaks? [Fisher] Well they are Slavs, peasants,
and about 2 million strong. [Lloyd George] Where are they?
I don't seem to place them. [Fisher] On the west of Hungary.
[Lloyd George] And where are the Ruthenians? [Fisher] On
the North.

Lloyd George also stated that 'The Austrian Empire must be
broken up' and expressed his support for a Yugoslav state,
characteristically adding: 'I am attracted by the Serbs. They are
like the Welsh.' These comments show where Lloyd George's
sympathy lay, but they should not be taken too seriously because
he ended the discussion by saying: 'I am against discussing the
settlement of Europe in public. The war spirit is a madness. While
it is on you cannot pledge yourself to anything profitably. You
must keep everything indefinite.[81]

The foreign office, but not the cabinet, was subject to influence
from the émigrés because it conducted relations with them.
Except for Grey and perhaps Balfour, members of the cabinet
were probably not aware of the co-operation that existed between
the émigrés and the various branches of the government.
Between 1914 and 1916, these relations were conducted entirely
by officials without reference to the cabinet. The war aims memoranda were the first occasion upon which the idea of national
self-determination officially reached the cabinet level. Cabinet
members were subjected to memoranda from various émigrés
which they undoubtedly left unread because their relations with
the émigrés lacked the ingredient of co-operation which existed
in those between the foreign office and the émigrés. A cabinet
member had no reason to read such memoranda, but an official

who wanted assistance from the émigrés had to take their political programmes seriously. It was therefore inevitable that the foreign office would be subject to far greater influence from the émigrés. This situation created the possibility that in the future a definite split might develop between the cabinet and the foreign office on the subject of war aims. Since the sympathy for the nationalities in the cabinet seemed, with the exception of Balfour, to exist among the Liberals but not the Conservatives, the possibility of a split would increase with the weakening of the Liberal element in the government.

In November 1916, Maurice Hankey, the secretary of the war committee, listed those war aims upon which there seemed to be general agreement. On eastern Europe the list included the following: '(iii) That some arrangement should be made in regard to Poland which is acceptable to Russia . . . (vi) That Serbia should be re-established.'[82] Hankey's memorandum cannot be considered a definitive statement of war aims but, because of his undoubted knowledge of the views of the cabinet, it is an indication of both the lack of support for national self-determination and the general desire in the government to avoid the subject of non-essential war aims. The government was only prepared to accept commitments under the greatest pressure. Hankey also wrote:

> it is impossible to contemplate with equanimity the prospect
> of a discussion of peace terms at any date, however remote,
> until the balance of advantage has inclined far more decisively
> than at present to the side of the Allies, . . .

Although some members of the cabinet were extremely pessimistic about the military and naval situation in the autumn of 1916, the majority of the cabinet, backed by the military authorities, agreed with Hankey that the unfavourable strategic situation made the prospect of peace negotiations highly undesirable.[83] It must be added that whenever peace was discussed, national self-determination was never considered a reason for rejecting negotiations. The war would not be continued for non-essential aims in areas of secondary importance. Despite the reluctance to negotiate, it was obvious that in the near future President Wilson would attempt some form of mediation. During the last six months of 1916, rumours to this effect were numerous although no one was certain when he would act.[84] In an attempt to forestall mediation, Lloyd George gave an interview in September 1916 to an American reporter in which he absolutely rejected the idea of outside interference in the conflict.[85] Nevertheless the Entente was still heavily dependent upon the United States for the maintenance of the war effort so that any attempted mediation would be most embarrassing because the negotiations would have to be avoided without giving offence to Wilson and the American public.[86]

On 5 December 1916, Asquith resigned and Lloyd George formed a new government dedicated to the more vigorous prosecution of the war. Runciman and Grey followed Asquith while Balfour became the secretary of state for foreign affairs. The change meant the decline of those who seemed most sympathetic to the nationalities, although this trend was offset by Balfour's appointment. But that sympathy had been of little value to the émigrés. The ultimate success of national self-determination depended not on the sympathy of British statesmen but on the course of the war. The destruction of the Central powers brought about by a more vigorous conduct of the war would contribute more to the cause, regardless of the intentions of the victors, than all the sympathy of all the Liberals.

On 20 December 1916, President Wilson addressed a note to the belligerents asking for an authoritative statement of war aims. The request could be answered by a simple rejection of outside interference, but if Lloyd George now acted on the views he expressed in September, he would seriously risk alienating the United States. On 22 December 1916, Cecil proposed that the reply should be a positive statement outlining Allied objectives and designed to appeal to Wilson and the American public. He warned that rejection of the note might alienate Wilson and lead to retaliation.[87] Cecil was acting on advice received by the foreign office from numerous sources, particularly Spring Rice, who was adamant that the reply had to be positive and designed to appeal to Wilson.[88] On 23 December 1916, the cabinet approved the proposal without opposition and asked Cecil and Balfour to submit drafts.[89]

To ensure that the reply would appeal to Wilson, Cecil, in writing his own draft, consulted the American ambassador in London and referred to the views expressed earlier in the year on the future of Europe by E. M. House, Wilson's unofficial adviser on foreign policy.[90] On 21 December 1916, Drummond suggested that Cecil should consult House's memorandum on peace terms and even suggested using secret service channels to consult House himself. On the same day Cecil circulated the House memorandum to the cabinet with an accompanying minute stating that it represented Wilson's own views. If necessary this could be verified: 'Secret means exist to communicate direct with Colonel House, and it would be possible, if thought desirable, to inquire of him whether the Memorandum of February 22nd still holds good in its entirety, and whether the President still concurs in its terms.'[91] The issue was again considered by the cabinet on 26 December 1916, but the actual drafting of the reply was referred to the Anglo-French conference meeting in London later that day.[92] At the conference: 'M. Ribot [French Minister of Finance] said it came to this: Was our reply to be a diplomatic Note or an answer to the American People? The Conference agreed that the essence of it was an appeal to democracy.'[93]

At a second session, on 28 December 1916, a preliminary draft was approved. Balfour later claimed that the reply was primarily a combination of his and Cecil's drafts.[94] A comparison of these drafts with the final text bears out Balfour's claim, with some exceptions, on those parts of the reply related to eastern Europe.[95] The reply, delivered to the American government on 10 January 1917, stated that Europe had to be reorganized on the basis of, among other things, 'the respect for nationalities'. In elaborating on this point the following terms were stipulated:

> the liberation of the Italians, as also of the Slavs, Rumanes, and Czecho-Slovaks from foreign domination; . . . The intentions of his Majesty the Emperor of Russia in regard to Poland have been clearly indicated by the manifesto he has just addressed to his armies.[96]

These statements, while very carefully phrased, sounded like an endorsement of national self-determination. Had there been a change in official war aims policy? Cecil, who disliked nationalism yet supported the inclusion of these statements in the note, stated on 26 December 1916: 'The probable result of the Allied discussions will be a formless note of no significance whatever.'[97] In referring to the note much later in the house of commons, Cecil stated that the government was not pledged to any particular form of liberation.[98] In the process of drafting the note, the sole consideration had been its potential appeal to American democracy. No one ever suggested that it was to be an accurate reflection of war aims policy, and no consideration was given to the real significance or possible interpretations of the terms. Although Balfour probably took the contents of the note seriously, as they reflected his own personal views, there is no evidence that anyone else agreed with him. Thus the note cannot be considered an accurate reflection of British war aims. The aims stated in the note would never have been publicly endorsed by the government without external pressure of the type that Wilson could exert upon the Entente. The note must be considered not as part of a war aims policy but as part of a strategic policy which allowed for the acceptance of commitments whenever necessary for the maintenance of the war effort.

The terms of the note, by their vagueness, did not commit the Entente to any specific solution to eastern European problems. Since liberation could mean autonomy as well as independence, the Entente's freedom of action to meet further contingencies was not unduly restricted.[99] But the note was important regardless of official intentions. As the first occasion upon which the government publicly referred to the Czechoslovaks, it was for them a form of recognition which drew public attention to their cause. The note also supplied ammunition to those, like Seton-Watson, who had always argued, regardless of the facts, that the government had been committed to national self-determination since 1914. Regardless of official intention, the note gave the impression and was widely interpreted as a commitment to national self-determination. If in the future the government failed to meet the expectations created by the note, it would inevitably be subject to accusations of bad faith.[100] The note also had an immediate effect on official British propaganda which now openly advocated national self-determination thus supplying even more evidence upon which to base future accusations against the government.[101] Since such accusations are always better avoided, the government had, by stating these aims, to some extent limited its future alternatives.

The reference in the note to Poland, insisted upon by Balfour and Cecil, was undoubtedly motivated by the desire to satisfy the American government as well as the Polish émigrés. The idea might have originated with House whose views Cecil used in writing his draft.[102] The well-known interest of the American government in this problem was confirmed on 28 December 1916 when Spring Rice telegraphed that a statement on Poland would have a good effect on Wilson.[103] The inevitable Russian objections to the reference were only overcome through the application of great pressure by the Allied ambassadors in Petrograd acting on Balfour's statement that 'the omission would probably produce a bad effect in the United States.'[104]

Since the Czechoslovaks and Poles were mentioned elsewhere in the note, it might be assumed that the reference to 'Slavs' meant Yugoslavs. Some have even assumed that 'Yugo' was deleted because of Italian objections.[105] The phrase originated in Cecil's draft as 'the liberation of the Slav peoples from German domination'.[106] There is no evidence of Italian objections although Cecil might have used this wording in anticipation of such opposition. Since Cecil had no sympathy for the subject nationalities, this phrase was undoubtedly motivated by his general aim of satisfying the United States.

Since it did not occur in either the Balfour or Cecil drafts, the reference to the Czechoslovaks is more mysterious. It does not appear to have been discussed at the sessions of the Anglo-French conference and it cannot be found in any of the English texts of the note. According to Eduard Beneš, Masaryk's lieutenant in Paris, Briand inserted it at the last moment.[107] The total lack of comment by the British on its insertion leads to the conclusion that they were consulted, for unilateral French action would have undoubtedly elicited some reaction. Almost twenty years later Cecil wrote: 'If I am right in my recollection, it was the first time that Czechoslovakia appeared in a diplomatic document and I am ashamed to say I had some doubts as to what it was.'[108] This statement suggests that Cecil was consulted on the insertion. On 13 December 1916, Wiseman, in reference to the reply to the German peace note, cabled to London:

> If British reply to German peace proposals contains no
> mention of Bohemian aspirations, it is probable that the work
> done for us here by Czechs will suffer, and possible that if
> too much discourages [*sic*] they might listen to bids from
> Central Empires. This might cause us considerable harm.[109]

Although it was an official cable, there is no indication to whom it was addressed – the secret service or the foreign office. A copy exists in the Wiseman papers but, not unexpectedly, cannot be found in the government records. If the secret service had some influence on the reference to the Czechoslovaks, it is unlikely that a record of that influence would survive, but it is as plausible an explanation of the reference as any other that has been offered. It could have been Voska's reward.

The reply included references to national self-determination in order to appeal to President Wilson and American democracy. The Allies, with justification, believed that Wilson was becoming interested in the nationalities, particularly the Poles. That interest was based largely on the political influence of the nationalities as well as the general public interest in national self-determination. These conditions in the United States to which the Entente responded were obviously related to previous British action. For almost two years British propaganda directed towards the United States had promoted the idea of national self-determination. At the same time, British officials had encouraged and supported the efforts of the various nationalities to acquire political influence through organization. In replying to President Wilson and in making references to national self-determination, the government was responding to a necessity which its agents had helped to create. The methods adopted by various branches of the government for the conduct of the war were beginning to influence the reasons for which it was being fought and, indirectly, its results.

5 : BRITAIN AND AUSTRIA-HUNGARY, 1917–18

In January 1917 the British government was committed neither to the preservation nor to the destruction of the Habsburg monarchy. To a government involved in a war for survival, and concerned with the immediate problems of its own preservation, the future of Austria-Hungary was an issue of at most secondary importance. The government was not totally indifferent to the future of eastern Europe but its aims in that area were of a general nature, and might be achieved by any one of a number of solutions proposed for the final settlement. Any solution which did not increase the military potential of the Central powers and which was conducive to peace and stability was acceptable. It could be argued that these aims would be satisfied by the preservation of the Habsburg monarchy, by the absolute application of national self-determination or by any one of a number of compromises between these two which in practice would mean self-determination for some nationalities but not others. While the relative merits of each solution were debatable, conclusive evidence did not and could not exist by which the policy-makers could predict which solution would best satisfy their general aims in eastern Europe. The solutions could be tested only by application. While the war was in progress and the future of Europe uncertain, there was no overwhelming need for the government to choose the programme for eastern Europe that it would favour during peace negotiations. Many officials, particularly in the foreign office, had their own preference, usually for national self-determination, but the government remained uncommitted and unconvinced. The government was prepared to accept binding commitments based on strategic calculations designed to promote the conduct of the war, but not prepared to accept commitments based on its own calculation of its long-term political interest in the future structure of eastern Europe. By avoiding commitments which were not immediately necessary the government was able to maximize its alternatives and use the resulting flexibility to increase its military potential. National self-determination, as an alternative to the status quo, had been considered by the foreign office during the first years of the war, but had never been discussed by the cabinet. The preservation of Austria-Hungary, in contrast, was not seriously considered by anyone in the government. Excluding the attacks by the exponents of national self-determination few references to the question of the future of the Habsburg monarchy appear in the existing records. In this case the lack of evidence of interest within the government, and particularly within the cabinet, cannot be attributed either to a conspiracy of silence or to the destruction of documents; it must be considered as evidence of indifference. Before 1917 no one in the government argued that Austria-Hungary ought to be preserved. No one argued that its existence would be the best solution to the problems of eastern Europe, that it was necessary for the balance of power or in the interest of Britain. No one suggested that any sacrifice however small should be made for the preservation of Austria-Hungary. Despite overwhelming provocation from the exponents of national self-determination, no one rose to the defence of Austria-Hungary. Despite the preferences within the foreign office, the government was indifferent to the future of the Habsburg monarchy. Its survival or destruction would be equally acceptable to the government as long as the settlement in eastern Europe tended to promote peace and stability while not increasing German power.

Although uncommitted on the future of Austria-Hungary, the government, acting on considerations of strategic necessity, had accepted binding and far-reaching commitments to Italy and Rumania which, if fulfilled, might well destroy the Habsburg monarchy. By the treaty of London Italy had been promised the Trentino, Cisalpine Tyrol, Trieste, Gorizia, Gradisca, Istria and northern Dalmatia. Rumania had been promised Transylvania, the Banat and Bukovina. There was good reason to assume that the monarchy could never survive such amputations. Any government which accepted such terms would risk extinction because of the internal reaction, particularly from the Magyars. The effect of such losses on the prestige of the monarchy might be more than it could stand. But as no Habsburg government could accept such terms, the Allies were committed, as long as Italy and Rumania continued to fight, to continue the war until the Habsburg army was destroyed. From that, Austria-Hungary could hardly survive. Remarkable as it may seem, in the negotiations with Italy and Rumania, the government had failed to consider the effect of these terms on the future of the monarchy. Since enemy territory was considered forfeit, the negotiations were conducted without reference to Austria-Hungary. Robertson, who assumed that it might survive, incorrectly concluded from the negotiations that the government intended to destroy Austria-Hungary.[1] Several comments, during the negotiations, show some awareness that these terms would necessitate the military defeat of the Habsburg army, but it seems to have been assumed that despite defeat and the anticipated amputations the monarchy could survive. Paget and Tyrrell would not have argued for its destruction had they believed that its fate had already been decided. Balfour assumed that a Habsburg monarchy comprising only those areas which were ethnically German-Austrian and Hungarian was a practical possibility, despite losses of territory so enormous as to change it beyond recognition. The significance of the agreements with Italy and Rumania was clearly misunderstood, and thought devoted to the future of the monarchy extremely confused, not because the situation was so complex as to be incomprehensible, for Robertson had recognized the significance, but because few addressed themselves to the problem. Those not interested in the survival of the monarchy had no reason to ponder its future. The government had always been extremely careful in its relations with the nationalities in order to maintain various alternative courses of action. But what it had guarded with its right hand it had, as subsequent events were to show, unwittingly given away with its left.

A separate peace with Austria-Hungary had always been a possibility and had been, on occasion, considered by the foreign office. Once, during the Balkan negotiations, the foreign office had rejected the idea of a separate peace, but there was no indication, after those negotiations had ended, that further Austrian approaches would be rejected. But in the absence of such approaches the possibility was not seriously considered. A separate peace which would enable Austria-Hungary to survive would not signify or necessitate any alteration in the war aims policy of the British government for, as has been explained, the government had no particular objection to its survival or desire for its destruction. A separate peace would, however, necessitate a fundamental alteration in British strategic policy because those anti-Habsburg elements which the government had always encouraged would have to be abandoned.

During 1917 government thought on the future of eastern Europe was dominated, almost to the exclusion of all else, by the possibility of a separate peace with Austria-Hungary. In this situation the policy-makers had to contemplate, for the first time, the problems of eastern Europe in an immediate and practical sense. As a result, the preferences for national self-determination which had emerged in previous hypothetical discussions receded into the background and little consideration was given to the cause of the nationalities. For the émigrés the year had begun with the reply to President Wilson. It had been the most significant statement by the Allied governments on the cause of the nationalities, and had justifiably created great expectations. But it was a false start, for nothing that followed during 1917 satisfied these expectations. No sooner had the reply been given than it was forgotten.

On 10 January 1917, the British minister in Christiania informed the foreign office that he had received approaches, apparently official, from Austrian agents on the subject of a separate peace.[2] Despite ample evidence that Austria-Hungary was labouring under such severe economic conditions as a result of the war and the blockade that it might desire a negotiated peace, the foreign office was quite sceptical about the feasibility of a separate peace because the agreements with Italy and Rumania seemed to be insurmountable obstacles to any negotiations.[3] Although, on 18 January 1917, the war cabinet instructed Balfour to follow up these approaches, and although a special emissary was sent to Christiania nothing came of this incident.[4] The cabinet's decision to respond to these approaches marked the beginning of a long and fruitless exploration by the British government, lasting well into 1918, for the illusory separate peace.

The immediately favourable reaction of the cabinet to the idea of a separate peace with Austria-Hungary must be seen within the context of the strategic position in 1917. The campaigns in the summer of 1916 in Galicia, in Rumania and on the Somme had been fought at great cost and with little success. The deterioration in Russian military strength, already apparent to the Allies, made optimism about the future course of the war difficult. In 1915 the Allies had sought a quick solution to the war in a Balkan league, in 1916 they placed their hopes on Rumania, and in 1917, with equal self-deception, they sought the solution to their military problems in detaching Austria-Hungary from Germany. On 18 January 1917, when the cabinet discussed the issue, the military advantages led Robertson to support the pursuit of a separate peace.[5] Throughout 1917 the war office never wavered in this support, which even increased as the strategic situation deteriorated with the collapse of Russia.[6] The military failures of 1917 so severely shook the confidence of the war office that by the end of the year it was ready to admit that total victory was unattainable. On 29 December 1917, Robertson wrote in a memorandum for the war cabinet:

> there is no prospect of ever acquiring all those vast enemy territories which the different members of the Entente have been promised or wish to acquire; and, therefore, leaving aside these ambitious territorial gains, the question is can we get what we must get if we are to secure the future peace of the world.[7]

On 21 January 1918, the commander-in-chief of the British Expeditionary force, Field Marshal Sir Douglas Haig, who was usually extremely confident, told General Jan C. Smuts, the South African representative on the imperial war cabinet, that there was little value in continuing the war as both the French and the Italians might soon collapse.[8] The war office was concerned solely with the military aspects of a separate peace, and showed no interest whatever in the terms upon which it might be negotiated. On a number of occasions Robertson argued that Allied aims should be moderated and that the agreements with the lesser Allies, Italy and Rumania, should be reconsidered. He believed that they had failed to contribute to the defeat of the Central powers, but was never able to suggest how the engagements could be renegotiated without fragmenting the Entente.[9] In essence, Robertson wanted the lesser Allies to abandon their aims without abandoning the war.

The only branch of the government which was unalterably opposed to a separate peace with Austria-Hungary was the intelligence bureau of the department of information. It was staffed by exponents of national self-determination like Namier and Seton-Watson. The head of the bureau, Major General Count Gleichen, and its other members, J. W. Headlam, R. Leeper and A. W. A. Leeper, were also supporters of the nationalities.[10] The bureau disagreed with government policy because it approached the problems of diplomacy in war from an entirely different basis.

Its officials, like Namier and Seton-Watson, based their advice on the assumption that the war aims of the government should be founded on calculations of the long-term political interests of the British government in eastern Europe. Overestimating the power of the government, they thought that it should set out its ideal aims and then fight until they were achieved. In contrast, the other branches of the government felt compelled to adjust war aims to a realistic analysis of the power of the British government. The war office overlooked political considerations; the intelligence bureau disregarded the dictates of military necessity. Since the intelligence bureau did not have to solve immediate strategic problems, military expediency did not play a significant role in its calculations. But since strategic necessity played a primary role in the formation of government policy, it was almost inevitable that the intelligence bureau would be in opposition now just as its members had opposed previous actions of the government based on similar considerations as in the case of the negotiations for the treaty of London.[11] Such disagreement had existed since the beginning of the war, but had had little or no effect on official policy. During 1917, while the government sought a separate peace with Austria-Hungary, the intelligence bureau campaigned against this policy with the only weapon at its disposal, the weekly reports it circulated to various branches of the government. Namier well represented the views of the intelligence bureau when he wrote in one of these reports:

> Austria-Hungary is bound to remain in international politics dependent on Germany because Germany is the only Power which defends the basis on which the Habsburg Monarchy rests – German preponderance in Austria and Magyar dominion in Hungary; and this is the only basis on which the Habsburg Monarchy can exist.[12]

But these reports had no discernible effect on British policy; they may not even have been read. The bureau certainly failed to divert the government from its chosen course of a separate peace.

The abortive attempt to initiate negotiations with Austrian agents in January 1917 inspired the members of the foreign office to consider, for the first time, the possibility and the repercussions of a separate peace with Austria-Hungary. Hardinge thought that the Allied agreements with Italy, Serbia and particularly Rumania might be insurmountable barriers to negotiations, an opinion almost universal in the foreign office. Nevertheless, he still favoured further investigation of the possibility of a separate peace because it would make the defeat of Germany 'comparatively easy'. He did not contemplate abandoning the solemn pledges the government had made to its lesser allies, but he believed that there was a slight possibility that they might reduce their war aims. Although he forgot the Czechoslovaks, he suggested that the other nationalities could be satisfied by giving Bosnia, Herzegovina and access to the Adriatic to Serbia, by ceding Galicia to the autonomous Russian Poland, and by establishing within the Habsburg monarchy an autonomous Yugoslav state made up of these South Slav areas not ceded to Serbia. The primary British objective in eastern Europe, the formation of a barrier to the German *Drang nach Osten*, would be achieved by a reconstituted Habsburg monarchy, which having deserted its allies and having made a separate peace, would be alienated from Germany.[13]

On 12 February 1917, Drummond expanded the ideas already suggested by Hardinge. He accepted the need for a barrier to the German drive to the East but believed that the Habsburg monarchy could be such a barrier if, by making a separate peace, it was alienated from Germany. It would be an even more effective barrier if it was reconstituted into four autonomous states of Austria, Hungary, Bohemia and Yugoslavia. Serbia would be given Bosnia, Herzegovina and part of Dalmatia, while Galicia would be ceded to Poland. Drummond admitted that Serbia, Italy and Rumania might block negotiations, but he was more optimistic than Hardinge that such obstacles could be overcome. He also believed that peace with Austria-Hungary would not affect Italy's belligerent status because of Italy's desire for territory in Asia Minor. The remarks with which he prefaced his memorandum clearly show his own preference for the future of eastern Europe and his reasons for supporting a separate peace:

> If the Allies were certain that the result of the war would be so decisive that they would be able to impose their own terms on the Central Powers. I still believe that the solution outlined in the Paget–Tyrrell memorandum is the best for the future of Europe. But if such terms are unlikely to be secured in their entirety, or if a different solution would materially shorten the war, the possible advantages of a

separate peace with Austria by some such scheme as I have ventured to outline somewhat roughly are, I think, worth careful consideration.[14]

Throughout 1917 Drummond consistently supported efforts to initiate negotiations for a separate peace, and within the foreign office remained one of its major advocates.[15] Although the others did not express their views in as much detail, it is apparent that Clerk, Gregory, Paget, Tyrrell, Sir Ronald Graham, an assistant under-secretary of state, and Lancelot Oliphant, an assistant clerk, all supported the general argument put forward by Hardinge and Drummond: not that a separate peace should be made to preserve Austria-Hungary but that, if a separate peace were a military necessity, as they all believed it to be, the continued existence of a Habsburg monarchy irreparably alienated from Germany would be consistent with British interests.[16] Graham, Clerk and Oliphant, however, doubted whether such a peace was possible.[17] Cecil was the exception in the foreign office. In his reply to Drummond's memorandum he stated that the preservation of a reconstituted Habsburg monarchy would be the best solution for the future of eastern Europe because it would prevent balkanization.[18] He added that a separate peace would almost certainly break the blockade of Germany, but in future deliberations within the government on the question of a separate peace this detail, along with so many others, was neglected when the military advantages of a separate peace were calculated. His general attitude towards the nationalities was best expressed in a letter he wrote in November 1917 to J. St Loe Strachey, the editor of the *Spectator*:

> I must honestly admit to you that I am to some extent a heretic. I recognize, of course, that we must do all we can for the Poles and the Yugo-Slavs and the Czechs, but I must add that I cannot look forward with much enthusiasm to the success of our efforts. As far as I can see the Slavs have never shown the slightest capacity for self-government. Steed and his friends would no doubt regard this as ignorant folly, but they will treat this aspect of European politics from a crusading point of view. They believe in nationality as if it were a religion. I can only regard it as one of the greatest international forces which it would be folly to disregard.[19]

Balfour, whose views had not changed since writing his war

aims memorandum in the autumn of 1916, thought that a separate peace was impossible and that negotiations with the Austrians were dangerous as well as useless.[20] In replying to Drummond's memorandum Hardinge wrote: 'It must be remembered, in considering this question, that no peace can be satisfactory for Great Britain which does not successfully bar the road to Germany towards the East.'[21] This idea which had been originally suggested by Masaryk was now accepted within the foreign office as an axiom of British policy in eastern Europe. But the foreign office, despite the preferences of many of its members, was at least prepared to attempt to achieve this aim by a method which would be fundamentally unacceptable to Masaryk and his colleagues.

The possibility of negotiations with Austria-Hungary rose again in April 1917 when Prince Sixte de Bourbon presented to the French government a letter from his brother-in-law, the Emperor Karl, expressing his desire for a negotiated peace.[22] The letter did not mention a separate peace, but was vague enough to allow that interpretation by those who had a weakness for wishful thinking. Lloyd George enthusiastically welcomed the opportunity presented by this letter, and at the Allied conference on 19 April 1917, at Saint-Jean de Maurienne, discussed the issue of negotiations for a separate peace with Austria-Hungary. His hopes that the letter might lead to negotiations were destroyed, however, by Sonnino's opposition.[23] Although Lloyd George at first refused to abandon this opportunity for negotiations, continued Italian opposition prevented any response to the emperor's letter.[24]

Like many others Lloyd George saw a separate peace as the solution to Allied military problems, but it is doubtful whether he saw it as anything more. On 9 May 1917, he told the war cabinet: 'If we failed to induce Austria to make a separate peace, he could see no hope of that sort of victory in the war that we desired.' At this meeting it was agreed that: 'our diplomacy should, if possible, be used to assist the military situation, and that if Russia should go out of the war, every possible effort should be made to secure compensation by a separate peace with Austria'.[25] Having stated his preference in 1916 for the destruction of the Habsburg monarchy, Lloyd George now showed no concern for its preservation.[26] At the same time he was equally unconcerned about the subject nationalities. At a meeting of the war cabinet on 8 June 1917, he stated, in reference to the possibility of detaching Bulgaria from the Central powers:

Peace with Bulgaria should not be difficult to arrange, if only
the Serbs would carry out their threat to walk into the Austrian
camp. Personally he would not regard this as a misfortune
if it resulted in Austria's dependence on Slav races
instead of on Germans, but he believed he stood alone in
this view.[27]

Lloyd George refused to recognize that the government had
any formal commitment to Serbia despite the promises Grey had
made in 1915. Since Grey had acted on his own authority without
consulting the cabinet, his promises could now be repudiated.[28]
If Lloyd George was indifferent to the cause of Serbia, that
country which, in his own words, was one of the 'vessels by
which . . . [God] . . . carries the choicest wines to the lips of
humanity', that nation which he so admired because it reminded
him of the Welsh, it is not surprising that he failed to consider
the other nationalities.[29] The factor that inspired Lloyd George's
enthusiasm about a separate peace was strategic necessity resulting from the decline of Russia.[30] On 21 June 1917, he told the
cabinet committee on war policy: 'If Russia went out of the war
while Austria still remained in we could not win. If the Eastern
Armies of Germany were released we should have no chance of
eventual victory.'[31] Although there were disagreements on how
the negotiations with Austria-Hungary should be conducted, most
of the individuals associated with the war cabinet, like Curzon,
Smuts, Hankey, Robertson, Major General Sir Frederick Maurice,
the director of military operations, and Admiral Sir John Jellicoe,
the first sea lord, agreed with Lloyd George on the need for a
separate peace.[32] None of these individuals had ever shown the
slightest interest in, or even knowledge of, eastern Europe, and
when a separate peace was first contemplated they showed no
particular interest in the terms upon which it might be negotiated.
Curzon thought that the only vital British interest in Europe was
the independence of Belgium.[33] The strongest advocates of a
separate peace were either military technicians like Hankey and
Robertson, or imperialists like Smuts and Curzon who believed
that the future of eastern Europe was one of the least important
considerations for the British government. Viscount Milner, a
member of the war cabinet, represented the imperialist position
and was the exception among his colleagues in considering the
subject nationalities. He supported endeavours to seek a separate
peace and like Cecil was dubious about the value of national

self-determination. According to the historian Sidney Low, Milner told him that:

> Regards the creation – as part of the war settlement – of Czechoslovakia, Jugoslavia, enlarged Rumania, as impracticable. Very doubtful if these changes are in themselves desirable, but if they are, should be left for a post-war settlement . . .
> We did not go to war for Czechoslovakia, Jugoslavia or Rumanians, or Poles. We ought to try to make arrangements for their autonomy and etc; but we ought not to insist that we will go on fighting till their aspirations are satisfied, that is till Austria, Turkey and Bulgaria are disintegrated.

After the conversation Low noted: 'I gather that this is Milner's personal view; but that he has not yet got his colleagues to agree to it.'[34] On 11 April 1917, Leopold Amery, the assistant secretary of the war cabinet, wrote a memorandum for the imperial war cabinet's committee on the territorial terms of peace. Amery was one of Milner's followers, but while agreeing with him that the British empire should be the primary consideration of the government, he did not share Milner's indifference to the future of eastern Europe. Amery pointed out that if Germany controlled eastern Europe it would have a stronger base from which to attack the Empire. He concluded, therefore, in reference to central Europe and the Balkans: —

> That the whole of this region should remain under the direct control of the enemy Powers is not consistent with our safety or with our obligations towards our Allies. But the particular mode in which the problems of this region are solved is not a vital British interest.

This was, in fact, a reasonably accurate statement of the policy that the government was in the process of following. Amery considered that the maximum realization of the wishes and the ideals of the Allies would include an independent Poland, a Yugoslav state formed by uniting the South Slav areas of Austria-Hungary to Serbia and the creation of a Czechoslovak state. He foresaw difficulties in carrying out this policy because of the impossibility of creating ethnically homogeneous national states in eastern Europe, and because these national states might not, in the existing economic and geographic situation, be self-sufficient. Since the Allies were unprepared to fight until these aims were achieved, and since failure to secure a complete victory might necessitate a compromise peace, these aims might have to be reduced or abandoned. Amery never doubted that if some aims had to be abandoned it would be in the best interests of Britain to abandon those in eastern Europe so that its aims elsewhere could be achieved. Although Amery did not specify to what extent the aims in eastern Europe should be reduced, he speculated that, if necessary, autonomy for Poland, Czechoslovakia and Yugoslavia would be acceptable.[35] In a later memorandum Amery developed further Drummond's idea of a reconstituted Habsburg monarchy by suggesting that Rumania and Serbia might be added to the Habsburg dominions to form a large middle European federation.[36] Although Amery considered such solutions acceptable in terms of British interests, he did not suggest that they were the most desirable solutions to the problems of eastern Europe. He was also extremely pessimistic about the possibility of negotiations for he saw no evidence that Austria-Hungary wanted a separate peace, and believed that as the situation in Austria-Hungary deteriorated that country would only become more dependent upon Germany.[37] The imperial war cabinet's committee on the territorial terms of peace accepted Amery's basic statement on British policy in eastern Europe, but carefully avoided any statement of specific aims. It concluded that:

> As regards the settlement of the Alsace-Lorraine, Polish and Austro-Hungarian questions, the precise mode in which the object is to be achieved is a matter which, in the main, concerns our Allies more than ourselves. The principle British interest in the settlement to be aimed at is that, while it should effectively reduce the military power and resources of the Central Powers, it should correspond as far as possible with the wishes of the populations concerned, and be inherently stable and calculated to promote a lasting peace.

This general statement left the government free to adjust its war aims whenever it chose to the realities of the strategic situation. The committee also stated: 'In Eastern Europe the Committee have been impressed with the extreme importance of securing an effective barrier to the extension of German power and influence, both political, economic and commercial, over the Near East.'[38] The editor of the *Manchester Guardian*, C. P. Scott, who was very close to Lloyd George, had his own opinion about the tendency of officials, like Drummond and Amery, to speculate on the terms of peace:

> My own view as to the government's policy was that all the talk as to particular terms was at bottom insincere and that the one condition which to the mind of the government was fundamental was a military victory – not necessarily the 'knock-out blow' of which Ll. G. prated, but still something sufficient to break the prestige of the German military autocracy.[39]

Failing to convince the Italians to agree to negotiations with Austria-Hungary, Lloyd George adopted a plan by which he believed that Italian objections could eventually be overcome. He proposed that the British and French armies should participate in a major offensive against the Austrians on the Italian front in order to wrest from Austria-Hungary those areas, like Trieste, most coveted by the Italians. The failure of the Nivelle offensive in the spring of 1917 undoubtedly reinforced the strategic arguments for a separate peace while increasing Lloyd George's dislike of the dominant view of the Allied strategists that the war had to be won on the western front. Once the areas coveted by Italy were in the possession of the Allies, the Austrians might be more willing to make concessions to Italy, and the Italians, with greater assurance that their essential desiderata would be fulfilled, might be more willing to undertake negotiations.[40] At an Allied conference on 26 July 1917, Lloyd George:

> pointed out that if the Russians collapse, Roumania's collapse was also inevitable, and that in such circumstances it would be very difficult to exact the claims of the *Entente's* Eastern Allies against Austria. This rendered it more desirable to concentrate on the claims of Italy, who was co-operating with us to her full extent . . . If we still continued in the expectation of winning Galicia, Bukovina, Banat, Temesvar, Transylvania, and all the Serbian claims, we really were lacking the courage to face the facts.[41]

The fatal flaw in the plan was that by subordinating military considerations to diplomacy, even if the diplomacy were ultimately based on strategic necessity, opposition from the war office was almost inevitable. Despite Lloyd George's vigorous campaigning for this change in Allied strategy, it was never accepted by the Allied governments because of the British and French military authorities' opposition to shifting the military emphasis away from the western front. As a result, one of the major obstacles to a separate peace, the incompatibility between Austrian and Italian aims, still could not be overcome. Any possibility that this solution might be adopted later was destroyed by the overwhelming defeat of the Italian army at Caporetto late in October 1917.

During the autumn of 1917 the strategic situation deteriorated further. The Russian offensive in Galicia which began in July 1917 had failed and it was obvious that little more could be expected from the Russian army. The British government now had to consider the possibility that Russia might withdraw entirely from the war. There was little doubt that such an act would make total victory, and possibly any victory, impossible.[42] The campaign on the western front which the war office had favoured in preference to a major offensive in Italy had failed to produce results which might offset the deterioration of the eastern front. During the late summer and autumn the government continued to receive reports about the worsening of conditions in Austria-Hungary and of the Austrian desire for a negotiated peace, but it received no actual approaches from Austrian agents.[43] In this situation the government avoided all statements of war aims and awaited Austrian approaches.[44] A certain reserve marked the government's relations with the various subject nationalities who vainly attempted to pressure it into making a statement on national self-determination.[45]

The degree of pessimism which existed in government circles about the future course of the war can be seen in the discussions of the war cabinet. At a meeting on 14 August 1917, Lloyd George explained how he would conduct negotiations with Austria-Hungary. According to Hankey's own cryptic notes, Lloyd George said: 'Begin with Italy; then Serbia; if you have agreement you put up your fight on Roumania. If it comes to pt [point] would have no hesitation.'[46] One must assume that Lloyd George meant that he would not hesitate to abandon Rumania. If he was prepared to overlook formal commitments, what could the Poles, Czechs and Yugoslavs expect from a separate peace? By September 1917 the government was so pessimistic that it began to consider negotiations with Germany in which it would have to abandon eastern Europe to the Central powers in exchange for concessions in western Europe. At a meeting of the war cabinet on 24 September 1917, at which it was decided to receive any approaches from the Germans, Lloyd George stated: 'If we came to the conclusion that the Soviet was going to destroy our prospects of success, then Russia ought to pay the penalty.'[47] Nothing came of this willingness to negotiate with Germany, but it was to remain a possible alternative which the government would not reject out of hand. There can be no doubt that in such negotiations conducted at the expense of Russia and eastern Europe, negotiations in which the British would have to abandon their one essential aim of a barrier to the German *Drang nach Osten*, the subject nationalities would also be abandoned.

During this period the foreign office became more sceptical about a separate peace. On 22 August 1917, Harold Nicolson wrote that a separate peace was impossible but recommended that:

> we should consider the possibility of entertaining negotiations
> with these Austrian Representatives from the point of view,
> not of detaching Austria from the Alliance (which is impossible)
> but of placing the German Government in a position which it
> would be difficult for them to justify either to their own people
> or to their Allies.[48]

Oliphant, Graham, Hardinge and Clerk shared Nicolson's estimate of the impossibility of a separate peace, and began to look upon negotiations not as a means to achieve a real settlement, but as a weapon to embarrass and weaken the Central alliance.[49] This idea had also occurred to the war office.[50] On 31 October 1917, the government was presented with another opportunity for negotiations with Austria-Hungary when it was informed by Horace Rumbold, the minister in Berne, of an Austrian request that the government send a representative for official conversations about peace.[51] The government responded by sending Smuts, one of the most enthusiastic advocates of a separate peace, to Switzerland in December 1917 for discussions with Count Mensdorff, the former Austrian ambassador in London. This opportunity did nothing to allay the pessimism of the foreign office. Nicolson, expressing the views of his colleagues, wrote that Austria-Hungary had only two alternatives – destruction or subservience to Germany. He added that while Austria-Hungary desired a negotiated peace it showed no desire for a separate peace.[52] Balfour was particularly concerned about the risks involved and for that reason opposed negotiations. On 15 December 1917, he explained the difficulty of conducting any negotiations:

If we make proposals fully satisfactory to all our Allies, they
will be regarded as utterly unreasonable by all our enemies.
If, on the other hand, we make tentative qualifications in their
extreme demands, and the negotiations nevertheless break
down (as I rather think they will), then we shall have given
a most powerful instrument into the hands of our foes for
making mischief between us and our friends.[53]

On 29 December 1917, Balfour wrote to Cecil about the cabinet
discussion of war aims:

There was the usual endless talk about defining War Aims, – a
problem in which I take no great interest, because, as it seems
to me, there is not the slightest difficulty in defining what ends
we want to attain by the war. [Balfour still adhered to the
views expressed in his war aims memorandum in 1916]. The
real difficulty is to find out how far we shall be able to attain
them, and how far our Allies are prepared to fight till they are
attained; – and no amount of defining will help us to solve these
problems.[54]

Balfour feared that the negotiations could not be kept secret
and that they would discourage the lesser Allies.[55] Subsequent
events showed that it was impossible to maintain the secrecy of
the Smuts–Mensdorff conversations.[56] He understood and sympathized with the attitude of the subject nationalities, later writing to House: 'Various Slav peoples have so often been fooled by
phrase "self-government" that they will be disposed to regard all
schemes which are so described as giving them old slavery under
a new name.' In the same letter he gave another reason for
opposing negotiations:

The future of the war largely depends on supporting Italian
enthusiasm and on maintaining anti-German zeal of Slav
populations in Austria. Both Italians and Slavs are very easily
discouraged and are quick to find evidence in foreign speeches
that their interests are forgotten or betrayed. I fear Austrian
statesmanship will not be above using any indication that
President had a tenderness for Austrian Empire as a means of
convincing Slavs that having nothing to hope for from the
Allies they had best make terms with Central Powers.[57]

Balfour's warnings were to no avail because the government, in
the pursuit of peace, was prepared to undertake such risks. His

opposition, justified by the information available to the foreign office and by subsequent events, only made him and the foreign office unpopular among the optimistic advocates of a separate peace, like Hankey and Milner, who thought Balfour incompetent.[58] Such optimism was not entirely dead within the foreign office for Cecil and Drummond still favoured negotiations.[59] On 10 December 1917, Drummond wrote another memorandum on possible terms of peace which showed that his views had changed since February 1917.[60] He now maintained that the establishment of independent Slavic states would no longer achieve the primary aim of barring the German *Drang nach Osten* since, with the complete collapse of Russia, they would lack support from the rear. Such a barrier could be established only by a reconstituted Habsburg monarchy which would include the autonomous states of Bohemia, Poland and Yugoslavia, including Serbia. Although anticipated in rather vague terms by Amery, Drummond's recommendation on Poland was an innovation because the Polish question had been considered, prior to the collapse of Russia, as separate and distinct from the Austrian question. Hardinge, Gregory and probably others in the foreign office found these terms acceptable, but there is no evidence that the foreign office agreed with Drummond that this was the best solution to the problems of eastern Europe.[61] Although Clerk did not express his opinion on the whole programme, he did comment on the Polish proposal: 'If the Poles themselves adopt this policy, well and good, but it is so completely opposed to all our public assurances – and in my humble opinion to our real interests – that any such move on our part would have a deplorable effect.'[62]

Regardless of the foreign office, the government was determined to send Smuts to Switzerland. The intention of the Bolsheviks to make peace undoubtedly contributed to the government's pacificism which now reached its zenith and increased the cabinet's desire to find a diplomatic solution to its strategic problems. On 28 December 1917, Lloyd George told Scott:

> I warn you that I am in a very pacifist temper. If people really knew, the war would be stopped tomorrow. But of course they don't know, and can't know . . . The thing is horrible and beyond human nature to bear and I feel I can't go on with this bloody business: I would rather resign . . .[63]

Before his departure Smuts set out the basis upon which he intended to conduct his discussions with Mensdorff.[64] His proposals were similar to those already made by Drummond as he believed that, in the absence of Russia, Austria-Hungary was a necessary counterweight to Germany. The reconstituted Habsburg monarchy envisaged by Smuts would include an autonomous Poland and possibly an autonomous Yugoslavia including Serbia. This last point would be reserved for discussions between Austria and Serbia and the latter would only be guaranteed restoration but not acquisition of Bosnia, Herzegovina or part of Dalmatia. Smuts forgot Bohemia. As the object of his mission he sought to split the Central powers so that Austria would either make a separate peace or support the Allies against Germany in negotiations for a general peace. At their meeting, when Mensdorff asked him about the implication in the reply to President Wilson that the Allies intended to break up Austria-Hungary, Smuts responded: 'that note never had had such an intention, and that its object, and still more our object now, was to assist Austria to give the greatest freedom and autonomy to her subject nationalities'.[65] The Smuts–Mensdorff conversations confirmed the foreign office's pessimism about a separate peace because Mensdorff refused to discuss the subject, confining his remarks exclusively to a general peace. Smuts, not permitted to discuss a general peace, had to confine himself to a very general statement of British intentions towards the future of Austria-Hungary, and so repeated the ideas set out in his earlier memorandum.[66] No progress was made towards a settlement and no basis established for further negotiations. The government had correctly assessed the Austrian desire for a negotiated peace but had misinterpreted it as the desire for a separate peace.

In response to the negotiations at Brest-Litovsk, the Smuts–Mensdorff conversations, and unrest in the labour movement, Lloyd George addressed to the Trades Union Congress, on 5 January 1918, the most important statement of war aims since the reply to President Wilson.[67] Smuts, Hankey, Cecil and Philip Kerr, a private secretary to Lloyd George, some of the major advocates of a separate peace and the representatives of the most pro-Austrian element in the government, devoted considerable effort to the text of the speech.[68] In their recommendations, Smuts and Hankey overlooked the subject nationalities.[69] Cecil suggested stating that the destruction of the monarchy was not a British aim but that the Poles should be given independence and the other nationalities should be given self-government.[70] All that Kerr recommended on this subject was a statement that:

They [the Allies] also feel that a settlement of the racial
problem of South Eastern Europe on the basis that the various
nationalities therein contained should be as far as possible
grouped in autonomous units with securities for religious and
language rights of minorities to be an essential of lasting peace.
As to the relations which exist between these national entities
they have no fixed ideas, provided they are not brought under
the political and military domination of Berlin.[71]

In the actual speech Lloyd George warned the Russians that if
they made a separate peace, Britain would not fight to restore
their losses. He also told the Austrians that his government had
no desire for the destruction of the Habsburg monarchy.[72]
According to the war cabinet minutes: 'His main object was to
give a clear indication to Austria that we did not wish to destroy
her, and to make her people lukewarm in the war, thus deterring
her from using her strength actively against us.'[73] A statement
that a strong Austria was desirable had been considered but
rejected. Following Cecil's recommendation Lloyd George also
stated: 'We believe, however, that an independent Poland, comprising all those genuinely Polish elements who desire to form
part of it, is an urgent necessity for the stability of Western
Europe.' At a meeting of the war cabinet on 3 January 1918, Lloyd
George said: 'Some reference ought to be made in our statement
to such races as the Italians, Croats, Slovaks, Czechs, and etc.
who are under Austrian rule, and who seek some form of autonomy.'[74] In the speech he stated:

> Similarly, though we agree with President Wilson that the
> breakup of Austria-Hungary is no part of our war aims, we
> feel that, unless genuine self-government on true democratic
> principles is granted to those Austro-Hungarian nationalities
> who have long desired it, it is impossible to hope for the
> removal of those causes of unrest in that part of Europe which
> have so long threatened its general peace.

If compared with the reply to President Wilson, this speech
gave the definite impression that the government was backtrack-
ing on its previous statements, and that it was prepared to
abandon the subject nationalities. The speech was so interpreted,
with complete justification, by the émigrés.[75] But the previous
statement had been propaganda, directed at the American public,
which reflected certain preferences within the government but

not a policy that it was determined to follow. If anything, it had represented the government's maximum programme but not one to which it was committed. The speech to the Trades Union Congress represented the government's minimum programme and was, therefore, more indicative of government policy. The statements in the speech on the subject nationalities involved no commitment, and Lloyd George made it quite clear that the destruction of the monarchy was not a British war aim. But neither did he commit himself to its survival. The speech accurately reflected the dominant trend of government thought throughout 1917 on the future of eastern Europe. It stands out because, following the reply to President Wilson, it was the first precise public statement by the government showing its willingness to accept less than national self-determination. The speech indicated the strength of the government's desire for a negotiated peace in that it risked alienating the subject nationalities whose support might be necessary for the successful conduct of the war.

Despite the failure of the Smuts mission the government did not, as shown by Lloyd George's speech, abandon the idea of negotiations with Austria-Hungary. Smuts, Hankey and Milner remained incurable optimists. Lloyd George, however, began to agree with the foreign office that a separate peace was impossible and that negotiations could only be used as a weapon to weaken the Austrian war effort.[76] After February 1918 many who had supported the pursuit of a separate peace became pessimistic and began to lose interest. On 15 February 1918, Cecil wrote: 'My own impression is that we should do well to hold our hands so far as Austria is concerned, and allow events to produce their inevitable effect in that country.'[77]

In March 1918 the government made another attempt to begin negotiations. Kerr was sent to Switzerland to meet another Austrian agent in an attempt to follow up the Smuts–Mensdorff conversations. As in the previous case, Kerr's mission failed to establish any basis for further negotiations because the Austrian agent refused to discuss a separate peace.[78] Kerr only succeeded in confirming the results of the Smuts mission. On 21 March 1918, the Germans launched their great offensive on the western front, and the sheer force of events began to overtake the idea of a separate peace. When Horace Rumbold, the minister in Berne, suggested, on 26 March 1918, that if approached again by an Austrian agent he should reject the idea of future conversations, the foreign office approved.[79] The British government now ceased to pursue actively negotiations with Austria-Hungary, although the desire and the willingness to make a separate peace on the terms already discussed still remained.[80] But the government, unable to solve its strategic problems by negotiations with Austria-Hungary, now began to turn to the alternative it had always maintained.

During 1917 the primary British policy relevant to the future of eastern Europe was the pursuit of a separate peace with Austria-Hungary. It was not a policy designed for the future of eastern Europe but one produced by military necessity. Since Austria-Hungary would never negotiate for a separate peace, the foreign office was correct in thinking the policy impossible. In seeking a separate peace the government was pursuing a mirage. But even if Austria-Hungary had wanted such a peace there is good reason to assume that it would not have been able to detach itself from Germany. For the Allies the problem of Italian opposition to discussions with Austria-Hungary remained unsolved. Even the military advantages of a separate peace, never disputed within the government, are subject to some doubt. If the Austrians withdrew from the war, the Yugoslavs, Czechoslovaks, Poles, Serbians, Rumanians and Italians might follow their example, and the blockade of Germany would be broken. The Allies would still be faced with the major problem of defeating the German army on the western front. Throughout the war the British government sought painless solutions which would produce a quick victory. This tendency was dangerous, involving as it did attempts to by-pass the unavoidable problem of defeating the German army on the western front. Such was the pursuit of a separate peace. But even had the policy been successful it is uncertain whether the Allies would have derived from it the benefit they supposed. The government did not have a good record, considering its previous expectations of Italy and Rumania, in estimating military advantages.

There can be absolutely no doubt that the strategic situation was the primary reason why the government sought a separate peace. Military considerations, as the determining factors, over-rode the preferences within the government. Many advocates of a separate peace, like Hankey and Robertson, showed no interest whatever in the future structure of eastern Europe. Others, however – Milner, Smuts, Cecil and eventually Drummond – did prefer maintaining the Habsburg monarchy. But they did not propose this as a solution to the problems of eastern Europe until after the government sought negotiations which would obviously result in the survival of Austria-Hungary. They might be suspected of merely rationalizing the anticipated results of a policy already agreed upon for other reasons. Never at any time did they suggest that negotiations should be conducted for the precise purpose of saving the Habsburg monarchy. Like those with a preference for national self-determination, they did not campaign enthusiastically for their preference, which in any case was conditional upon a definite assurance that the monarchy would become anti-German. That assurance could only be given by Austria-Hungary deserting its ally, and if that did not happen, even the pro-Austrian advocates of a separate peace assumed that Britain would let events take their own course. Those who stated a preference for the survival of Austria-Hungary were influential within the government, but not decisive. In a government headed by Lloyd George, who did not share this preference, the pro-Austrian group cannot be said to have determined policy. During 1917 the discussions on the future of eastern Europe show that the government was not in favour of preserving the Habsburg monarchy but was conditionally willing to accept its survival as being consistent with British interests. That position can be seen in British policy from the very beginning of the war, and was precisely expressed in Lloyd George's speech to the Trades Union Congress. The preference within the government for the maintenance of the Habsburg monarchy had as little influence on British policy during 1917 as the much stronger preference for national self-determination had had between 1914 and 1916. The government remained uncommitted to either the preservation or destruction of the Habsburg monarchy, and prepared to accept whichever alternative contributed most to the conduct of the war.

Most of those who preferred national self-determination accepted the idea of a separate peace because it might shorten the war. Only the intelligence bureau opposed a separate peace because of national self-determination, but it had no significant influence on policy. Opposition within the foreign office was based not on national self-determination but on other considerations. Among the policy makers, the cause of the subject nationalities was never considered or suggested as an obstacle to a separate peace. The speculation on the possibility of autonomy for these nationalities must be dismissed as fantasy designed either to save the government's face or soothe guilty consciences. It is more than probable that the Habsburg government would never have accepted dictation on its own internal affairs and that the Allies would not have insisted on autonomy had agreement been reached on other issues. Even if Austria-Hungary had accepted such conditions there is no reason to assume that they would have been implemented. The Allies would not have resumed hostilities with Austria-Hungary for the sake of the subject nationalities. On 2 January 1918, Cecil wrote:

> I am afraid I attach very little importance to the Emperor
> Karl's alleged Liberal leanings. Even supposing them to be not
> only sincere but enduring, Autocrats and their Ministers have
> very little power. The policy of Austria-Hungary will always be
> the policy of its German and Magyar populations.[81]

During 1917, while the government sought a separate peace, its relations with the nationality organizations continued along lines already well established by the end of 1916. In most cases the pursuit of a separate peace, which definitely had priority over the cause of the nationalities, did not affect relations between the government and the nationality organizations. The government continued to use the nationalities as weapons of war, and in some cases, developed what were already standard practices even further. The major effect of the pursuit of a separate peace on the government's relations with the nationalities was that of reinforcing the quite natural desire to avoid commitments on national self-determination. As long as a separate peace seemed possible the government would not undertake commitments which would hamper or preclude negotiations. This unwillingness to undertake commitments limited but did not prevent the use of the nationalities. By maintaining its close relationship with the nationalities the government reserved the alternative of using them against the Central powers if it failed to use Austria-Hungary against Germany.

By the end of 1916 the government was using the nationality organizations extensively in the production and distribution of propaganda, particularly in the United States. In January 1917, following his return from the United States where, on behalf of the government, he had worked on the recruiting of American Poles for the Canadian army and the political organization of the Polish-Americans, Horodyski recommended to Drummond that greater organization was needed in the distribution of propaganda in the United States.[82] At this time Wellington House was distributing propaganda through the Bohemian National Alliance, the Polish National Alliance, the Polish Information Committee and possibly other organizations. To some extent these activities were supervised by Gaunt in New York and by Namier in London.[83] Probably as a result of this suggestion, although evidence on this subject is extremely scarce, the Bohemian National Alliance established the Slav Press Bureau under the directorship of Voska sometime before June 1917.[84] It seems that this organization was designed to co-ordinate the distribution of British propaganda among the nationality organizations in the United States. It would be reasonable for the government to use the Czechs, the most trusted and reliable of the nationalities, for work among the other nationalities in the United States. Although it is impossible to determine precisely when the organization was established, it had already, by June 1917, distributed at least 40,000 pamphlets.[85] During this period the Czechs continued to be a useful source of information and even expanded their distribution of pamphlets to include various eastern European communities in South America.[86]

The American election in November 1916 showed that a counterweight to the German-American vote was no longer necessary, and the later American declaration of war ended the problem of German plots in the United States. Nevertheless, British propaganda in the United States continued; first to maintain public support to reinforce the government's benevolent neutrality, and later to promote American determination to fight the war vigorously to its conclusion. But the propaganda changed in two important respects. During the first years of the war British propaganda was directed against Germany but had the effect, though not the aim, of bringing eastern Europe to the attention of the American public. In 1917 educating the Americans on the problems of eastern Europe became a primary aim of British propaganda in the hope that American interest in eastern Europe would lead to involvement.[87] Before 1917 British propaganda had helped the cause of the nationalities without explicitly advocating national self-determination. Following the Entente's reply to President Wilson, which the war cabinet instructed the propaganda agencies to publicize to the fullest extent, and in line with the text of that note, Wellington House now began to campaign for the cause of the nationalities.[88] The text of the reply was used as a basic guide for the contents of future propaganda, and was interpreted in its maximum sense so that liberation meant complete liberation and not autonomy. For this reason the pamphlets

produced during 1917 were far more explicit than their pre-
decessors on the subject of national self-determination: it was
now openly advocated as the best solution for the problems of
eastern Europe. In *A Lasting Peace*, G. W. Prothero wrote: 'We
have therefore stipulated for the emancipation of the Czechs of
Bohemia and Moravia, the Slovaks of Northern Hungary, the
Slavs of Croatia and other districts, and their formation into
independent States.'[89] This pamphlet was only one of a number
in which the change in the contents of British propaganda can
be seen.[90] Since the government was pursuing a separate peace
with Austria-Hungary which would necessitate abandoning
national self-determination at exactly the same time that Wellington House was campaigning for that cause, there was an obvious
divergence between policy and propaganda which is best explained by insufficient political control over a department in part
staffed by sympathizers of the nationalities.

The government's use of émigrés in espionage also continued
according to established patterns. In addition to his work in Polish
affairs, Horodyski continued as a trusted agent of the foreign
office, gathering political information in Europe.[91] Through
sources in Switzerland he supplied the government with information on Austria-Hungary and was at times involved in the
attempts to initiate negotiations for a separate peace.[92] The foreign
office considered Horodyski a reliable and useful agent while
Drummond, his contact, considered him a personal friend.[93]
Although some, like Hankey, disagreed with this estimate, there
can be no doubt that in the closeness of his relations with the
foreign office Horodyski had a position that was unique among
the émigrés.[94]

In the United States the Czechs under Voska continued to
work for Wiseman although there is little documentary evidence
as to their activities.[95] In May 1917 Wiseman proposed sending
American Czechs, Slovaks and Poles to Russia in a joint British
and American sponsored venture to combat pacifist propaganda.[96]
The American government immediately accepted the plan, but
the foreign office hesitated, hoping that the American government
would act alone and thereby incur all the risks of exposure. On
19 June 1917 it informed Wiseman: 'Dual control is difficult, and
we feel it would be better that we should not in any way appear
even unofficially.'[97] After being informed that Wilson was interested in the project, and that the Americans would not proceed
alone, the foreign office gave its approval and placed $75,000 at

Wiseman's disposal.[98] In trying to convince the foreign office to co-operate Wiseman wrote: 'I do not think that they [the Americans] will proceed unless we participate, because the scheme depends on the help of certain Slav Societies here, with whom the United States Government have no means of dealing without me.'[99] Although he was probably exaggerating his own importance, the statement is a reflection on the intimacy that existed between Wiseman and the nationality organizations.

The mission to Russia was headed by W. Somerset Maugham (code name Somerville), who had been working for M.I.1c in Switzerland, and included Voska, two members of the Bohemian National Alliance and one member of the Slovak League of America.[100] Receipts show that Maugham received at least $21,000 and Voska $4,000.[101] Through Masaryk, who, assisted by the British government, had travelled to Russia in July 1917 to organize a Czechoslovak army from the Czechoslovak prisoners of war, the mission established contact with the extensive Czechoslovak organization in Russia.[102] In this organization which comprised an estimated 1,200 agencies with an approximate membership of 70,000 the mission had at its disposal a large and well-disciplined apparatus for the collection of information and distribution of propaganda. Earlier action might have produced worthwhile results but it is probable that when the mission arrived in Russia on 2 September 1917, it was already too late. Maugham was able to indulge in some espionage, but by the time a comprehensive programme was formulated for the distribution of propaganda it was too late to act: the Bolsheviks had seized power.[103] On 4 November 1917, Maugham left Russia convinced that the tide in favour of the Bolsheviks was so strong as to make the mission's original aim of counteracting pacifist propaganda in Russia no longer possible.[104] This particular episode but not the use of Czechs in espionage and propaganda came to an end with Maugham's departure.[105] There is some evidence which suggests that the government might have made even more extensive use of the émigrés in espionage and propaganda.[106]

In the first months of 1917, while the United States was still neutral, the arrangements established in 1916 for recruiting Yugoslavs in America for the Serbian army continued to function. In the United States the recruiting was done by South Slav and French agents who sent their recruits to Canada. The British government agreed to share the costs with the French government and were responsible for the recruits from the time they entered

Canada until they reached the Serbian army. Because of the danger of alienating the American government, however, the British government absolutely refused to be involved in any manner whatever with the actual recruiting in the United States.[107] After the American declaration of war British officials in the United States began to assume a more active role in Yugoslav recruiting. On 5 September 1917, Balfour, hoping that the American government would accept, if not participate in, the recruiting of Yugoslavs of both Austrian and American nationality, asked Spring Rice to bring the matter to the attention of the American authorities.[108] Having difficulties organizing its own army, the government of the United States refused to participate in such recruiting but it agreed to allow recruiting of Yugoslavs not subject to service in the American army.[109] On this basis the original arrangements continued but now with the open support of the British government.[110] Unfortunately there are no reliable figures on the numbers recruited.

Yugoslav recruitment was not a peripheral issue because the continued existence of the Serbian army depended upon securing replacements. For that reason Balfour told Spring Rice: 'The matter is of considerable urgency and importance.'[111] Italy had the greatest potential for supplying replacements for the Serbian army because of the number of its Yugoslav prisoners of war, but Sonnino was reluctant to release them. Although he claimed that there was a danger of Austrian reprisals it is obvious that he had no desire to strengthen Italy's potential rival on the Adriatic.[112] The placing of Yugoslavs in the Serbian army might be interpreted as acceptance of the idea that the South Slavs were one nation, and that was unacceptable to Sonnino. The war office considered the matter significant enough to be brought to the attention of the war cabinet and, after the original request for the release of Yugoslavs was rejected, Rodd was instructed to apply pressure on Sonnino.[113] But such measures failed to move the Italian foreign minister whose obstinacy considerably annoyed the British government. Cecil noted on one despatch: 'I wonder if the presence of Baron Sonnino at the Ministry of Foreign Affairs is really an advantage.'[114] Both the British and French governments continued to pressure Sonnino to change his attitude but without success.

During 1916 the Czechs in England, who, because of the recommendation of the London Czech Committee, were not subject to internment were singled out by the war office for the distinction of being allowed to serve in the British army. The authorities did not directly recruit Czechs but worked through the London Czech Committee.[115] In fact the Czechs were given a choice between military service, national service or internment.[116] By the end of May 1917 at least 321 had been recruited from the Czech community in Britain, which numbered approximately 1,000, and at least six who opposed military service were interned on the recommendation of the London Czech Committee.[117] In July 1917 the French government began to establish a separate Czech army for which it hoped to gain recruits from all the Allied countries.[118] Recruiting began by November 1917, and, as in the case of the Yugoslavs, French and Czech agents worked in the United States where they got an estimated 30,000 volunteers.[119] On 16 December 1917, the French government officially announced the creation of a Czechoslovak army under the political authority of the Czechoslovak National Committee but under the military command of the French army.[120] The British government eventually co-operated in the formation of this army by releasing for service its Czech prisoners of war.[121] The French also wanted the Italians to release their Czech prisoners for this army, but instead the Italian government followed the French example and established its own Czech army.[122] In March 1918 the Italian government agreed to establish this army on the same terms as the army in France in that while under Italian military command it was subject to the political authority of the Czechoslovak National Committee.[123] While serving on different fronts the Czechoslovak military forces were recognized as one army with one political allegiance.

Early in the war the Russian government had formed Czech military units from the Czech communities in Russia. In 1916 these had been expanded by recruiting the Czechs who had deserted in large numbers from the Austro-Hungarian army. After the revolution in March 1917 these forces had been expanded even further by the Provisional government until they reached the size of an army corps.[124] In July 1917 Masaryk travelled to Russia with the assistance of the British government to work on the organization and expansion of this army.[125] It has been claimed that he went at the request of the British government and as its paid agent, but this cannot be substantiated by documentary evidence.[126] There can be no doubt that the government would not have hesitated to use Masaryk in this fashion had its interests been at stake, but in July 1917 it showed no interest in the formation of Czech units in Russia. As president of the Czechoslovak National Committee Masaryk was able to establish his authority over the Czech army in Russia so that by the spring of 1918 the committee possessed the allegiance of all Czechoslovak forces fighting for the Entente.[127]

The British government was in no way involved with this Czechoslovak army until November 1917, when the French government suggested supporting it and other military units in Russia prepared to continue the war against the Central powers.[128] The collapse of the Russian army after the failure of the July offensive in Galicia exposed the right flank of the Rumanian army and relieved the enemy of pressure on the eastern front. The proposal to support a number of military units in Russia determined to continue the war was designed to organize these forces and so reconstruct an eastern front. The proposal appealed to the foreign office but Clerk warned:

> As regards the Czechs, the risks they run if captured by the enemy are obvious, but if they are willing to incur them, we need not worry. But in return the Allied Govts. will be considered pledged to support Czech aspirations to the best of their power. Bohemia is the buckle of the Slavonic belt which we need to draw across Eastern Europe, but her liberation involves highly complex political and military problems, which cannot be lightly undertaken.[129]

The declared intention of the Bolshevik government to make peace with the Central powers weakened the strategic position of the Allies even further, and intensified the need to organize whatever forces were available in eastern Europe to combat the enemy. On 14 December 1917, the war cabinet decided that:

> Any sum of money required for the purpose of maintaining alive in South East Russia the resistance to the Central powers, considered necessary by the War Office in consultation with the Foreign Office should be furnished, the money to be paid in instalments so long as the recipients continued the struggle.[130]

Arrangements to carry out this policy in conjunction with the French government were worked out at a conference in Paris on 23 December 1917, attended by Cecil, Milner and General G. M. W. Macdonogh, the director of military intelligence.[131] From this time the Czechoslovak army in Russia was financially supported by the French and British governments and according to one source, by June 1918 it had received £80,000 from the British representatives in Russia.[132] By the end of March 1918 there were about 42,000 men in the first Czechoslovak corps and a second was being formed.[133]

Before 1917 the British government had used the émigrés primarily in espionage and propaganda. Although émigrés had been recruited in 1916, that policy was not fully developed until 1917 when military service became the major form of co-operation between the government and the nationality organizations. This use of the Yugoslavs and Czechoslovaks was the direct outgrowth of the co-operation which had existed in the early years of the war. In most cases it was carried out by the same officials, both in the government and the nationality organizations, and was the logical extension of their earlier policies. Once the government had begun to use the nationalities in espionage and propaganda, it was natural and probably inevitable that it would use them to form military units.

The successful use of the nationalities depended upon the willingness of the émigrés to co-operate with the government. In fact the leaders of the nationality organizations not only volunteered their services, but also suggested many of the forms of co-operation which were later adopted. For example, the idea of creating Czechoslovak military units originated with the émigrés who had campaigned for such a policy long before it was adopted. Once the Allied governments agreed to form such units their success depended almost entirely upon the émigrés who undertook the task of recruiting. In his memoirs Beneš explained the émigrés' willingness to co-operate:

> The Allies could desert us only if we ourselves were to desert beforehand. This meant a perpetual struggle, and the general establishment of our independence during the war by means of our own work and the sacrifice of our own blood.[134]

The political influence of the émigrés increased because the more the Allies used them, the more dependent upon them they became. By the spring of 1918 the Czechoslovak National Committee had political control over three Czechoslovak armies. The possession of such military force was one step on the road to statehood and it increased enormously the political influence of the Czechoslovak émigrés in Allied countries. Now the Czechoslovaks could, if they chose, make demands upon the Allied governments which could not be easily brushed aside. The

Yugoslavs were not so fortunate since Yugoslav volunteers had always been sent to the Serbian army over which the émigrés had no control. There was no separate Yugoslav army and therefore no lever with which the Yugoslavs could pry concessions from the Allied governments.

The pursuit of a separate peace obviously did not cause the government to abandon the nationalities who were indeed used more than before. If a separate peace with Austria-Hungary proved impossible, the government could always intensify its use of the nationalities in political warfare against Austria-Hungary. The government's attitude towards the émigrés and their British supporters reflected the contribution of the nationalities to the war effort rather than the desire for a separate peace. During 1917 good relations existed between the officials and the émigrés, as one might expect in view of their co-operation, and the government did what it could to assist them. There were a number of incidents which reflected government support for the nationalities despite the fact that the government was seeking a separate peace. The foreign office, for example, facilitated the transfer of funds to Masaryk from the Bohemian Alliance and made the arrangements for his trip to Russia.[135] In February 1917 Supilo, who in October 1914 had been exempted from the restrictions which applied to enemy aliens, got into difficulty with the Special Branch of Scotland Yard.[136] Both the police and the home office wanted to treat him like any other enemy alien but were prevented from doing so by the foreign office.[137] In fact, Clerk and Harold Nicolson, who were responsible for the intervention of the foreign office, were considerably annoyed by the police harassment of Supilo.[138] According to Clerk:

> . . . Mr. Supilo is none the less a serious leader of the
> Jugo-Slavs and should be treated with all possible consideration,
> as not only is he heart and soul with the Allies, but he has more
> common sense and more idea of what is practical than any of
> the other members of the Jugo-Slav Committee.[139]

The government also assumed a very lenient, if not protective, attitude towards Seton-Watson, despite his criticisms of the policy of the government and its allies. While not protecting itself from the attacks of Seton-Watson, it often protected him from the attacks of his many enemies. In March 1917 one of his severest critics was interned, apparently on his recommendation.[140] On 30 March 1917, Seton-Watson was called up for military service and it appeared as if his political and journalistic activities had come to an end. It is possible that the call-up was arranged by his political opponents, for on 4 March 1917, J. King, a member of parliament associated with the Union of Democratic Control, noted: 'Seton-Watson has now joined the R.A.M.C. – thanks to me. I hope this may curb his baneful activities.[141] If this was an attempt to neutralize his influence, it failed because, according to the minutes of the war cabinet:

> The War Cabinet had under consideration the case of Mr. Seton-Watson, the authority on Serbian affairs, who was serving as a private in the Royal Army Medical Corps, and whose services as an expert were required by the Information Department. The War Cabinet decided that – Private Seton-Watson should be attached for duty to the Information Department.[142]

The government took no action against Seton-Watson's periodical *The New Europe*, even though it received complaints that some of the articles were anti-Italian.[143] It also adopted a similar attitude towards Yugoslav propaganda. When the director of special intelligence requested permission from the foreign office to prohibit the export of Yugoslav propaganda, the latter refused except in those cases where the propaganda included direct attacks on the Italian government, and reserved for itself the right to decide in all cases whether the offending pamphlet should be prohibited.[144] Within Britain, the Yugoslavs remained free to publish without restriction. The Russians or the Serbians usually assumed the responsibility of protecting Yugoslavs in neutral countries but since neither had representatives in Peru, the foreign office accorded unofficial protection for the Yugoslavs in that country.[145] These incidents are of little importance in themselves, but they do reflect the government's support, and possibly sense of responsibility, for the nationalities.

During 1917 the relations between the government and the nationality organizations centred almost exclusively on their co-operation in espionage, propaganda and the formation of military units. There was little interchange of ideas between the officials and the émigrés. During 1915 and 1916 the émigrés had presented their political programmes to the foreign office and had won at least the limited support of a number of officials. But the period of proselytizing in official circles was past. There was little to be gained by the resubmission of the same programmes since the fate of the nationalities depended more on the success of their efforts to co-operate with the government and upon the course of the war. During 1917 the Czechoslovaks and Yugoslavs did not press their views on the government, did not try to prompt discussion in official circles of their political programmes and did not attempt to force the government to adopt a policy favouring national self-determination.

The Yugoslavs had the least contact with the government for reasons peculiar to their own movement. The connection that was weakened by Supilo's resignation from the Yugoslav Committee in June 1916 was severed by his death in September 1917.[146] Since the Yugoslav Committee subordinated itself to the Serbian government, the British government tended to deal with South Slav affairs through the latter. The subordinate relationship of the committee to the government, the reason for Supilo's resignation, was confirmed in June 1917 when Pašić and Trumbić signed the declaration of Corfu which announced their support for the union of the Serbs, Croats, and Slovenes under the Karageorgević dynasty.[147]

Had the nationalities seriously attempted to promote the discussion of national self-determination within official circles, they would have had little success. The attention of the government was obviously devoted almost entirely to a separate peace with which national self-determination was utterly irreconcilable. Even if the Allies achieved their maximum aims in a separate peace, the Czechoslovaks and Yugoslavs would gain nothing more than autonomy, a solution totally unacceptable to the émigrés who had staked everything on national self-determination. Indeed, they might even be entirely abandoned. Since national self-determination for the Yugoslavs and Czechoslovaks now seemed impossible there was little desire or inclination within the government to discuss it. Whenever the issue was brought up, it was only within the context of a separate peace and, therefore, on terms which were a negation of the principle itself.

In October 1917, following the recognition of the Czechoslovak National Committee by the Italian and French governments, Beneš sought some act from the British government to reaffirm its support of the Czechoslovak cause. Approaches on his behalf were made to Balfour and, on 25 October 1917, he submitted a memorandum to the foreign office after discussions with Clerk on the subject of recognition.[148] It is important to note the manner in which Beneš approached the government because the tactics of Beneš and Masaryk probably explain, to some extent, why the British officials tended to prefer the Czechs to the other émigrés. In his discussions with Clerk, Beneš began by stating that the Czechs were united and committed to the Entente. Their support was absolute not conditional. He then reminded Clerk of the Czech contribution to the struggle and requested that some encouragement be given to the Czechs in the form of a public statement alluding to their desire for independence.[149] The significance of his approach is that, unlike the Polish émigrés, he neither made demands upon the government nor threatened it with loss of Czechoslovak support if it failed to act upon his suggestion. Clerk agreed that something should be done to encourage the Czechs and added: 'I believe that we are under a great obligation to Czech organizations in America, both for information, documents, and frustration of acts of violence and sabotage.' Balfour brought the issue to the attention of the cabinet on 21 November 1917, and stated:

> As far as his personal sympathies were concerned, although he did not in any way wish to minimise the efforts of many of the Poles, he thought the Bohemians were deserving of the greatest consideration from the Allies. They had made great sacrifices for the Allies, but he feared that, owing to their geographical position, the ideal of independence appeared chimerical; the utmost that they could hope for being home rule within the Austro-Hungarian Empire.[150]

But the Czechs received no public encouragement whatever, for the government did not even consider accepting a commitment to their cause; neither they nor the Yugoslavs were mentioned in the speech to the Trades Union Congress. The British government was under no compulsion to recognize the Czechoslovak National Committee since, unlike the French and Italian governments, it was not forming a separate Czechoslovak army in Britain. As long as the government was intent on a separate peace it would not create unnecessary obstacles to negotiations with Austria-Hungary and could, therefore, scarcely satisfy the émigrés. By pursuing a separate peace while using the nationalities as a weapon of war, the government was following a policy that was ultimately contradictory. But it was free to follow this policy without resolving the contradiction because the Yugoslavs and Czechoslovaks did not demand a commitment in exchange

for their services. This situation could not, however, last indefi-
nitely. As the émigrés' contribution to the war, and hence their
power, increased, they would be in a better position to make
demands and would almost inevitably do so.

The government's failure to give any public assurance to the
Czechs was certainly not the result of any ill-will. Not everyone
in the government was pro-Czech but, on the other hand, it is
remarkable that no one in the government ever seems to have
commented adversely about them. Statements like Cecil's 'The
Poles always were a most unreliable people', of which numerous
examples can be found in the official documents, never appear
to have been made in reference to the Czechs.[151] The undeniable
popularity of the Czechs in British official circles probably
resulted in part from the personal qualities of their leaders, particularly Masaryk, and in part from their services to the Entente.
In any case, among the various nationalities, they made the
greatest positive impression on British officials. Maugham's
opinion of the Czechs, formed when he worked with them in
Russia, may not have been typical but is worth quoting:

> here I see a patriotism that fills me with amazement. It is a
> passion so single and so devouring that it leaves room for no
> others. I feel that awe rather than admiration is due to these
> men who have sacrificed everything for the cause, and not in
> twos or threes, fanatics among an apathetic herd, but in tens of
> thousands; they have given everything they had, their peace,
> their home, their fortune, their lives, to gain independence for
> their country.[152]

The lack of comment on the fate of the nationalities in Lloyd
George's speech to the Trades Union Congress caused a resur-
gence of Yugoslav activity. On 9 January 1918, Jovan Jovanović,
the Serbian minister and a supporter of the Yugoslavs, asked
Cecil if the speech meant that the Yugoslavs had been abandoned.
Cecil, although not a supporter of national self-determination,
replied that:

> if we had a complete victory and were able to dictate any
> terms we pleased I should favour the establishment in some
> form or other of a Yugo-Slav state as also the granting of
> independence to the Czechs; though how far any such object
> would be obtainable depended on the future of the war.[153]

The Serbian government did not find such statements reassuring and continued to press for a British pronouncement on the future of Yugoslavia.[154] There was, of course, no possibility that the government would make any meaningful statement on the future of the Yugoslav cause as long as a separate peace with Austria-Hungary seemed possible. Even if the lack of action annoyed the South Slavs and weakened their war effort, the government would not create new obstacles to a separate peace.[155] In response to one request by Jovanović, Hardinge commented: 'This sort of "demarche" is in reality "window dressing" for Serbian consumption. The Minister must know that under present conditions such aims cannot be realized.'[156]

It might appear as if during 1917 the government was following two separate and contradictory policies on the future of eastern Europe. If the government's action is analysed on the assumption that it reflected the government's political aims in eastern Europe then that action becomes incomprehensible: the pursuit of a separate peace gives the impression that the government desired the maintenance of the Habsburg monarchy, while its support of the nationalities gives the impression that it favoured national self-determination. The apparent contradiction cannot be explained in terms of the structure of the government or the confusion that undoubtedly existed within it during the war because the actions giving the impression that there were two policies were carried out by the same departments and often by the same men. The assumption that government action in these affairs reflected its political aims must, therefore, be rejected. If, however, it is assumed that the government's action was based on immediate strategic calculations, then that action at once appears consistent and comprehensible. The pursuit of a separate peace and the government's relations with the nationalities were two aspects of a policy designed to derive the maximum strategic advantage from the political problems of eastern Europe, which were, in any case, of secondary importance to the British government.

In March 1918 the government was still prepared to accept either the survival of the Habsburg monarchy or national self-determination, as long as neither solution increased German power. But it was not committed to either solution and was not absolutely convinced that one was intrinsically better than the other. During 1917 it had pursued a separate peace in preference to, but not to the exclusion of, national self-determination because this course of action seemed to offer the maximum strategic advantage. But the government was still prepared to accept national self-determination and, because it had maintained its relations with the nationalities, was still in a position to do so.

6 : THE RECOGNITION OF THE POLISH NATIONAL COMMITTEE, 1917

During 1917 the Poles were in a position entirely different from that of the Yugoslavs and Czechoslovaks. The declaration of the Central powers on 5 November 1916, of the creation of an independent kingdom of Poland internationalized the Polish problem by altering the territorial settlement of the Congress of Vienna. This act escalated the competition among the belligerents for Polish support and focused that competition, hitherto restricted to the Polish community in America, on Poland itself. The Russian government might still refuse to recognize that Poland was an international problem, but it could not overlook the military significance of this declaration.

Before November 1916 the British government considered the Polish problem primarily as an aspect of Anglo-American relations. The foreign office had avoided involvement in Polish affairs in Europe, but had sought the support and the assistance of the Polish-American community. Anglo-Polish relations, insofar as they existed, developed within the context of the political warfare in the United States but divorced from the Polish problem in Europe. That problem remained frozen as long as the Russian, German and Austro-Hungarian governments maintained the Polish settlement by treating it as an internal problem and avoiding any action which would constitute internationalization. The political warfare which made the Polish issue important in Anglo-American relations continued after 1916, but ceased to supply the context in which Anglo-Polish relations developed. The emergence of the Polish problem in Europe now supplied that context while the Polish aspects of Anglo-American relations became less important and relatively unimportant.

Changes in the nature of the Polish problem did not change the British approach to Polish affairs: it remained as it had been since 1914. Since the Polish nation was a weapon which could be used by either side, the primary concern of the British government was to maximize its military advantages from the Polish situation, while minimizing those of the Central powers. On one hand the Allies were under constant pressure, created by enemy initiatives, to undertake measures to counteract German attempts to win Polish support while, on the other, the worsening strategic situation forced the Allies to use every means available, including the nationalities, to increase their military strength. These two factors motivated almost every British action in Polish affairs during 1917. While the government used the Polish nation as a weapon of war, it remained determined to avoid embarrassing commitments on the future of Poland. Such commitments had always been avoided because of the attitude of the Russian government, and because, by limiting future alternatives, they were always inexpedient. During 1917 the natural desire to avoid commitments was reinforced by the Entente's loss of faith in its ability to win the war and by the possibility which now emerged of a separate peace with Austria-Hungary. But in contrast to Czechoslovak and Yugoslav affairs, Polish affairs were not significantly influenced by the possibility of a separate peace until December 1917, when Poland ceased to be in any sense whatever a Russian problem.

British policy was determined by basic military considerations and not by any desire for Polish independence. In fact almost no thought was given to independence, the form it might assume, or its potential significance for European relations. As that independence became more likely, the desire developed within the British government for a Poland consistent with British interests and therefore hostile to Germany. But this desire must not be mistaken for a desire for an independent Poland, for it could be satisfied by a number of alternatives not involving independence. Although personal preferences existed, the government remained uncommitted to any particular solution to the Polish problem and prepared to accept any of the alternatives as long as it did not involve an increase in German military potential. In fact, the government was prepared to accept whatever alternative produced the greatest immediate strategic advantage. The general policy of using the Poles as weapons of war was never clearly enunciated and did not entirely represent the views of those officials who were pro-Polish. But the following analysis of British action in Polish affairs shows clearly that the government supported action designed to thwart German policy in Poland, that it initiated and supported other attempts to gain military advantages from the Polish situation, that it consciously and assiduously avoided commitments on the future of Poland and that it was prepared to barter the future of Poland in exchange for immediate strategic advantages.

Before November 1916 the British government had ample warning that the Central powers were considering the establishment of an independent kingdom of Poland and the creation of a Polish army.[1] The attitude of the Russian government made action to forestall this threat impossible but the foreign office could at least take comfort in the thought that it might finally force the Russians to assess the Polish situation realistically. According to Clerk: 'Any interference by us would be resented in Petrograd and might easily make things worse. The best hope is that the Austro-German offer, when made, will force even the reactionaries to see that Russia must make a counterbid.'[2]

In the latter half of 1916 developments in Russia caused a considerable degree of uneasiness within the foreign office and strengthened the resolve of the government to maintain its reserve on the Polish issue. The dismissal of Sazonov in July 1916 was attributed to his liberal attitude towards Poland.[3] The appointment of Boris Stürmer, a reactionary hostile to Polish reform, as his successor justifiably reinforced the ever-present fear within the foreign office that Russia might agree to a separate peace with the Central powers rather than continue a war which might eventually result in the loss of Poland.[4] Grey was particularly apprehensive and wrote on 14 October 1916: 'The Germans are no doubt holding up the proclamation of an autonomous buffer state of Poland because it would be fatal to separate peace with Russia.'[5] When the Central powers finally acted, the foreign office, primarily concerned about a separate peace, reacted almost with relief, despite the military advantages the Central powers might gain from this proclamation. Seeing the proclamation as a tactical error Hardinge wrote to Bertie: 'I think that the fears held in high quarters of a separate peace between Russia and Germany are now greatly diminished . . .'[6]

Following the proclamation of an independent kingdom of Poland, the Central powers began to work on the formation of a Polish army.[7] Unless the Poles were to be totally abandoned to the Central powers the proclamation necessitated some response from the Entente. Although the initiative had to come from the Russian government, there was never any doubt that the British would co-operate. The military significance of enemy policy in Poland was clearly understood when Robertson reported to the cabinet that there were about 700,000 men in occupied Poland available for military service.[8] Following a request by the Russian government on 12 November 1916, the foreign office issued a statement charging that the proclamation was a violation of international law.[9] From Paris Asquith, in concert with Briand, also issued a protest which included, at his insistence, a reference to the Grand Duke's promises of 1914.[10] This reference, which might have annoyed the Russians, was probably suggested by Clerk. He had accompanied Asquith to Paris and on 6 November 1916, had written: 'I believe that the German proclamation will be the best form of Allied propaganda, especially if followed, as it should be, by Russia renewing the assurances of the Grand Duke's Manifesto.'[11] By protesting against the action of the Central powers the British government was acting according to Russian policy. Even though something more than a protest was obviously necessary if the Central powers were to be deprived of Polish support, the British government, passively hoping that the Russians would themselves respond to the challenge more decisively, and afraid of offending the Russian government, still refused to take the initiative in Polish affairs.[12] The Russians were not unaware of the military significance of German policy and, like the British, realized that some positive action was necessary. The tsar's Order of the Day of 25 December 1916, stated that peace negotiations were impossible because Russian aims, such as the creation of a free Poland consisting of its three component parts, had not yet been achieved. On 5 January 1917, the tsar told Count Wielopolski, the leader of the Polish Realist party, that 'free' as used in his Order of the Day meant a Poland with a constitution, diet and army.[13] It certainly appeared as if the Imperial government was moving in the direction, long desired by the British government, of an autonomous Poland.

Despite these measures the British government was losing patience with the Russian attitude towards Poland. When Mikhail Pokrovskii, the Russian foreign minister, was shown the text of the Entente's reply to President Wilson, which had been drafted at the Anglo-French conference in London, he protested that the reference to the tsar's Order of the Day tended to give the Polish issue an international character. Buchanan replied to Pokrovskii that: 'So far as Posen and Galicia were concerned that question could not be divested of its international character . . .'[14] He also wrote to Hardinge the next day: 'I think that we ought to tell the Russians quite plainly that that question has now assumed this character.'[15] The foreign office, now directed by Balfour, who does not appear to have shared Grey's fear of Russia, was no longer prepared to accept objections of this type from the Russian government and, following Balfour's instructions, Buchanan continued in league with Maurice Paléologue, the French ambassador, to insist upon the original text of the note.[16] In finally accepting the text, however, Pokrovskii warned the Allies that there were limits to what his government would accept: 'I must however make it quite clear that my Government expressly understands that elaboration of future status of Poland must be reserved exclusively to Russia and that question cannot form subject of International discussion.'[17]

In January 1917, despite this warning and unaware of Wielopolski's interview with the tsar, the cabinet instructed Milner, who was about to embark for Russia:

> to exercise his discretion as to the extent to which he might be able to urge upon the Russian authorities the importance of conciliating Polish opinion, from the point of view both of Germany's efforts to organize a Polish army, and of the influence of the large Polish element in the United States.[18]

On 14 January 1917, the Central powers established a Polish Council of State and pressed forward their plans for a Polish army. The foreign office was kept informed of these events by Polish émigrés, who constantly warned that the dangers presented by enemy action in Poland could only be averted by the Entente's open and declared support for Polish independence.[19] The émigrés did not hesitate to take advantage of the opportunity, presented by the action of the Central powers, to play one side off against the other. But the foreign office did not immediately respond to these warnings because the Russian government was already acting on the Polish question. Following the interview of 5 January 1917, the tsar set up a special commission under Wielopolski to work out plans for the future structure of Poland.[20] After discussions with Wielopolski and other Polish émigrés when he accompanied Milner to Russia, Clerk concluded that:

> the first essential in any advance towards Polish unity and independence, [is] namely, that the initiative depends on, and must come from, the Russian Government. Unless Russia herself of her own volition, and *without* pressure from other Powers, offers all the Poles a measure of independence, such as

that outlined in the Emperor's announcement to Wielopolski, Poland can never start on her progress to self-Government.[21]

Shortly after this reaffirmation of the policy of non-intervention in Polish affairs the entire situation changed because of the outbreak of revolution in Russia. Between November 1916 and March 1917 the British government had remained passive in Polish affairs while welcoming Russian attempts to win Polish support. The foreign office had hoped for Russian action on this problem since 1915. For the future of Poland, the foreign office still preferred autonomy within the Russian empire, as set out by Balfour.[22] Even Drummond, who was particularly pro-Polish, admitted that a united Poland under the Russian crown would be the best solution since Polish independence as advocated in the Paget–Tyrrell memorandum was, under existing circumstances, quite unattainable.[23] The Balfour solution would weaken Germany by making Poland, beyond any doubt, an internal Russian question. It would be an innovation in Russian internal affairs, but would not introduce a new factor into international relations. But the future structure of Poland and its potential role in international relations were not considerations, in any sense, for the British government. Its desire for Russian action on the Polish issue and its exasperation at the failure of the Russian government to act quickly and decisively to satisfy the Poles was based upon the fear, clearly shown in the cabinet's instructions to Milner, that the Central powers would win Polish support and use it against the Entente.

The establishment of a liberal government in Russia after the revolution gave the Entente the opportunity to act on the Polish issue. Possibly sensing the weakness of the Provisional government, the British government now acted on the warnings from Polish émigrés about the progress of the enemy's Polish policy. On 22 March 1917, Dmowski submitted a memorandum to the foreign office in which he claimed that German efforts to create a Polish army had met with some success and that, freed from their oath of allegiance by the abdication of the tsar, the Poles might turn to the Central powers if the Provisional government continued to treat Poland as an internal problem.[24] While probably not swallowing Dmowski's nonsense about the oath of allegiance, Balfour forwarded this report to Buchanan with the comment that it was worth consideration.[25] On 25 March 1917, in conversation with Paul Miliukov, the new Russian foreign minister, Buchanan tried to overcome Miliukov's misgivings about Polish independence by claiming that: 'Such a proposal would win over Poles at once to side of the Allies and would be received with enthusiasm in America.'[26] In reporting this conversation to the foreign office, Buchanan asked permission to raise the question again and to point out to Miliukov the serious danger of the Poles turning to the Central powers. Clerk greeted Buchanan's suggestion enthusiastically, supported the idea of Polish independence, and stated that Russian fears as to the future policy of an independent Poland could be overcome by a military alliance between the two countries.[27] Hardinge fully realized the military necessity of some act to appease the Poles but was more hesitant than Clerk about independence because he shared Russian fears that an independent Poland might be drawn into the German orbit. He suggested, therefore, that Russia be urged to go as far towards independence as possible while establishing guarantees as to future Polish policy.[28] On 28 March 1917, Balfour wrote to Buchanan:

> I agree that in our treatment of the Polish question we must keep Russia with us. But it is very important that Russian Government should bear in mind certain aspects of that question which deeply affect the allies. (1) The Poles have it in their power to add enormously to Germany's strength by joining the German forces either as soldiers or as workmen . . . (2) The re-creation of Poland in any satisfactory shape must affect Austria and Germany as well as Russia. In other words the Polish question is necessarily international and not merely Russian. Bearing these two points in mind would it not be desirable to sound the Russian Government as to policy of making some declaration about Polish freedom which would give reasonable satisfaction to the Poles and making this declaration not merely in the name of Russia but in fact of the Allies generally?[29]

Balfour was cautious enough to refer to Polish freedom, not independence. Although Buchanan's comments of 25 March 1917, may have influenced Miliukov's declaration on Poland of 29 March 1917, Balfour's telegram probably arrived after his decision.[30] Nevertheless the telegram was significant in showing that the British government was no longer prepared to treat Poland as an internal Russian problem, that it was primarily concerned about the military aspects of the problem and that, while hoping to avoid a breach with Russia, it was no longer prepared to leave the initiative entirely to the Russian government.

On 29 March 1917, Miliukov declared that the Russian government intended to create an independent Poland comprising those areas inhabited by Poles, possessing its own constitution and army, and linked to Russia by a military alliance. He added the reservation, however, that this programme would be subject to revision by a future Russian constituent assembly.[31] This solution was called independence although it sounded more like autonomy. According to Drummond the declaration satisfied Balfour, whose original fear that an independent Poland would release Germany from Russian pressure was mollified by the proposed military alliance.[32] Once Dmowski and Horodyski had expressed their approval, the foreign office seemed satisfied with the declaration. Hardinge commented: 'On the whole, it gives the impression of a generous and statesmanlike measure.'[33] Since the Russian government had acted independently, the original suggestion for a joint declaration was abandoned.[34] But the ever-present Polish émigrés informed the foreign office that unless the British government associated itself with the declaration, it would have no effect in Poland.[35] On 5 April 1917, the foreign office instructed Buchanan to inform Miliukov that:

> His Majesty's Government are happy to give their complete adherence to the principle of an independent and united Poland, which they recognize has now been rendered possible by the liberal and statesmanlike pronouncement of the Provisional Russian Government and Great Britain is ready to make every effort in unison with Russia to secure its attainment.[36]

Had the original Russian declaration not been somewhat equivocal, and had this statement, drafted by Clerk, been without the phrase 'in unison with Russia', it might have committed the government to a great deal.[37] On 26 April 1917, Andrew Bonar Law, the chancellor of the exchequer, in reply to a question in the house of commons, welcomed the Russian proclamation with a statement that had been approved by the cabinet: 'Our efforts in the war will be directed towards helping Poland to realize her unity on the lines described in the Russian proclamation, that is to say, under conditions which will make her strong and independent.'[38] The original text of this statement had been suggested by Clerk after a conversation with Dmowski and was worded: 'The efforts of Great Britain in the war would be directed to helping Poland to realize her union and independence under conditions which would make her a strong and independent State . . .'[39] Following a request by Miliukov this text was modified and considerably weakened, so that the final statement delivered to the house of commons was far less committal than the one originally proposed by Clerk.[40] Nevertheless the government seemed committed to work with the Russians for the fulfilment of the promises to Poland.

Following the pattern established in 1916, the British government continued to prefer the conservative Poles of Wielopolski's Realist party and Dmowski's National Democratic party, with whom Horodyski, Alma-Tadema, Smulski and Paderewski were associated, to the left wing represented by Zaleski and the Polish Information Committee. This preference was clearly shown by most of the officials in contact with Poles, and in the government's daily handling of minor aspects of Polish affairs.[41] In those areas where Namier had influence there were exceptions, but these were insignificant and can be explained in part by the confusion and lack of co-ordination, resulting from overwork, which existed within the government and which gave Namier some freedom of action.[42] Since the foreign office refused to have any relations whatever with Polish émigrés in Britain not associated with Dmowski, most of its information on developments in Poland came from Polish conservatives, who were thus in an ideal position to influence the development of foreign policy. Dmowski and Ladislas Sobanski passed information directly to the foreign office, while two of Dmowski's lieutenants, Maurice Seyda and Erazm Piltz, channelled information through Rumbold.[43] The one exceptional source of information was Esme Howard, the minister in Stockholm, who established contact with representatives of the Polish left-wing in German-occupied Poland.[44] Information that German policy was achieving some success in Poland and that action was necessary to prevent the Poles from supporting the enemy invariably came from Polish émigrés who stood to gain the most from Allied countermeasures. The fact that Dmowski's followers, who were widely dispersed throughout Allied and neutral countries, were permitted to communicate through the facilities of the British government is an indication of the strength of their position.[45] Among Dmowski's supporters Horodyski's influence on the British government was the greatest, greater even than Dmowski's. Because of his work for the government, he, more than any other Polish émigré, was trusted and respected by the foreign office.[46] As Polish fortunes improved Dmowski's aims increased. In March 1917, following the abdication of the tsar, he informed the foreign office that Polish autonomy within Russia was no longer sufficient, and that he was now working for a large, independent Poland with access to the sea.[47]

Dmowski's rise was accompanied by the eclipse of Namier, his most bitter antagonist in official circles, whose slight influence on the foreign office disappeared during 1917. As an employee of Wellington House Namier never had official access to the foreign office, but when Polish affairs were discussed his views were presented and defended by Percy. Since Percy, as an expert on America, dealt with Polish affairs only when they were part of Anglo-American relations, his involvement declined when the centre of attention in Polish affairs shifted to Europe. This development limited Namier's unofficial access to the foreign office and his reports for Wellington House, although circulated, appear to have had little influence.[48] In reference to the conflicts between Namier and Dmowski, Drummond wrote:

> Of course I know about Namier, and Eustace Percy vouches for his absolute honesty. At the same time I regard him with considerable suspicion. I disagree with a great deal of what he writes . . . his attack on Dmowski and other Poles is, in spite of what he says, purely personal and quite unjust.[49]

In answer to similar charges Namier once wrote to Kerr:
> You know me well enough to believe me that I am not actuated here by personal resentment against Dmowski and his whole Polish Black Hundred crew. After all from the very beginning it was not a personal question. I have never known any of their leaders personally and merely distrusted them as one disliked and distrusted their Russian reactionary confrères.[50]

Despite his lack of influence in the foreign office, Namier did not lose all possibility of influencing foreign policy, his friendship with Kerr gave him at least potential access to the prime minister. When Wellington House was merged into the new department of information in February 1917 Namier began to write weekly reports on Polish affairs for its intelligence bureau. Regardless of the foreign office, and much to its annoyance, these reports were circulated to the secretary of the war cabinet.[51] This practice gave Namier access to the centre of power and he remained at least a potential threat to Dmowski.

After the Russian proclamation, which momentarily satisfied the Polish émigrés, the foreign office was able to devote its attention to the military aspects of Polish affairs. In October 1916 Horodyski was sent to the United States as a paid agent of the British government to recruit American Poles for the Canadian army – a task at which he seemed to achieve some success.[52] The records show that he received a payment of £2,000 in May 1917. Probably influenced by the example of the Central powers, Horodyski submitted a memorandum to the foreign office on 7 March 1917, in which he recommended the formation of a Polish army recruited in neutral countries, under British command and recognized as an ally.[53] Although interested, the foreign office rejected the proposal as being too far-reaching in the existing circumstances.[54] But the formation of a liberal government in Russia on 12 March 1917, and the American declaration of war on 6 April 1917, removed the two major obstacles to the creation of such an army.

On 22 April 1917, Balfour embarked for the United States on a mission to establish closer relations in the conduct of the war.[55] In an interview with Balfour shortly after his arrival, Horodyski again raised the proposal for a Polish army and acquired Balfour's approval for submitting a memorandum on the subject to the American secretary of war.[56] It was now proposed, in the slightly altered plan set out in the memorandum, to establish a separate and distinctive unit within the American army of about 100,000 Poles recruited in America. To avoid confusion in American military planning, it was also suggested that this unit could be trained in Canada where adequate facilities were available.[57] On 21 May 1917, General G. T. M. Bridges, the military representative of the Balfour mission, explained the plan to House and urged its immediate acceptance.[58] On the following day Balfour, in an interview with Robert Lansing, the secretary of state, argued in favour of the proposal, for, as he wrote to the foreign office:

Quite apart from the fighting value of such an army its creation ought to have a very favourable effect upon the international situation in central Europe and it would greatly hamper if not entirely defeat any German attempts to get an important section of the Poles either to fight for them or to work for them.[59]

During this interview Lansing informed Balfour that his government approved the plan in principle. Between that approval in principle and the commencement of recruiting, there were about three months of negotiations, in which the plan was fundamentally altered. The French government immediately complicated the situation by announcing on 28 May 1917, the formation of a Polish army in France.[60] This independent French action, which had not been preceded by consultation with the British government, was probably the result of simultaneous approaches to the Allied governments by Dmowski's subordinates. Horodyski caused further confusion with a proposal, entertained by the American government, for the creation of a Polish army, not as part of the American army, but as a separate legal entity in international affairs.[61] The foreign office disliked both developments because, while having no particular preference for the type of army created, it wanted immediate action before the military and political advantages evaporated. On 21 June 1917, Drummond telegraphed Horodyski: 'Present proposal that Polish army should become legal international affair . . . seems to offer endless possibilities for delay and friction and I know that our people would much prefer original scheme.'[62]

As the negotiations continued it became obvious that the French government wanted all available Polish recruits in the French-Polish army, that the Poles disliked the idea of exclusive French control, and that the American government was having second thoughts about the formation of a Polish army as part of the American army.[63] By August 1917, the British government, probably following the path of least resistance in an attempt to settle the affair quickly, began to favour the French programme. The first steps in that direction came when the government arranged to ship Polish volunteers from Holland to France and to allow recruitment among the Poles interned in Britain for the French-Polish army. By the end of the war 1,588 Polish civilians and prisoners of war had been released for service in this Polish army.[64] On 28 August 1917, Drummond, Clerk, Horodyski and Macdonogh met and worked out a compromise in which a Polish army financed by the Entente would be formed in the United States, trained in Canada and put under French command.[65] This plan was slightly modified after Spring Rice informed the foreign office that while the American government would permit recruiting in the United States for the Polish army, it would not assist in its creation because of the confusion this would cause in

American military planning.[66] In October 1917, after arrangements had been made with the Canadian authorities and with
the sanction of the American government, recruiting for the Polish
army began.[67] By February 1918 there were about 6,000 Polish
recruits in Canada awaiting transport to France and by the end
of the war 22,000 had been sent.[68] This recruiting was organized
by Paderewski, Horodyski, Smulski and other Polish leaders in
co-operation with the French authorities in the United States.[69]
It was to be of the greatest political significance that the Poles
involved were all followers of Dmowski.

The extent to which the British government was motivated to
support the Polish army by purely military considerations should
not be underestimated. The advantage of the army was that it
allowed access to hitherto untapped sources of manpower such
as Polish prisoners of war, enemy alien Poles and Poles in the
United States not subject to conscription. While interested in
the political advantages, such as the effect it would have on
German attempts to create a Polish army, the British government
was not prepared to release Poles already enlisted in the British
and Canadian armies.[70] In terms of Anglo-Russian relations, it is
also significant that the Russian government was informed but
not seriously consulted about the creation of this army. At one
point the Russian government was asked to supply experienced
Polish officers, but after this request was refused it was not consulted again.[71] The Polish army as it finally emerged was recruited
by the Poles, trained by the Canadians, transported by the British
and commanded by the French. These arrangements tended to
give France the most important role and created the impression
that the Polish army was exclusively a French affair. Although
Wiseman objected to the prominence this gave the French in
Polish affairs, the foreign office was completely satisfied to allow
France to appear to play the leading role.[72] The British government was not solely responsible for the creation of the army, but
it played a key and far more decisive role than has been indicated
in any previous account. Its involvement can be traced back
directly to the decision to send Horodyski to the United States
in October 1916.

The development of this Polish army, associated exclusively
with the National Democrats, had important consequences for
subsequent relations between the British government and Polish
émigrés. Possessing the political allegiance of this army, the
National Democrats' position in Allied countries vis-à-vis their

political opponents was enormously strengthened because they could now approach the Allied governments, not as supplicants, but as men of authority. Early in these negotiations it became evident that the creation of an army almost necessitated the creation of some complementary political organization. Proposals for the recognition of a Polish committee arose from the negotiations, and, as in the case of the army, could be justified by political as well as military considerations. The long and difficult process which led to the recognition of the Polish National Committee began, however, on 30 April 1917, when Dmowski suggested to Clerk that Polish committees be formed in Allied countries to carry out consular functions. He argued that this step was necessary because, since the Russian declaration of Polish independence, the Russian officials were beginning to treat all Poles as foreigners. The foreign office referred the proposal to the home office, where it disappeared for two months.[73]

On 15 June 1917, while the home office was pondering the question, Spring Rice informed the foreign office that the American government was considering the establishment of a Polish provisional government, an act of far greater political significance than the recognition of consular committees.[74] The foreign office disliked the idea, for reasons which were not yet evident, but seemed hesitant to oppose it.[75] In July 1917, Clerk revived Dmowski's original proposal, possibly in an attempt to forestall the creation of a provisional government, by suggesting that the Allies be consulted on the recognition of consular committees. He argued that the recognition of a Polish committee would have beneficial political repercussions in Poland but added, possibly in reference to the proposal for a provisional government: 'It is not necessary as yet to go further than to create Polish Committees in the various Allied countries which should . . . be allowed to protect, and vouch for, individual Poles in those countries, whatever their technical nationality.'[76] The foreign office accepted Clerk's proposal and instructed its representatives to consult the respective Allied governments to which they were accredited on the recognition of committees charged with consular responsibilities. Following the text of Clerk's original proposal, the communication stated:

> From such information as His Majesty's Government possess of recent events in Poland it is clear that the situation in that country has been the cause of serious preoccupation to the

Central Powers, and it seems to His Majesty's Government that the Poles should be stiffened in their demands for liberty and independence and encouraged by all possible means to refuse all promise from our enemies of a mock independence, ... His Majesty's Government would therefore propose that the Allied Governments should henceforth openly recognize as friends and potential allies all Poles in their respective countries, ... This would not only be an earnest to the Poles themselves that the Allies supported their claim to an independent Polish State but it would also tend to bring home to public opinion in Allied countries the conception of a separate and independent Polish State and nation. These ends would be greatly furthered if there were set up in each country a representative Polish Committee, which, if approved by the Government, might be treated as the main channel of communication with Polish patriots.[77]

With the exception of the Russian government, which feared that the Polish situation was getting out of control, the Allies responded favourably to the British proposal.[78] At the suggestion of the French government, however, further action was postponed, pending the results of a conference of Polish conservatives in Lausanne. In August 1917 representatives of the National Democratic and Realist parties met in Lausanne, and created the Polish National Committee, under the presidency of Dmowski.[79] They undoubtedly anticipated Allied recognition of some committee and were confident that it would be their organization. Although Dmowski later made the ridiculous claim that the committee represented ninety per cent of Polish opinion, it was in fact entirely conservative and largely National Democratic.[80] Other than Dmowski, its more prominent members were Paderewski, Seyda, Piltz and Sobanski.

Dmowski's supporters could be optimistic about recognition because the foreign office never seriously considered recognizing any other Polish organization. The conservatives were the only Poles with whom the government conducted any relations, and Allied attempts to create a Polish army depended upon their support. There was, however, a possible drawback to giving the conservatives official recognition. Despite Dmowski's extravagant claims, the foreign office suspected that he represented only a minority of Poles.[81] The suspicion was unsubstantiated but, if it was accurate, there might be little political advantage in recognizing the Polish National Committee. One of the original aims of recognizing a committee had been to thwart German attempts to win support in occupied Poland, but this aim might be jeopardized by recognizing a committee which did not represent Polish opinion. The alternative to the Polish National Committee seemed, however, even more unacceptable.

On 14 January 1917, as part of their plan to establish a Polish army, the Central powers created the Council of State as an advisory body on government in Poland. The Polish left-wing, never averse to limited co-operation with the Central powers, supported the council and participated in it.[82] Zaleski and Aleksander Lednicki, the leaders of the Polish left-wing in England and Russia respectively, recognized the Council of State as the nucleus of the future government of Poland, adhered to its pronouncements on policy, and sought recognition for it from the Allied governments.[83] In the European conflict the Council of State claimed to follow a policy of neutrality, but was obviously willing, and had little choice but, to undertake limited co-operation with the Central powers. Within Poland itself the council agreed to the formation of a Polish army to be used exclusively against Russia but only if it was created under a Polish government. In an attempt to enforce a policy of neutrality on those Poles beyond its reach, the Council of State opposed active Polish participation in the war against the Central powers, and the formation of Polish armies outside of Poland.[84] Although it was always impossible to verify the claims of Polish politicians, the Council of State could claim, as convincingly as the Polish National Committee, to represent the majority of Poles. The Allies could, therefore, recognize either the Polish National Committee or a committee associated with the Council of State. The political advantages of recognizing the former were debatable, since it might not represent Polish opinion, but at least it represented those Poles who, having clearly shown their commitment to the Entente by supporting the creation of a Polish army, were trusted by the Allies. A committee associated with the Council of State might represent Polish opinion, but it would not be committed to the Entente and could be suspected of being pro-German or pro-Austrian. Its recognition might hamper German attempts to exploit the Council of State, but it would mean abandoning plans for a Polish army.

When Zaleski sought Allied recognition for the Council of State, in July 1917, Clerk admitted that that organization might have the support of the majority of the Poles, but attributed this to the conditions of war which made it difficult for the National Democrats to remain in contact with the people of Poland.[85] He argued that, as an instrument of the Central powers, the Council of State could not be recognized by the Entente, and proposed:

> that His Majesty's Government should whole-heartedly support the policy of M. Dmowski and his helpers, and should recognize them as the people to whom . . . the destinies of Poland are entrusted until a reconstituted, free and independent Polish nation has the opportunity of deciding its own fate.[86]

Hardinge agreed with Clerk, and Drummond wrote: '. . . I think we ought to be very careful of accepting any views expressed by M. Zaleski on the war. The Council of State is after all a purely Austro-German institution.'[87] The foreign office also reacted unfavourably when it learned that Zaleski was planning to give a public lecture at King's College.[88] On this subject Drummond wrote to Kerr: 'We do not think that the people who are getting up this meeting should be encouraged. I am rather doubtful as to their pro-Ally sentiments.'[89] Instead of sanctioning the meeting, the foreign office asked the director of military intelligence to investigate Zaleski's activities.[90] In October 1917 Macdonogh sent the foreign office the results of this investigation, along with a recommendation for legal action against the *Polish Review* published by Zaleski. The investigation presented no positive evidence that Zaleski was pro-German, despite the numerous accusations levelled against him by the National Democrats. But, accepting these accusations, the investigators remained convinced that Zaleski was pro-German because they did have evidence that he was in contact with other Poles suspected of being pro-German or pro-Austrian. One report ended with the statement: 'Meanwhile we are continuing the check on Zaleski's correspondence in the hope that it may yield useful results.'[91] Military intelligence failed to realize that almost all of the Polish émigrés, including Dmowski, were in contact with, or even in some cases related to, pro-Austrian Poles. Obviously influenced by the accusations of Horodyski and Alma-Tadema, military intelligence acted on the incredibly stupid assumption that anyone opposed to Dmowski was pro-German, an assumption which led them to make the preposterous accusation that Seton-Watson was publishing pro-German articles in *The New Europe*. One of the reports ended with the recommendation that Zaleski be removed from politics by deportation or conscription. The foreign office accepted the views advanced by military intelligence, but after momentarily considering conscripting Zaleski into the British army, rejected the idea because such action might make him a martyr.[92] With Balfour's approval, however, legal measures were initiated to suppress the *Polish Review*.[93] There was obviously never any question of giving official recognition to Zaleski or anyone associated with him.

In contrast, Lednicki in Russia was far more successful. When, as a result of the revolution, Wielopolski and Dmowski lost their influence in Russian official circles, they were replaced by Lednicki and his Polish Democratic Club, whose views were in far greater harmony with those of the Provisional government.[94] Shortly after the revolution, the government appointed Lednicki chairman of the Liquidation Committee charged with formulating plans for the separation of Poland and Russia.[95] When Dmowski's supporters in Russia began to agitate for the creation of Polish military units within the disintegrating Russian army, the Provisional government rejected the idea because of the danger that such troops might be used for counter-revolution. Following the policy of the Council of State, Lednicki supported the government in its opposition to Polish military units.[96] The divergence between the Russian government and its allies on the Polish issue was obviously growing and it was unlikely that the Russian government would look with favour on Allied recognition of a Polish committee dominated by conservatives who had previously supported Russian autocracy.[97]

The foreign office considered Lednicki no better than Zaleski. Although Howard, the only British official in contact with the Polish left-wing, sent the foreign office favourable reports about Lednicki, these had no effect upon its attitude and his recommendations were never accepted.[98] When he stated in one report that recognition of the Polish National Committee would cause dissension among the Poles, Clerk wrote in reference to the Council of State: 'But their whole attitude . . . has been one of compromise and making terms with the occupying Power and neither the Regency nor the cause of Poland would be safe in their hands.' He went on to attack the council's policy, adhered to by Lednicki, against the formation of Polish armies, and concluded: 'I entirely agree with Sir Esme Howard that it is undesirable to sow dissension among the various Polish parties, but I submit that to support those whose policy helps our enemies is even worse, . . .'[99] Subsequent events showed that Clerk expressed the view of the foreign office.[100] It is obvious that Zaleski and Lednicki were never considered an alternative to the Polish National Committee. That committee might not have the support of the majority of the Poles, its recognition might not produce all of the anticipated political advantages but, especially if the Allies wanted a Polish army, there was no alternative.

When the Polish National Committee, on 28 August 1917, officially informed the British government of its creation, the foreign office immediately wanted to recommend its recognition to the Allies.[101] It hesitated, however, because the American ambassador, Walter Hines Page, had again raised the proposal for a Polish provisional government. On this occasion the opposition of the foreign office to the idea of a provisional government was clearly explained by Cecil in the description of his conversation with Page:

> I said that it seemed to me a very difficult thing to create a Provisional Government of Poles in the United States without consulting the people of Poland, and I took the opportunity of pointing out that any such Government would necessarily define what it conceived to be the future limits of Poland and that these would include, among other things, the port of Dantzig. If we recognized a Provisional Government claiming the port of Dantzig, we should be more or less bound to struggle for the inclusion of Dantzig in the future Poland, and that, I thought, would be a great burden on the Allies. I therefore thought the proposal, in itself, of doubtful advisability.[102]

Instead of a provisional government the foreign office still preferred the politically less significant recognition of the Polish National Committee although now the original proposal for an organization charged only with consular functions was altered to include representation of Polish interests in Allied countries and responsibility for political issues arising from the Polish army.[103] On this basis, the committee would carry out many of the functions of a provisional government without being recognized as such. The problem of possible Russian opposition was solved simply by not consulting the Russian government.[104] After some delay over the actual formula of recognition, the French government recognized the Polish National Committee on 20 September 1917, and the British government followed suit, in similar terms on 15 October 1917.[105] The American government, having abandoned the proposal for a provisional government yet alone among the Allies intent upon consulting the Russian government, delayed its recognition until 10 November 1917.[106] By that time the provisional government, opposed to the Polish National Committee until the end, no longer existed.

In view of the opposition of the foreign office to the proposal for a Polish provisional government, it is necessary to examine the terms on which it recognized the Polish National Committee, and the interpretation it placed on the act of recognition. The actual letter of recognition to Sobanski, the representative of the Polish National Committee in London, stated: 'I am to inform you . . . that His Majesty's Government are very willing to recognize this official Polish organization and that they note that the headquarters of the Committee are in Paris.'[107] Clerk later explained this rather vague statement:

> as regards recognition, this has, for practical purposes, been accorded to a Committee of Poles working in the Western Capitals of Europe, but neither gives that Committee the status of representing all Poland nor excludes recognition of other equally pro-Ally organizations.[108]

In other words the committee had been recognized as nothing more than an official Polish organization. In practice the government, showing no inclination to recognize any other Polish organization, treated it as the only official Polish committee. Nevertheless, it had minimized its commitment to the Polish National Committee and had retained the option of recognizing other Polish organizations in the future.[109] In addition the foreign office did not consider that recognition implied any commitment on the future of Poland. When Cecil expressed his apprehension about recognition Drummond replied: 'I agree with Lord R. Cecil as to the inadvisability of making the reconstruction of Poland . . . an allied war aim on the same plane as Belgium or Servia, but I do not see that the recognition of the Polish National Committee commits us to this in any way.'[110]

Great significance might be read into the act of recognition by others, particularly Poles, but it is obvious that the foreign office did not agree. This conclusion is borne out by the arrangements which followed the recognition of the committee and which indicate the degree to which the government was prepared to allow the committee to act as a provisional government. On 8 January 1918, at a conference attended by Clerk, Sobanski,

Stanislas Kozicki and representatives of the war office and home office, arrangements were made to give the Polish National Committee consular privileges.[111] The foreign office had already rejected a politically more significant proposal put forward by Gregory to give the committee full diplomatic privileges.[112] As a result of this conference the government agreed to recognize Poles, regardless of their origin, as alien friends if they possessed a certificate issued by the committee. These certificates could be used as passports but, in return, the holders were obliged to volunteer for national service.[113] Sobanski wanted the certificates to state that the holder was of Polish nationality, but this was rejected by the officials who preferred that the certificates state simply that the bearer was a Pole.[114] At the conference Clerk explained to Sobanski that until an independent sovereign Poland existed it was impossible to recognize Polish nationality.[115] Sobanski was obviously trying to derive the maximum political advantage from these arrangements, but the government, while prepared to grant convenient privileges to the committee, was equally determined to minimize the legal significance of both recognition and the arrangements which followed.

The manner in which consular privileges were given to the committee also showed that the officials suspected that the National Democrats would use these privileges against their political opponents. For that reason the government reserved the right to issue certificates to Poles not approved by the committee. The home office report on the conference stated: 'It was further made clear that the Polish National Committee was only *an* official Committee, and that there might be others, and that the National Committee had not, therefore, the exclusive right of issuing the certificate in question or similar certificates.'[116] Although British officials tended to accept the accusations made by the National Democrats against their opponents, they obviously did not trust the committee to use its power with impartiality. On this point Clerk wrote: 'This is of course necessary to ensure that the Committee should not use its certificates as a means for political pressure and to maintain the position we have consistently adopted, namely that the Committee is an official Polish Organization but not necessarily the only one.'[117]

Although in practice the government treated the committee as the only Polish organization, it obviously intended to maintain its freedom of action. It also wanted to protect itself from the attacks of Dmowski's opponents by not appearing too closely associated with the National Democrats. To some extent these arrangements represented no more than official recognition of existing practices. Since 1916 the Polish Exiles Protection had exercised to a lesser degree similar consular privileges. Another existing practice was given official recognition when the foreign office agreed to allow Sobanski to send correspondence through British diplomatic pouches.[118]

The recognition of the committee led, however, to one very significant innovation. The committee needed funds for propaganda, intelligence, administration and recruiting, but wanted to avoid being charged by its opponents as being paid agents of the Allies.[119] It therefore asked the Allied governments for a loan of £12,000 per month, presumably to be repaid after the establishment of a Polish government. In January 1918 the British government agreed to pay its share of £3,000 per month with payments beginning in February 1918.[120] These payments were unrelated to the cost of the Polish army which was also a responsibility of the Allied governments. The appointment by the Allied governments of agents to supervise the finances of the Polish National Committee show that repayment of this so-called loan was not expected.[121]

With the formation of a Polish army in France and the recognition of the Polish National Committee, Dmowski and the National Democrats had achieved a position of some importance. They reached the zenith of their influence on the British government, however, at the beginning of 1918, as a result of developments in Russia following the Bolshevik revolution. Despite the opposition of the Provisional government, the Russian military authorities, in collusion with the National Democrats, had created by August 1917, a Polish corps, under General Jozef Dowbor-Musnicki, within the Russian army.[122] The British war office, after initially disapproving of the disruption of the Russian army in order to create national units, began to take an interest in the Polish corps as the Russian army disintegrated after the failure of the Galician offensive in July 1917.[123] By November 1917 the government was seriously considering the possibility of supporting a Polish army in Russia directed against the Central powers.[124] Just before the Bolshevik seizure of power, Horodyski suggested the formation of Polish and Cossack units to assist the Rumanians, whose right flank was exposed by the collapse of the Russian army.[125] The plan was not unanimously supported by the military experts; the military attaché in Petrograd thought it would only lead to civil war and wrote to Macdonogh: 'I believe Poles simply wish to organize force to protect Polish landlords against their Russian peasantry.'[126] But such opinions had little effect on the British government once it became apparent that the Russian government intended to make a separate peace which might end all resistance to the Central powers in eastern Europe.[127] As already explained in the previous chapter in reference to the Czechoslovak army, the war cabinet decided on 14 December 1917, to support all military units in Russia prepared to continue the war against the Central powers. The Allies sought to reconstruct some form of eastern front without the aid of the Bolsheviks by using the existing Polish, Czechoslovak, Cossack and Rumanian military forces. Dowbor-Musnicki's Polish corps was one of these units and on 4 January 1918, Bertie reported that the French government had allotted to it ten million roubles.[128] On 9 January 1918, the foreign office asked the treasury to agree to share these costs with the French government.[129] The establishment of this Polish army particularly enhanced the political influence of the National Democrats because, as one of the few armies on the eastern front still prepared to fight the Central powers, it appeared to be of major strategic importance. Frequent discussions about this army in the war cabinet, which almost never discussed other aspects of Polish affairs, are an indication of its importance.[130]

In the negotiations which led to involvement in Polish affairs, the British government was primarily motivated by strategic considerations and not by the desire to pursue any particular programme for the future of Poland. Each initiative by the government was inspired by the need either to thwart German policy in Poland or to use the Poles, particularly in military units, as weapons of war. Despite this opportunistic approach to the Polish issue, however, the government was not totally devoid of attitudes and even intentions on the future of Poland.

By making Polish independence possible, the Russian revolution added to the uncertainties of the Polish problem, uncertainties which reflected those within Russia itself. In the Provisional government's proclamation of 29 March 1917, the idea of autonomy within Russia was abandoned in favour of an independent Poland linked to Russia by a military alliance. The British government welcomed and supported the proclamation as it represented a solution to the Polish problem which would win Polish support while being consistent with British interests and on lines favoured by those in the government involved in Polish affairs. The officials, when dealing with Polish affairs, now began to speak in terms of independence, but never made any attempt to explain the meaning of that term as it would actually be applied in the geographic area of Poland. Such problems, not clearly understood and complicated by uncertainty, were easier to avoid than solve. In any case the issue was not of immediate importance, as it was by no means clear that independence could be achieved.

During 1917 Dmowski presented the foreign office with his programme for the future of Poland, setting out territorial claims to which the Poles had only a debatable ethnographic case.[131] Namier attacked the claims of the National Democrats, whom he labelled 'Polish Imperialists', on the grounds that many of the areas were inhabited predominantly by Lithuanians, Byelorussians or Ukrainians.[132] Although the foreign office, with a weakness for the nationality principle, thought of Poland in ethnographic rather than historic terms, there is no evidence that it paid anything more than scant attention to these numerous memoranda about problems obviously not of immediate importance.[133] Within the foreign office, the only branch of the government in which the proposition was seriously discussed, opposition to a more forward policy on Polish independence was based almost entirely on the practical difficulties and not on any theoretical objections to independence. To varying degrees Balfour, Hardinge, Drummond, Clerk and Gregory all preferred the independence of Poland, not as an essential war aim of the British government, but as the best solution to the Polish problem.[134] The one exception was Cecil, who supported the government's policy of using the nationalities as weapons of war while disliking nationalism and national self-determination.[135] In essence the government seemed prepared to accept any solution to the Polish problem which did not increase German strength and which was acceptable to both the Poles and the Russians. But no one ever suggested continuing the war for the sake of Poland. For that reason the government scrupulously avoided commitments on the future of Poland during the negotiations of the formation of a Polish army and the recognition of the Polish National Committee.

During 1917 the war cabinet was hardly concerned with the negotiations on Polish affairs conducted, with its general approval, by the war office and the foreign office. The members of the cabinet, faced with a multitude of more important problems, showed little interest in Poland. The foreign office and the war office could do as they liked with the Poles as long as they made no commitments. Only then would it become a cabinet issue. The government's reluctance to accept commitments on the future of Poland resulted from the commonly held belief that if Russia collapsed such commitments could never be fulfilled. Even if the Allies achieved victory in the west, itself by no means certain, the possibility of influencing, let alone dictating, the settlement of eastern Europe without an army there loyal to the Entente seemed remote indeed.[136] According to Amery: 'without Russia we are powerless to dispute the settlement of the Polish, Roumanian and Serbian problems according to the wishes of the Central powers . . .'[137] Similar pessimism inspired Cecil to write: 'At this stage in the war to adopt and proclaim as one of our war aims, as essential as the restoration of Belgium, the creation of an independent Polish Kingdom which would cut Prussia in two seems to me sheer lunacy.'[138] In September 1917, Lloyd George explained the problem quite clearly to Scott:

> Who is going to restore it [Poland]. The Soviet and Russian government will not or cannot lift a finger and are we to do the work for them. We cannot be more Russian than the Russians. If Germany is asked to surrender all her gains on the East as well as to retrocede Alsace-Lorraine she will fight on for years and, with access to certain cornlands of Russia, she can do it.[139]

The seriousness of the situation was evident when the war cabinet, on 24 September 1917, considered the possibility of peace negotiations with Germany and expressed its willingness to consider any offer put forward by the Germans. The cabinet was fully aware that in such negotiations the only real inducement they could offer Germany for the restoration of Belgium was a free hand in eastern Europe.[140] Whether the cabinet would have ever made such an offer in actual negotiations is debatable but the proposition certainly was considered. As long as victory was in doubt, the government could not undertake commitments on Poland which it might never have the power to honour and which would make a negotiated peace impossible. There is insufficient evidence to reveal the cabinet's attitude, if such existed, on the future of Poland. If the cabinet had a preference it might have agreed with the foreign office in sympathizing with the cause of Polish independence. But, above all, it had no intention of continuing the war for the sake of Poland.

Yet the government could not entirely avoid the question of some commitment to the Polish cause unless it was prepared to abandon the Poles to the Central powers. In September 1917, the Central powers replaced the Council of State with a Regency Council designed to act as the head of state of the kingdom of Poland. They also delegated to the Regency Council the administration of certain aspects of Polish internal affairs and pushed forward their own plans for a Polish army.[141] The émigrés who kept the government informed of these developments continually emphasized the need for some new Allied declaration on the future of Poland.[142] On 3 October 1917, Gregory explained, in a long minute, that the Polish National Committee wanted a declaration that: 'we consider the restoration of United Poland with free access to the sea as one of the essential objects of the war and an indispensable condition of peace and the balance of Europe'. He argued that such a declaration was impossible because: 'As things are at present, the prospect of our wresting Posen from Germany is not a good one, and it is clear that not one of the Allies would be willing to prolong the war by a day in order to do it.' He concluded, reluctantly, that the only declaration possible would be one expressing nothing more than a pious aspiration which would carry little conviction, have little effect on the Poles and do nothing to prevent them from supporting the Central powers.[143] More optimistically Clerk maintained that a pious statement involving no commitment would satisfy the Poles, and Hardinge concluded: 'So long as it is only a pious aspiration it does not much matter what is said.'[144] On 15 October 1917, with the permission of the foreign office and, in this case, of the prime minister, Buchanan associated himself at a public meeting with a statement by the Russian foreign minister that the creation of an independent and indivisable Poland was one of the conditions of a solid and just peace.[145] The Poles had received their declaration of pious aspiration and, as intended, it was worthless.

As Gregory had so easily predicted the Poles found the statement completely unsatisfactory and continued to press for a commitment on the future of Poland. Howard, relying on his Polish sources, continued to report on the enemy's progress in forming a Polish army and urged that some Allied declaration was necessary to counteract what appeared to him a very real danger that the Central powers would gain Polish support and successfully form a Polish army.[146] Balfour opposed issuing another declaration and commented on one of the reports: 'I do not understand why our recent very definite statements about Poland are systematically ignored.'[147] Further action on the question was postponed until the meeting of the supreme war council in Paris at the beginning of December 1917. Since the beginning of the war the British government had followed, in its relations with the nationalities, the policy of using them while maintaining the option, by avoiding commitments, of pursuing such other alternatives as a separate peace with Austria-Hungary. At first the idea of a separate peace was totally unrelated to British policy in Polish affairs because Poland was still considered a Russian sphere, and it was naturally assumed that in a separate peace the Habsburg monarchy would have to cede Galicia to Russia, whereupon it would be included in whatever form the new Poland assumed.[148] In August 1917 the government learned, through unofficial contacts, that the Emperor Karl was interested in a Habsburg confederation which would include a re-united Poland.[149] This knowledge gave the government an additional reason for avoiding commitments, for concessions on the future of Poland might prove useful in negotiations with Austria-Hungary. The announcement of an armistice between the Bolshevik government and the Central powers on 30 November 1917, by releasing the Allies from their obligations to Russia, made such concessions possible. When the supreme war council met in Paris on 1 December 1917, the British government was about to embark on the Smuts–Mensdorff conversations. These conversations represented the greatest opportunity yet presented to the Allies for a negotiated peace with Austria-Hungary, and as such undoubtedly influenced the British contribution to the discussion of a declaration on the future of Poland.[150]

At the meeting of the supreme war council Stéphane Pichon, the French foreign minister, proposed issuing a declaration on Polish independence and was supported by House, the American representative. According to the minutes, after Balfour raised some objections to the proposal:

> Mr. Lloyd George said he was sorry to differ from his colleague [Pichon], but he hoped we would not increase our obligations at the very moment when our military strength was debatable . . . the present moment was most unpropitious, when we had almost broken with Russia and had some hopes from Austria. He could understand the United States taking some such

action, because they had a large Polish population, but he asked: Was the United States prepared to send an army to Poland? It was impossible to contemplate keeping the war going for two years to set up a Polish State.[151]

The proposal was dropped at this meeting but was raised again by Balfour at a conference of Allied foreign ministers on 3 December 1917. Balfour presented the text of a declaration which he believed would have a good effect in Poland without adding to Allied war aims: 'The creation of a Poland, independent and indivisible, constitutes one of the conditions of a solid and just peace, and of the regime of right in Europe. The proper development of an independent State requires unrestricted access to the sea.' The statement was absolutely worthless as Balfour himself admitted when he added: 'The propositions contained in it were undeniable, and would not be embarrassing to us in the future.' He also explained, although it was hardly necessary, that access to the sea did not necessarily imply possession of part of the Baltic coast because it could be achieved by making the Vistula an international waterway. After some modifications because of objections from Sonnino, the following text was accepted by the conference: 'The creation of a Poland, independent and indivisible, under such conditions as will ensure her free political and economic development, constitutes one of the conditions of a solid and just peace, and of the regime of right in Europe.'[152]

Allied agreement on this proposal left the problem unsolved because the text was unacceptable to the Polish National Committee. The committee claimed that its publication would only have an adverse effect in Poland, and after consultation the declaration was not published.[153] The Poles wanted a clear, unmistakable commitment and were not stupid enough to be deceived by a statement which entailed no obligation whatever. Despite continued warnings that some statement on Poland was necessary, however, the government could not bring itself to issue a more explicit declaration.[154] On 7 December 1917, Hardinge wrote to Howard: 'Our principal object has been to encourage as much as possible those elements which we know to be in favour of the defeat of the Central Powers, but we have never been able to see our way sufficiently clear to adopt publicly a definite line.'[155]

Until 1917, because the émigrés were not powerful enough to make demands on the government and because the alternatives to national self-determination were as yet only hypothetical, the government had encountered little difficulty in using the nationalities while maintaining its freedom of action. But the use of the nationalities implied, at least to the émigrés, support for national self-determination. If the émigrés decided to make their support contingent upon the government's acceptance of a commitment, the latter would have no choice but to forego that co-operation or risk destroying the possibility of a separate peace with Austria-Hungary. This problem did not arise with the Yugoslavs and Czechoslovaks because they made no demands on the government and maintained that their support was not conditional but absolute. By the end of 1917 the Polish émigrés were in a position, because of the existence of two Polish armies, to make demands which the government could not ignore. The Polish leaders did not make direct demands upon the government, or threaten to withdraw their support, but they constantly warned the government, probably quite correctly, that if it did not accept a commitment it would definitely lose the support of the bulk of the Poles. However much the government might prefer to seek a separate peace with Austria-Hungary while simultaneously using the Poles, the course of events and the pressure from the Polish émigrés for a commitment forced it to make a choice between a negotiated peace or the use of the nationalities in total war.

The government chose a separate peace, accepting the risk of losing Polish support. The terms upon which it would have made peace, given the opportunity, can only be a matter of speculation. But there can be no doubt that in December 1917 it considered terms that were absolutely unacceptable to the Polish National Committee. On 10 December 1917, in his memorandum on possible terms of peace, Drummond recommended negotiating on the basis of a reconstituted Habsburg monarchy which would include a re-united Poland. He maintained that this solution would be in the best interests of eastern Europe and consistent with the interests of the British government.[156] On 13 December 1917, in setting out for the cabinet the basis upon which he thought his discussions with Mensdorff should proceed, Smuts accepted Drummond's suggestion and, in reference to Poland, wrote: 'Cession of Galicia to Russian Poland: Poland thus reconstructed as Independent State to be linked in personal and commercial union to Austria-Hungary as third state of Empire.'[157]

During 1917 the government was under constant pressure,

created by the Central powers and magnified by the émigrés, to adopt measures to counteract enemy policy in Poland. It responded with a number of measures designed to show its interest in the future of Poland, but stopped short of any firm commitment. It also sought, through the formation of military units, to use the Polish situation to increase Allied military strength. Although British policy in Polish affairs was thus determined by military considerations in an attempt to increase its own strength and reduce that of the Central powers, the pursuit of this policy led to unprecedented involvement in Polish politics. In responding to enemy policy and in attempting to use Polish support, the British government assisted the cause of Polish independence by playing a leading role in the formation of the Polish army and the recognition of the Polish National Committee. But this assistance was the by-product, not the aim, of British policy. The government's willingness to use Poland in the negotiations with Austria-Hungary and unwillingness to accept commitments on Poland showed that it had no particular aims for the future of Poland other than depriving Germany of its support. British policy in the conduct of Anglo-Polish relations, in the public statements on Poland, in the formation of the Polish army, in the recognition of the Polish National Committee, was determined by immediate strategic considerations resulting from the war.

7 : COMMITMENT BY IMPLICATION, 1918

On 13 November 1917, Sobanski suggested to Balfour that the Allies launch a political offensive against Austria-Hungary in order to drive her out of the war. The methods used by the Germans to create chaos in Russia might be used with equal success against the Habsburg monarchy.[1] The government did not seriously consider the proposal at this time because a programme designed to promote internal disorder within the Habsburg monarchy appeared to necessitate a commitment to the nationalities incompatible with the pursuit of a separate peace. As Gregory pointed out: 'There are only two apparent forms of "political offensive" possible, a separate peace with the lesser Powers of the enemy coalition or the stirring up of nationalist strife within the Dual Monarchy.'[2] Should a separate peace prove to be unattainable, the use of the nationalities in a total war against Austria-Hungary was the obvious alternative. If Austria-Hungary could not be used against Germany, then the nationalities would be used against Austria-Hungary. If Austria-Hungary would not leave the war, she would be driven out.

The government did not realize at any decisive moment that a separate peace was impossible but only came to this conclusion gradually. In the same way it did not decide at any particular moment to use the nationalities in a total war against Austria-Hungary. Such significance cannot be attributed to any one decision. The more extensive use of the nationalities during 1918 developed gradually, simultaneous with the realization that a separate peace was impossible, and as the direct outgrowth of the earlier co-operation between the government and the nationalities. While a decision to use the nationalities to destroy Austria-Hungary was never taken, a host of less significant decisions, when combined in their historical context, had the same effect.

The change in British policy was a shift in emphasis rather than the complete abandonment of one course of action and the acceptance of another. In 1917 the government had not completely committed itself to the policy of a separate peace and had maintained its relations with the nationalities. During 1918 it did not totally abandon the idea of a separate peace, but instead, it gradually shifted the emphasis in its general policy, which was to use the problems of eastern Europe to its own strategic advantage, away from a separate peace and towards the disruption of the Habsburg monarchy. The shift went so far by November 1918 that the government was in essence supporting national self-determination in eastern Europe without ever having made a formal decision to do so.

As the government realized between December 1917 and April 1918 that a separate peace was impossible, it gradually began to consider negotiations not as an honest attempt to make peace with Austria-Hungary but as a means to weaken the Austrian war effort and embarrass the Central powers.[3] In December 1917 this view prevailed in the foreign office, but by March 1918 it prevailed throughout the government. According to the minutes of the war cabinet for 1 March 1918:

> Mr. Balfour said he was certain that Austria would not accede to a peace such as we wanted. The Prime Minister agreed, but pointed out that, by continuing conversations a very important secondary object might be achieved, namely Austria might be deterred from making an attack and gradually reduced to a state of inactivity . . .[4]

This attitude towards negotiations was the first discernible step in the shifting of emphasis in British policy; the second can be seen in the changes in Allied propaganda. Before 1918 British propaganda had been directed entirely at Allied and neutral opinion, and no attempts had been made to influence public opinion in enemy countries. Offensive propaganda was impractical at the beginning of the war because it could only be effective when the enemy was almost exhausted. In December 1917 Christopher Addison, the minister of reconstruction, urged Lloyd George to adopt this type of warfare.[5] The suggestion was not original – Tyrrell was thinking along similar lines – and sufficient records would probably show that, as a result of the apparent effects of German pacifist propaganda in Russia, the idea had a certain common currency.[6] In February 1918 the government established the department of Propaganda in Enemy Countries with its headquarters at Crewe House, Curzon Street, and under the directorship of Lord Northcliffe, the newspaper publisher.[7]

It was almost inevitable that this department would attempt to influence foreign policy and that it would disagree with the foreign office. Northcliffe was responsible only to the prime minister, and while his department was expected to co-operate with other branches of the government it was subservient to none of them.[8] Combined with this freedom of action, not unusual for a propaganda agency, Crewe House had its own opinion, different from that of the foreign office, on what British war aims in eastern Europe should be. Northcliffe appointed Wickham Steed and Seton-Watson as the co-directors of propaganda against Austria-Hungary, and their views on war aims became those of Crewe House.[9] Since, by the very nature of the situation, effective propaganda against Austria-Hungary had to be based on national self-determination, it was quite reasonable that the two foremost exponents of that doctrine should be appointed to conduct such propaganda. Had Crewe House been as willing as Wellington House to accept dictation from the foreign office on matters of foreign policy, there would have been fewer problems. But Northcliffe, Wickham Steed and Seton-Watson, a dangerous combination of megalomania, self-righteousness and crusading spirit, were reluctant to accept dictation from the foreign office, and, because of their independence, not obliged to do so. According to Peter Chalmers Mitchell, the liaison officer between Crewe House and the war office, Northcliffe was responsible for a major innovation in Allied propaganda in that: 'The inspiring principle of the new operation was that propaganda should depend upon policy.'[10] This claim is not strictly accurate because Wellington House had always sought to tailor its propaganda to the government's policy and had only failed to do so, as in the case of national self-determination, when that policy was not clearly defined. Northcliffe's innovation was not that he made propaganda consistent with policy but that he tried to alter foreign policy to make it consistent with propaganda formulated by Seton-Watson and Wickham Steed.

On 24 February 1918, Northcliffe informed Balfour, in a letter drafted by Wickham Steed, that Austria-Hungary was the best target for propaganda and enquired as to the nature of Allied policy towards her.[11] He suggested that his department (and the government) had two alternatives: '(a) To work for a separate peace . . . or (b) To try to break the power of Austria-Hungary, as the weakest link in the chain of enemy States, by supporting and encouraging all anti-German and pro-Ally peoples and tendencies.' Northcliffe himself was certain which policy should be followed: 'The (a) policy has been tried without success . . . It remains to try the (b) policy.' The ultimate aim would be 'not to form a number of small disjointed States, but to create a non-German Confederation of Central European and Danubian States'. In order to carry out this policy it would be necessary for the Allied governments to state clearly their determination to secure 'government by the consent of the governed' for the subject nationalities, to avoid all statements which might give substance to the belief that they did not wish to dismember Austria-Hungary, and to work for a reconciliation between the Yugoslavs and the Italians. Through the Bohemian National Alliance, the Yugoslav Committee and various Polish organizations, Crewe House already had at its disposal the facilities to disseminate propaganda in Austria-Hungary. All that was necessary was official approval.[12]

This letter, which Drummond considered 'pure Steed', tried to force on the foreign office the dilemma of having to make a clear and irrevocable choice between Austria-Hungary and the subject nationalities.[13] The foreign office had always sought to avoid this decision because, as long as a separate peace was possible, any choice would limit the government's freedom of action. In Cecil's opinion: 'The (b) policy as stated seems to involve an indefinite prolongation of the war.'[14] But, as Drummond suggested to Balfour, the two courses of action proposed by Northcliffe were not necessarily, in the initial stages, mutually exclusive. For the moment Crewe House could base its propaganda on national self-determination without any decision from the government on the fate of Austria-Hungary. Following this suggestion, Balfour replied to Northcliffe:

> As you point out with unanswerable force, everything which encourages the anti-German elements in the Habsburg dominions really helps to compel the Emperor and the Court to a separate peace, and also diminishes the efficiency of Austria-Hungary as a member of the Middle-Europe combination. The Emperor, by these means, might be induced or compelled, fundamentally to modify the constitution of his own State. If he refused to lend himself to such a policy, the strengthening of the non-German elements might bring about the same and even more effectually than if he lent his assistance to the process. But in either case the earlier stages

of that process are the same, and a propaganda which aids the struggle of the nationalities now, subject either to Austrian Germans or to Magyar Hungarians towards freedom and self-determination must be right, whether the complete break-up of the Austrian Empire or its de-Germanization under Habsburg rule be the final goal of our efforts.[15]

Not unnaturally Northcliffe was dissatisfied with this decision and he replied:

The two policies may not be mutually exclusive, in the last resort, but it is very important that one or the other of them should be given absolute precedence. It would place me in an awkward predicament if, after basing vigorous propaganda on the (b) policy, I were confronted with some manifestation of the (a) policy on the part of the British or other Allied Government.[16]

On 5 March 1918, the war cabinet settled the issue by authorizing Northcliffe's plan for a propaganda campaign on condition that:

a. No promise should be made to the subject races in Austria which we could not redeem: for example, we must not promise complete independence if the best we could get was autonomy. b. Lord Northcliffe agreed to show the Secretary of State for Foreign Affairs the leaflets he proposes to issue, in order to ensure that it might not be possible later on to charge the British Government with a breach of faith.[17]

Crewe House began the campaign against Austria-Hungary by concentrating its efforts on the Italian front where the Austrians were most accessible. Before the major enemy offensive expected within two months, Crewe House hoped to weaken the enemy's military capacity through propaganda aimed at the subject nationalities within the Austrian army, particularly the South Slavs. But this propaganda could only be conducted success-fully with the co-operation of the Yugoslav Committee and the Italian propaganda authorities. Before the actual campaign could begin, therefore, Crewe House had to reconcile these two hostile groups so that they would be able to work together. Steed had, in fact, been working on such a reconciliation for some time, but now, with his appointment to Crewe House, these activities became quasi-official.[18] In March 1918, at the instigation of Crewe House, representatives of the Yugoslav Committee and the Italian department of propaganda met in London and worked out an agreement later entitled the pact of Rome. In the agreement, signed on 7 March 1918, the Italians accepted the unity and independence of Yugoslavia, the Yugoslavs accepted the completion of Italian unification, and both accepted the division of Habsburg Adriatic territories according to the principle of nationality.[19] The agreement was the first step in a superficial reconciliation, but it lacked official significance because the participants had no authority to speak for anyone other than themselves. On 9 March 1918, when Trumbić presented the agreement to the foreign office at an interview arranged by Steed, Cecil stated that the British government was pleased that the Italians and Yugoslavs had agreed but was careful to avoid any further comment on the pact.[20] Seton-Watson and Wickham Steed might be employed by the government, but the foreign office did not consider that their action reflected or affected foreign policy. Since the Italian government took the same attitude towards its propaganda agents, any agreement between them and the Yugoslavs, considered operative only in the field of propaganda, in no way affected either Italian war aims or the treaty of London.[21]

The initial agreement between the Italians and the Yugoslavs was followed by the Congress of Oppressed Nationalities – the Czechoslovaks, Yugoslavs, Poles, Rumanians and Italians – which took place in Rome in April 1918. Seton-Watson and Wickham Steed participated in the calling of this congress, and both attended supposedly as representatives of Great Britain, but not of the British government.[22] When questioned in the house of commons about their presence at the congress, Cecil replied: 'Lord Northcliffe, after consultation with the Foreign Office, delegated Mr. Steed to proceed to Italy as his representative to study there certain aspects of questions relating to propaganda.'[23]

The Congress of Oppressed Nationalities was an affair in which Crewe House alone was involved; the foreign office was scarcely interested. It was considered an aspect of Allied propaganda but not otherwise related to foreign policy. On 29 April 1918, Balfour told the house of commons that 'the conference was not official, there has been no question of the adoption of the resolutions by the Allied Government'.[24] The Italian government adopted a similar attitude by refusing either to appoint official representatives to the congress or to recognize its resolutions.[25] The congress did, however, achieve its immediate aim of a reconciliation between the Yugoslav émigrés and the Italian propaganda authorities sufficient to enable them to co-operate in the anti-Habsburg propaganda campaign. But the real differences remained unresolved.

While in Italy Steed assisted in the creation of the Inter-Allied Propaganda Commission to co-ordinate the attack on Austria-Hungary and arranged for the production of propaganda leaflets.[26] After consultation with the Italian authorities and the British military representatives, it was agreed that the best way to appeal to the subject nationalities in the Habsburg army would be for the Czechoslovaks, Poles and Yugoslavs to issue proclamations of independence which would be recognized and publicized by the Allied governments.[27] On 4 April 1918, the foreign office, acting on a request from Steed, agreed to recognize such declarations but added that it could not undertake to fulfil them.[28] This decision signified a slight modification of the restriction placed on Crewe House by the war cabinet that it was not to promise independence to the subject nationalities, but it does not appear to have been taken very seriously by the government. It was certainly never invested with the importance that Steed attributed to it. The foreign office never referred to it again, and did not consider it either as a reflection of foreign policy or as an act involving a commitment. Crewe House could embarrass the government by making promises that could not be fulfilled or by misrepresenting British policy, but it had no power to commit the government.

The campaign against Austria-Hungary began in April 1918 and consisted largely of the dissemination of leaflets, either smuggled across the lines or dropped from aircraft, through the Austrian army.[29] This propaganda was designed to appeal to the separatist tendencies within Austria-Hungary so as to demoralize the army and encourage the desertion of soldiers belonging to the subject nationalities. In May 1918 Seton-Watson was sent to Switzerland to arrange for the smuggling of propaganda into Austria-Hungary through the Czechoslovak system of communication which offered extensive facilities for the dissemination of propaganda.[30] In reporting to Lloyd George, Northcliffe stated:

> Though no binding assurances have been given, or
> engagements entered into, a very precise impression has been
> conveyed, under my responsibility, that this country, at least,
> favours a policy of liberation of the Habsburg subject races
> with a view to their constitution, in the event of an Allied

victory, into a non-German polity, or Danubian Confederation.[31]

It has always been believed that the campaign against the Austrian army substantially contributed to the failure of the Austrian Piave offensive in June 1918.[32] The government's decision to use the nationalities and to appeal to their separatist tendencies through propaganda against Austria-Hungary illustrates the shifting of emphasis during the spring of 1918 away from the idea of a separate peace and towards the destruction of the Habsburg monarchy. Balfour's reply to Northcliffe on 26 February 1918 on the subject of offensive propaganda clearly reflects the official attitude of the moment. Determined to avoid an absolute and possibly irrevocable decision on the future of Austria-Hungary, the government would not completely abandon the prospect of a separate peace but was prepared to sanction greater use of the nationalities. This shifting of emphasis in official policy continued after February 1918 as the course of events seemed to confirm the impossibility of a separate peace. After the failure of the Kerr mission in March 1918 and after the French government published the Sixte letter in April 1918, only the most die-hard optimist could still advocate negotiations.[33] On 21 May 1918, the foreign office, with Lloyd George's approval, informed Lord Derby, the new ambassador in Paris, that:

> We feel that policy of trying to detach Austria from Germany
> must be abandoned as both inopportune and impracticable . . .
> We think that best plan is to give all possible support to
> oppressed nationalities in Austria in their struggle against
> German-Magyar domination. Austria may thus be reduced to
> a reasonable frame of mind.[34]

The Allies encountered some difficulties, however, in giving all possible support to the nationalities, and, in return, using them against the Central powers. On 26 January 1918, Dowbor-Musnicki's Polish army in Russia, which the Allies had agreed to support if it continued to fight against the Central powers, came into conflict with the Bolsheviks.[35] According to the minutes of the war cabinet Lloyd George was not interested in paying Poles to fight Bolsheviks:

> In regard to the Polish movement, he gathered that the Polish
> armies in question were engaged not in fighting the Germans
> and Austrians, but in fighting the Bolsheviks. This was no

concern of ours, and they could only be regarded as our
friends if they diverted their armies against the Germans or
Austrians or, as was suggested, to the assistance of our
Roumanian Allies.[36]

On 25 February 1918, Dowbor-Musnicki signed an agreement
with the Germans which ended his army's involvement in the
conflict.[37] In the words of General Sir Henry Wilson, the chief
of the imperial general staff, it was an act 'tantamount to joining
the enemy'.[38] For the National Democrats who had urged the
government to support this army, Dowbor-Musnicki's desertion
was a setback because it gave their opponents an opportunity to
cast doubt on their loyalty to the Entente. For the foreign office,
which had always supported the National Democrats against
their critics, it was, to say the least, an embarrassment. The
foreign office had good reason to look upon this incident with
chagrin because if it had understood Polish affairs, it might have
predicted Dowbor-Musnicki's desertion. Before deciding to support this army the government had been warned by its military
attaché in Petrograd that the Poles were not interested in fighting
the Germans but only in protecting their own property. On 27
December 1917, Howard had written to Hardinge:

> I am afraid the Poles, that is to say all the propertied classes,
> are rapidly drifting away from us. If the Russian revolution
> has brought the working-classes closer to Russia it has
> certainly had the effect of making the propertied classes look
> to Germany as their only hope for saving something out of the
> general wreck . . . I have been told that even Mr. Dmowski
> now shares this view, but this of course may be only a canard.[39]

Before the Russian revolution the conservative Poles had supported Russia, and therefore the Entente, while the Polish left-
wing, inspired by a hatred of reactionary Russia, had gravitated
towards the Central powers. But the Russian revolution, by
replacing Europe's most reactionary government with its most
radical, turned Polish politics upside down, reversing what had
come to be accepted as a static pattern. The natural political
affinities of the conservatives now lay with the Central powers
while those of the Polish left-wing with Russia. As successive
Russian governments became more radical, the various Polish
political parties gradually adjusted their positions according to
the new situation. In Russia, Lednicki replaced Wielopolski as

the Polish leader most closely associated with the Russian government. In Poland, Pilsudski withdrew his support from the Council of State in July 1917 while the National Democrats gradually began to co-operate with it.[40] The British government was aware of the changes in Polish politics in Russia but does not appear to have understood the situation in Poland. For that reason, the action of National Democrats in Poland never caused it to doubt the loyalty of the Polish National Committee. Since the army had been formed by the National Democrats, it had a definite conservative bias which made conflict with the Bolsheviks more likely than conflict with the Germans. Dowbor-Musnicki's apparent desertion to the Central powers was perfectly reasonable given the situation in which he, a former tsarist officer, operated. As Namier explained:

> They have formed that Army under conditions and on lines which in the long run could lead to one result only. Nature takes its course, politics have their iron laws no less than physics. The Polish National Democrats stand for social Conservatism and Polish Imperialism. Since the Russian Revolution Germany has been the stronghold of social Conservatism in Eastern Europe, and conquests at the expense of Russia can obviously never be made otherwise than with German help . . . Considering the interests for which the Polish Army stood and was meant to stand by its organisers, the compromise which they have concluded with Germany must be described as the logic, and not as an irony, of history.[41]

The foreign office had no immediate reason to distrust the Polish National Committee because the Russian revolution did not cause the Poles to reverse their positions. Before 1917 the Polish left-wing in Britain under Zaleski had not strictly adhered to the policy adopted by its counterpart in Poland which co-operated with the Central powers. Zaleski had to adopt a position more favourable to the Entente or risk internment. After the revolution the National Democrats in western Europe maintained their commitment to the Entente regardless of the actions of their supporters elsewhere. Dmowski and his associates on the Polish National Committee were too involved in the war against Germany to change their position. Nevertheless, the British government, without fully comprehending recent developments in Poland, gave official recognition to a Polish committee dominated by conservatives at almost the precise moment that political developments were occurring elsewhere which might weaken their support for the Entente or cause them to change their political allegiance.

Dmowski and Horodyski made a mistake by maintaining overt contact with their associates in Russia who were unable, because of local conditions, to follow the policy of the Polish National Committee. Since Horodyski had convinced the British government to subsidize Dowbor-Musnicki's army, its actions could not but reflect unfavourably upon him and the Polish National Committee.[42] Dowbor-Musnicki's timing was unfortunate for he acted just when the foreign office was having second thoughts about its recognition of the committee. In the latter part of 1917 the foreign office had been criticized for its close association with the National Democrats by a number of groups who preferred Zaleski and the Polish Information Committee. On 6 September 1917, Seton-Watson had, in the *New Europe*, warned the government of the dangers of accepting Dmowski's Polish policy with its extensive territorial aims.[43] In July and November 1917 similar warnings had come from the Jewish community which could not approve of the government's close relations with a political movement openly and rabidly anti-Semitic, and on 7 December 1917, the *Manchester Guardian* criticized the government's official recognition of the Polish National Committee.[44] This opposition had no effect on the government's decision to recognize the committee or on those officials, like Gregory, who were such partisans of Dmowski that they considered his opponents the enemies of the Entente.[45] But it seems to have affected Cecil who had never been enamoured with Dmowski and who found anti-Semitism extremely distasteful.[46] He could not accept the accusation that Dmowski's opponents were necessarily pro-German and on 27 December 1917, wrote:

> The whole question seems to me to be whether Lednicki or Dmowski represents the majority of the Poles. My own impression is that Lednicki does and if so I see no sense in our putting ourselves in opposition to him – though I have no wish to quarrel with Dmowski either – unless his plans will really help our enemies.[47]

It appears that Cecil was not alone in suspecting the National Democrats and that such suspicions prevented the foreign office from completely committing itself to the Polish National Committee. It had only recognized the committee as an official Polish organization and had carefully reserved the right to recognize other Polish organizations. A number of incidents show that the foreign office had no desire to eliminate completely its contact with Dmowski's opponents. On 24 December 1917, the foreign office rejected a request from the war office to deport Zaleski.[48] On 26 December 1917, in reference to the problem of aid for Polish refugees in Russia, Balfour decided that it should be given to all refugees regardless of their political affiliations:

> Such action might give an opportunity for the Council of Regency and Poles in Poland itself to try to get into closer touch with Allies than they have hitherto done. It would also tend to counteract belief that we were backing one party only and not Poland as a whole.[49]

Dowbor-Musnicki's desertion was a setback for the National Democrats but, despite the doubts expressed about them in the foreign office, it did not substantially weaken their influence on those government departments with which they had always had close relations. The monthly payments to the Polish National Committee were continued, and the foreign office assured Reading that: 'We have every reason to maintain our confidence in the Committee and give it our support. Its policy is entirely favourable to the Allied Cause and is constantly directed towards keeping the Poles from a compromise with the Central Powers.'[50] Horodyski's relations with the foreign office remained unimpaired as is indicated by the fact that when the ministry of information was seeking a Polish agent, in March 1917, Drummond recommended him and praised his work for the Entente.[51] When the leaders of various Polish organizations associated with Zaleski formed the Council of the Polish Community in Great Britain and protested against the privileged position of the Polish National Committee, the foreign office supported the home office in opposing any changes in the consular privileges of the Polish National Committee or the recognition of any other committee.[52] The home office, which had long been under the influence of the National Democrats, was convinced that Dmowski's opponents were both corrupt and pro-German.[53] Military intelligence also continued to support the National Democrats and in May 1918, with the approval of the foreign office, banned the export of Zaleski's periodical *The Polish Review*.[54] When the foreign office received reliable reports about the fate of Dowbor-Musnicki's

army, Gregory wrote, with greater charity than had ever been
shown towards Zaleski:

> It is evidently impossible to judge the action of these
> independent and isolated corps by our standards. They appear
> to be full of inconsistency and compromise. But the Poles are
> very subtle and have got their own ideas as to the line they
> intend to pursue – which will probably be neither pro- nor
> anti-German. At all events we ought to suspend judgement and
> revise our conclusion that Dowbor-Musnicki has gone
> irrevocably over to the enemy.[55]

The cabinet which, unlike the foreign office, had never had
close contact with the Polish émigrés was not as willing to excuse
Dowbor-Musnicki's desertion. On the next occasion upon which
Horodyski presented proposals to the war cabinet, they were not
well received. According to its minutes:

> In the one matter in which Count Horodyski had been tried he
> had failed us. The Prime Minister referred to a Polish army
> which Count Horodyski had induced us to support and which
> had eventually turned around and joined with the enemy. That
> was the one real test we had of his *bona fides*.[56]

Although Horodyski's relations with the foreign office remained
unimpaired, he was discredited in the eyes of the cabinet. With
such a scapegoat, however, the cabinet did nothing to alter the
official relationship with the Polish National Committee. There
were, however, some developments at this time which might,
over a long period, weaken the position of the National Democrats.

In 1918 criticism of official policy surpassed anything experienced by the government in the first years of the war. The
Union of Democratic Control was particularly active in attacking
official policy on peace negotiations, war aims and Anglo-Russian
relations.[57] Noel Buxton found the government's association with
the National Democrats an obvious target when, on 16 April
1918, he asked Cecil in the house of commons: 'Can the Noble
Lord explain how it came about that Mr. Dmouski's [*sic*] party,
which proved to be the most disloyal section of the Poles, was
selected by the Foreign Office as the most loyal section?' Cecil
replied: 'I do not think it would be fair to Mr. Dmouski [*sic*] to
identify him with the most disloyal section.'[58] There is no

evidence that such criticism had any positive effect on foreign policy in the sense of causing actions or decisions in relation to the National Democrats which would not have otherwise been taken. This criticism certainly did not cause the government to withdraw support from the Polish National Committee. But it is evident that the foreign office now, for the first time during the war, became sensitive to public opinion and to attacks on it in parliament. It now felt constrained to avoid actions which would obviously provoke further criticism.[59] It is possible that in the absence of such criticism the government would have associated itself even more closely with the Polish National Committee.

In February 1918 the intelligence bureau of the department of information was transferred to the foreign office and became, under Tyrrell, the political intelligence department.[60] The significance of this reorganization should not be overestimated as the personnel, powers and functions of this department remained largely unchanged. During the rest of the war it produced more verbiage than almost any other department of the foreign office without causing substantial changes in policy. But, as part of the foreign office, it was at least in a better position to work for a reorientation of British policy. This reorganization helped Zaleski because the department, under Namier's influence, opposed Dmowski and for the first time gave Zaleski support within the foreign office. Namier continued, as he had always done, to attack Dmowski's territorial aims in eastern Europe which he contended included areas inhabited by Lithuanians, Byelorussians, and Ukrainians.[61] He argued that it was not in British interests to support Dmowski because Polish expansion at the expense of Russia would necessitate Polish dependence on Germany:

> Poland lies between Germany and Russia and never can be
> equal in strength to either, still less superior to both together.
> She can make conquests only in one direction. Any
> aggrandisement at the expense of Russia implies therefore
> dependence on German protection.[62]

The foreign office disapproved of Polish expansion at the expense of Russia as much as Namier. As the Balkan negotiations had shown, it believed in the nationality principle – the drawing of frontiers according to nationality – and had always thought of a reconstructed Poland in ethnic terms. It had never sanctioned Dmowski's territorial claims, and Balfour himself was adamantly opposed to Polish acquisition of non-Polish areas. But while fundamentally agreeing with Namier, the foreign office did not accept his assessment of the National Democrats. As it appeared to involve long-term British interests, Namier considered Dmowski's territorial claims the fundamental issue in Anglo-Polish relations, but the foreign office, more concerned about immediate problems in the conduct of the war, considered the territorial question of minor importance. None of Namier's arguments could outweigh the fact that the Polish National Committee was apparently following a more anti-German policy than its opponents and, above all, that it was making a considerable contribution to the war effort. Just as Dmowski was too committed to the Entente to reverse his policy, the Entente was now too committed to the Polish National Committee to abandon it in favour of its opponents.

Even if the foreign office had considered the territorial question as seriously as did Namier, it probably would not have accepted his conclusions. In formulating its Polish policy the foreign office was always plagued by its failure to find an adviser whose knowledge and objectivity inspired it with confidence. Those, including Namier, who knew something about Poland seemed biased, while those who were 'objective' were ignorant of Polish affairs. As Clerk explained:

> There is unfortunately no prominent authority on whom one can rely for accurate information as to political sentiments in Poland. There is no one from whom we can derive information as to the cross currents of Polish politics and the underlying aims of Polish political leaders, as for instance Dr. Seton-Watson has enabled us to do in the case of the Jugolsavs: nor is there any Pole in a position in any way analogous to that of Professor Masaryk among the Czechs, who can speak with recognized and impartial authority.[63]

In practice the foreign office and military intelligence often relied upon Horodyski for advice on Polish politics and particularly for his judgement on the *bona fides* of other Polish émigrés. This practice gave Horodyski immense influence and, in part, explains why the National Democrats were able to win the good opinion of the government while blackening their opponents' reputations.[64] On 8 February 1918, acting on Balfour's instructions, Drummond sought an independent opinion by asking the director of naval intelligence to undertake a study of Polish politics.[65] Military intelligence had already been so influenced by the National Democrats that it was incapable of objectivity. But, since the results of the investigation by naval intelligence were not complete until June 1918, the foreign office had to work until then with advisers and information in which it lacked complete confidence.[66] It was therefore unlikely to sacrifice the immediate advantages of Polish co-operation because of Namier's possibly faulty calculations of long-term British interests. Even if Namier's facts were accepted, the most ardent of Dmowski's supporters in the foreign office, like Drummond, were prepared to argue that his fears were groundless because as long as a reconstituted Poland included Posen it would be estranged from Germany.[67]

The incorporation of the P.I.D. into the foreign office did not affect a reorientation of Britain's Polish policy, but it did afford Namier greater protection from the attacks of the National Democrats. When Dmowski's organ, the *Tygodnik Polski*, attacked Namier, the foreign office warned Dmowski that further attacks on officials of the foreign office would result in the discontinuation of financial support for the Polish National Committee.[68] It also resulted in the establishment of contact between the foreign office and the *Bureau Polonais de Presse* in Berne which was associated with the Council of Regency in opposition to Dmowski's *Agence Polonaise Centrale*.[69]

During the first half of 1918 the National Democrats were able to maintain their predominant position in Allied countries, although in the defection of Dowbor-Musnicki's army they lost one of their greatest assets. They came under increasing public criticism and even attack from within the government itself, but they were reasonably secure as long as they were useful to the Allies in the conduct of the war.

The shifting of emphasis in British policy away from a separate peace is clearly evident in the government's relations with the Yugoslavs and Czechoslovaks. In April 1918 British interest in the Yugoslavs centred on the problem of recruits for the Serbian army. The French and British governments had been attempting to pressure Sonnino into releasing Yugoslav prisoners of war for this army since December 1917 but without success. As an alternative the Entente began to recruit Yugoslavs in Canada, but this was an inadequate and unfeasible solution to the problem of replacements for the Serbian army.[70] Allied tonnage was so limited that if Yugoslav recruits were shipped from Canada, they would displace American troops destined for France.[71] Since there were an estimated 18,000 potential Yugoslav volunteers in Italian prison camps, the Allied governments continued to press the Italian government for their release. The Italian decision to form Czechoslovak units gave some reason to hope that Sonnino would adopt a more reasonable attitude on the question of Yugoslav recruits.[72] On 5 April 1918, at the height of the Ludendorff offensive, the foreign office instructed Rodd:

> Present situation of all the Allies is so critical that political considerations cannot be allowed to override military necessities, and you should therefore, as soon as your French colleague receives similar instructions, urgently press the Italian Government to reconsider their previous attitude.[73]

The Italian government finally conceded to Allied demands only after Pichon raised the issue of replacements for the Serbian army at a meeting of the supreme war council on 4 July 1918.[74] It agreed to release Orthodox Serbs for the Serbian army but refused to release Croats and Slovenes whom it now planned to form into a separate Yugoslav unit. The Yugoslavs were not averse to the proposal to form a separate army, as it would increase their bargaining power vis-à-vis the Serbian government, but the British government was dissatisfied because, since most of the prisoners were Croats or Slovenes, it would leave the problem of replacements for the Serbian army unsolved.[75] As Macdonogh pointed out, the intention was obvious: '. . . Sonnino's suggestion would, if put into practice, defeat the aim of Jugo-Slav unity by separating Serbs from Croats and Slovenes'.[76] In August 1918 the Italians released four hundred Orthodox Serbs, but after that Sonnino would make no further concessions and the war ended before the Italian government was able to form a Yugoslav army.[77] If such an army had been created, the Yugoslavs might have been able to wring political concessions from the Allied governments, but without it they were never very successful at converting their services to the Entente to their own political advantage. Their only influence stemmed from their importance in anti-Habsburg propaganda.

The government encountered fewer difficulties in the more extensive use of the Czechoslovaks but found that this entailed, at the insistence of the émigrés, irrevocable steps towards national self-determination. The more the Allies used the Czechs, the more they became committed to the cause of Czechoslovakia. The Czechoslovaks were in a more powerful position than the

Yugoslavs because they represented an army of an estimated 100,000 men. In addition to the army in France, there were about 70,000 troops in Russia and about 12,000 in the army being formed in Italy.[78] Difficulties arose between the Allies over the fate of the Czechoslovak army in Russia because the French government wanted it transferred to France under French command while the British government preferred to leave it in Russia.[79] The French plan was fraught with difficulties because of the shortage in Allied tonnage and was obviously motivated by political rather than military considerations because tonnage allotted to the Czech army would have to be diverted from the transport of American troops to France.[80] Although Balfour thought the French plan absurd, the British government reluctantly agreed, on 2 May 1918, at a meeting of the supreme war council at Abbeville, to transport the Czechoslovak army to France.[81] Despite its acceptance of the French plan, the British government was still extremely dissatisfied and sought to circumvent it by appealing to the émigrés to leave their forces in Russia.[82]

At the beginning of May 1918 the British government was already involved in negotiations with the Czechs arising from the formation in Italy and France of Czechoslovak armies under the political jurisdiction of the Czechoslovak National Council.[83] On 24 April 1918, Colonel Milan Štefanik, the Slovak member of the National Council, asked the British government to recognize the Czechoslovak army under the political authority of the National Council, to give it all possible moral and material assistance and to appoint a military attaché to its headquarters.[84] Since the Italian government had just signed a similar agreement, made necessary by its use of Czech forces, an Anglo-Czech convention as suggested by Štefanik would merely bring British policy in line with the position adopted by the other Allies.[85] Štefanik's proposal was supported by the war office and strongly endorsed by the chief of the British military mission in Italy, General Charles Delmé-Radcliffe, who, under the influence of Wickham Steed, had become a supporter of the nationalities.[86] On 4 April 1918, Delmé-Radcliffe had suggested the creation of provisional governments for each of the nationalities because they would facilitate both the use of Czechoslovak troops and the campaign of offensive propaganda directed against the Habsburg army.[87] The foreign office saw no objection to Štefanik's proposals and did not seem to consider them particularly significant.[88] But the issue arose just when it was seeking some way to circumvent the Abbeville agreement on the fate of the army in Russia.

At a meeting arranged by Steed on 10 May 1918, Beneš followed up Štefanik's initiative by presenting Balfour with proposals that the British government should:

> (1) . . . reserve to the National Council the same treatment as has been accorded to it by the French, Italian and the ancient Russian Governments, that is to say . . . in so far as its action concerns British interests and territory;
> (2) take account of the existence of a national Czecho-Slovak Army, . . . and to give adhesion to its constitution both from the political and military point of view;
> (a) by recognising the Czecho-Slovak National Council as the supreme political organ not only of the Czecho-Slovak movement for independence, but also of the national Czecho-Slovak Army; (b) . . . by appointing an officer of liaison or a military attaché . . . (3) . . . give to the National Council certain political rights concerning civil affairs of our compatriots, *similar to those* already accorded to the *Polish National Committee*.[89]

Nothing was decided at this meeting, but Beneš records that Balfour expressed the desire to retain the Czechoslovak army in Russia.[90] In giving the council consular privileges, these proposals were more comprehensive than Štefanik's, and, in the wording of the second point proposing the recognition of the council 'as the supreme political organ not only of the Czecho-Slovak movement', they might be politically more significant. This wording could be interpreted as meaning more than the recognition of the council as the political authority of the army and the representative of Czechoslovak interests in Allied countries.

On 17 May 1918, the war cabinet again discussed the question of the Czechoslovak army and instructed Cecil to ascertain from Beneš whether the National Council would agree to its retention in Russia.[91] On 18 May 1918, Cecil explained to Beneš the reasons for wanting to keep the army in Russia, and, according to Cecil, Beneš stated that the army would obey the orders of the National Council. He added, however, that if the army was asked to remain in Russia:

> the Allied Governments should take an opportunity of recognising in public the Cecho-Slovak [*sic*] movement and

their National Council. He did not ask that any promise should be made, but he did wish that they should be acknowledged as a nationality with just claims to independence.[92]

The foreign office favoured Beneš proposals and wanted immediate action because a solution to the problem of using the Czechoslovaks in Russia could not be postponed.[93] There was little discussion of the details of these proposals because they did not seem to involve any commitment for the government. As Cecil noted: 'The Czechs do not desire any promise or guarantee which they recognize to be useless.'[94] Namier alone commented extensively on the proposals, and he argued that since the other Allies had already made similar agreements with the Czechoslovaks, these proposals, which might otherwise have been significant, were not particularly important.[95] On 27 May 1918, at a meeting of the war cabinet, Cecil proposed addressing a letter to the Czechoslovak National Council which 'while giving them the measure of recognition desired, would not commit the Government to any increased War obligations'.[96] With the cabinet's assent Balfour wrote to Beneš on 3 June 1918, that the government:

> will be glad to give the same recognition to this movement as has been granted by the Governments of France and Italy. His Majesty's Government will thus be prepared to recognise the Czecho-Slovak National Council as the supreme organ of the Czecho-Slovak movement in Allied countries, and they will also be prepared to recognise the Czecho-Slovak Army as an organised unit operating in the Allied cause and to attach thereto a British liaison officer as soon as the need may arise. His Majesty's Government will at the same time be prepared to accord to the National Council political rights concerning the civil affairs of Czecho-Slovaks similar to those already accorded to the Polish National Committee.[97]

It is interesting to note that in condensing and revising Beneš' original proposals Cecil eliminated the clause which might have been interpreted as recognition of the council as the supreme political organ of the Czechoslovak movement in all countries. Before 1918 the Czechoslovaks had had the least success among the émigrés in gaining political recognition from the Allied governments. But by June 1918, because of the formation of Czechoslovak armies, they gained the success that eluded the

Yugoslavs and almost equalled the success of the Polish National Committee. The foreign office explained its decision by saying:

> we have been obliged to take this action in view not only of active co-operation being afforded to Czecho-Slovaks on Italian and Western Fronts, but also of the fact that there are some 50,000 Czecho-Slovaks in Russia composed partly of prisoners and deserters, whom we have every hope of organizing into an effective force to combat the enemy either in the Eastern or Western theatre of war.[98]

It is doubtful whether the issue of the army in Russia was decisive in prompting the government to recognize the Czechoslovaks. Since the foreign office did not exhibit at any time during the negotiations the slightest opposition to such recognition, the government probably would have eventually followed the example of France and Italy regardless of the situation in Russia. But this situation probably explains the timing of this recognition. It was hardly a coincidence that Cecil raised the issue in the cabinet and that it agreed to recognition on the day prior to an Anglo-French conference in London at which the fate of the army in Russia was to be discussed. At that conference the British representatives tried to use Beneš' assent to the maintenance of the army in Russia in order to convince the French government to alter its decision to transfer the army to France.[99] Although the French representatives adamantly refused to alter the Abbeville agreement, the fate of this Czechoslovak army was no longer at the disposal of the Allies. On 25 May 1918, it came into conflict with the Bolsheviks making its evacuation from Russia difficult if not impossible.[100]

By May 1918 the government was willing to give general recognition to the aspirations of the subject nationalities. The Polish National Committee, with the support of the American and French governments, had been seeking an Allied declaration on Poland since the autumn of 1917. Pašić, obviously worried about the danger of a peace with Austria-Hungary at the expense of Serbia, had sought reassurances about Britain's intentions on the South Slav question.[101] On 18 May 1918, Beneš had requested public recognition of the Czechoslovaks as a nationality with just claims to independence. These requests had been vigorously but unsuccessfully supported by the British military representatives in Italy and by Crewe House whose campaign to disrupt the

Habsburg monarchy necessitated a forthright statement by the British government in support of national self-determination.[102] British resistance to such declarations, based primarily on the desire for a separate peace, would have been important had it prevented the other Allies from recognizing the aspirations of the subject nationalities. But, on 9 January 1918, Wilson announced, as one of his fourteen points, that:

> An independent Polish State should be erected which should include the territories inhabited by indisputably Polish populations, which should be assured a free and secure access to the sea, and whose political and economic independence and territorial integrity should be guaranteed by international covenant.[103]

As hope for a separate peace faded, the foreign office began to consider a similar declaration and, on 8 March 1918, it instructed its representative in Rumania to inform Polish émigrés, in reference to the Brest-Litovsk negotiations, 'of the determination of His Majesty's Government to support all Polish attempts to obtain union and independence for Poland'.[104] Despite the government's willingness to consider stronger declarations on the subject nationalities, however, it was still unprepared to undertake commitments. When Pichon, at an Anglo-French conference on 28 March 1918, proposed the recognition of Polish and Bohemian independence, Lloyd George still insisted that the Allies avoid pledges that might be unredeemable: 'We would try to free them, but we could not say that the independence of Bohemia and Poland was one of our war aims.'[105]

The issue was not considered again by the Allies until the supreme war council met in June 1918, and, by this time, if any opposition to such declarations existed within the British government, it remained passive. On 21 May 1918, the foreign office had informed Derby that: 'policy of trying to detach Austria from Germany must be abandoned as both inopportune and impracticable . . . We think that best plan is to give all possible support to oppressed nationalities . . .'[106] The American government even increased the pressure on the Allies to make a declaration by announcing, on 30 May 1918, its earnest sympathy for the freedom of the Czechoslovaks and Yugoslavs.[107] On 3 June 1918, the supreme war council declared that:

> (1) The creation of a united and independent Polish State

with free access to the sea constitutes one of the conditions of
a solid and just peace, and of the rule of right in Europe.

(2) The Allied Governments have noted with pleasure the
declaration made by the Secretary of State of the United States
Government and desire to associate themselves in an expression
of earnest sympathy for the nationalistic aspirations towards
freedom of the Czecho-Slovak and Yugo-Slav peoples.[108]

Among the émigrés, only the Poles found the declaration satisfactory. Although weaker than Wilson's thirteenth point, it did
contain the phrase 'free access to the sea', considered of the
greatest importance by Polish émigrés. But, contrary to Polish
expectations, the declaration was carefully worded, as in the past
to avoid any specific pledge.[109] The real significance of the
declaration, however, was that it was interpreted by the British
government as a limited commitment to the Polish cause. On 2
July 1918, Balfour wrote to Rumbold: 'This declaration should
place beyond doubt once and for all the decision of the Allied
Governments to see Poland's national aspirations fully satisfied,
so far as lies within their power, . . .'[110] In the past, when issuing
similar declarations on the Polish issue, the government had
always interpreted them so as to minimize their significance. The
Versailles declaration was the government's most important statement during the war on the future of Poland precisely because it
interpreted the declaration as a commitment to work for Polish
independence so far as it lay in its power. It was also the government's last significant act on the Polish issue prior to the
armistice.

After this declaration the P.I.D. – Tyrrell, Namier and Headlam
– intensified its efforts to reorient Britain's Polish policy by attacking the National Democrats and by attempting to rehabilitate
Zaleski and the Polish Information Committee.[111] The P.I.D.
argued that the charges of being corrupt and pro-German, levelled
against Zaleski and his colleagues by the National Democrats,
were totally unfounded.[112] Although these charges had been
accepted by the foreign office and military intelligence, the P.I.D.
was supported by naval intelligence which in June 1918 completed the report on Polish politics requested by Balfour in
February 1918. The report maintained that these charges were
merely unscrupulous libels perpetrated by the National Democrats and concluded, after examining this type of conduct in
Polish politics, that 'it is difficult sometimes for the casual

observer to avoid the uneasy suspicion that the whole of Polish politics is incredibly crude and raw, and has a general character of brutality and stupidity which make all parallels and analogies hopelessly misleading'. The report also pointed out, contrary to the belief of the foreign office, that the National Democrats in Poland were co-operating with the enemy and that the Socialists were the only group in Polish politics unalterably opposed to the Central powers.[113]

On 31 May 1918, Zaleski informed the foreign office that he had been appointed the representative in London of the Polish provisional government in Warsaw and requested the initiation of informal discussions between the two governments.[114] Although the foreign office opposed this request, Tyrrell was able, by arguing that it was necessary to expand the sources of information on Polish politics, to convince Balfour, Hardinge and Clerk to allow at least informal contact with Zaleski.[115] On 26 July 1918, the foreign office even agreed, at Tyrrell's instigation, to allow Zaleski to travel to Switzerland where it was expected he would have greater access to information on developments in Poland.[116] It was agreed, however, that he would travel only as a private citizen and not as a recognized representative of the Polish provisional government.[117] This decision marked a change in the official attitude towards the various Polish factions, and it was significant that Clerk, who had previously accepted the views of Drummond and Gregory, was now sufficiently satisfied that Zaleski was a supporter of the Entente that he was willing to sanction official contact with him. In September 1918 the foreign office also lifted the embargo on the export of Zaleski's *Polish Review* which had been previously banned for attacks on the Polish National Committee.[118]

As the war approached its end, the influence of the P.I.D. increased, and these measures, carried out at its instigation, were symptomatic of the decline of the Polish National Committee. Since that committee had achieved its predominant position in Anglo-Polish relations for strategic not political reasons, these measures indicated that its influence might not outlast the end of the conflict. The trend of events in Poland also worked against the committee because, as the foreign office gradually realized, there was a danger that when German authority in Poland collapsed, the vacuum would be filled not by the Polish National Committee but by those opponents of the National Democrats with whom the government had no contact except through

Zaleski. Despite the views of the P.I.D. which were shared, to some extent, by Cecil and Clerk and despite the danger that it might be supporting the wrong faction, the foreign office would not abandon the Polish National Committee.[119] As long as hostilities continued and as long as the Polish army fought in France, the original reasons for recognizing the committee remained valid. The foreign office could not replace the faction responsible for the creation of the army, which by November 1918 contained 100,000 men, with another faction known to be conducting relations with the Central powers.[120] In the uncertainties of Polish politics it seemed of questionable value to abandon one faction for another. On 4 September 1918, Clerk wrote: 'I am quite clear that we must not be drawn into any negotiations direct or indirect with the so-called Polish Government. If we were we should risk the sympathies of all other Polish opinion.'[121]

To avoid being caught at the end of the war backing the wrong horse, the foreign office sought to expand the Polish National Committee to make it more representative of Polish opinion. Although a committee representing all Polish parties seemed to be an ideal solution, the nature of Polish politics, as the foreign office quickly learned, made it impossible. On 15 August 1918, Drummond wrote: 'I naturally agree that a Polish Committee representative of all Polish parties would be most advantageous. Unfortunately I fear that it is not practicable to constitute such a committee under present conditions. We must I think therefore make the best of what material we have.'[122] Despite reservations, the foreign office did not abandon the Polish National Committee but continued, as long as the war lasted, its attempts to make it more representative.[123] For that reason, even though Gregory admitted that the committee 'will soon have outrun its utility', the Polish National Committee was able to maintain its predominant position until the armistice.[124] It still received its monthly payment from the British government for October 1918, and at the armistice it was the only Polish organization recognized by the government.[125]

The British position on the Polish issue at the time of the armistice had been determined by the Versailles declaration of 3 June 1918. The government was not committed to the Polish National Committee which had only been recognized as an official Polish organization and not as a provisional government. Although the government considered itself committed, in a limited sense, to the independence of Poland, this commitment did not have the legal force of, for example, British obligations to Italy under the treaty of London. The government also had no specific territorial commitments to the future Polish state for even its endorsement of Polish access to the sea only committed it, by its own interpretation, to internationalization of the Vistula.[126] The government had not even decided on what areas should be included in the Polish state, although it was determined that Poland should only comprise those areas inhabited by Poles. At a meeting of the supreme war council on 2 November 1918, Balfour replied with some annoyance to a suggestion by Pichon that Poland be given the frontiers of 1772: 'that he had listened to this proposal with some anxiety. The suggestion was that the Poland of 1772 should be that of 1919. That was not what we had undertaken to bring about.'[127]

The Poles had fared better in the Versailles declaration than the Czechoslovaks and Yugoslavs who, expecting more, were left extremely dissatisfied. Balfour later explained to Northcliffe that the British and French had wanted to issue a stronger declaration but had been opposed by the Italian government. Sonnino did not object to a stronger declaration on the Czechoslovak issue, but, since it was generally agreed that both nationalities had to be included in the same declaration, the Czechoslovaks suffered because of Italian opposition to the Yugoslavs.[128] Balfour justified the inadequacy of this declaration by saying that while the French and British governments were willing to make stronger declarations, they were also unwilling to advertise a 'fundamental difference of opinion between Italy on the one side and France and England on the other about an important point of policy'.[129] In order to overcome the limitations imposed upon them at Versailles by the attitude of the Italian government, however, the French and British governments had reserved for themselves the right to make supplementary declarations on the Yugoslavs and Czechoslovaks.

No sooner had the declaration been published than the foreign office began to receive indications of the amount of dissatisfaction it created among the supporters of national self-determination. On behalf of Crewe House Northcliffe wrote to Balfour:

> May I therefore impress upon you very earnestly the
> expediency of making some public statement without delay . . .
> in such terms as may reassure our Czecho-Slovak and

Yugo-Slav friends and encourage them to persevere in the
valuable work they have been doing, and are disposed
increasingly to do.[130]

In response to Northcliffe's appeal, Balfour asked Beneš to
publish the letter of recognition addressed to him on 3 June 1918,
and, on 11 June 1918, Cecil stated in the house of commons:

> It will be for the liberated Czecho-Slovak and Yugo-Slav
> peoples themselves to determine their future status. His
> Majesty's Government fully recognise the many proofs given
> by these races of intense national feeling, and cordially
> acknowledge the assistance which the national troops of the
> Czecho-Slovaks and Jugo-Slavs are rendering to the Allied
> cause.[131]

Despite this statement, the Yugoslavs and their supporters
remained dissatisfied as is evidenced by the number of representations made by them and on their behalf to the foreign office
appealing for a stronger declaration on the Yugoslav question.[132] On 21 June 1918, during the Austrian Piave offensive,
Delmé-Radcliffe informed Macdonogh:

> It is essential that strong action by the Allied Governments to
> bring all the oppressed nationalities of Austria more
> completely over to our side should be delayed no longer. The
> importance of such a result as affecting the military situation
> cannot be exaggerated.[133]

The foreign office clearly recognized the value and necessity of
a further declaration but had to find a suitable opportunity and
formula which would not upset the Italian government.[134] Sonnino
had justified his opposition to Yugoslav aspirations by claiming
that, since the majority of South Slavs wanted only autonomy
within the Habsburg monarchy, a declaration in favour of a
Yugoslav state would only alienate them and inspire them to
greater efforts on behalf of the Central powers.[135] The foreign
office doubted this interpretation of the Yugoslav situation, as it
contradicted most of its previous information, but, before taking
further action, it requested military intelligence to undertake
a thorough analysis of the whole situation. On 17 June 1918,
Hardinge wrote to Rodd:

> Bye the bye Baron Sonnino has really been extremely tiresome
> over the Yugo-Slav question. We are being bombarded by the

Serbians and Yugo-Slav committees protesting against the weakness of our Declaration and comparing it with that made regarding the Poles. I understand that Sonnino maintains that the Yugo-Slavs do not want independence but merely autonomy, and that to declare for independence would be to throw the bulk of the Yugo-Slavs into the arms of Austria. Our information is totally opposed to this, and we are working it out.[136]

The report, completed by military intelligence on 28 June 1918, repudiated Sonnino's interpretation and, as the foreign office expected, supported the Yugoslav claims.[137] The P.I.D. agreed with the report and the foreign office accepted it as an accurate and unbiased analysis of the Italian–Yugoslav problem.[138] The opportunity and even necessity of a further act of recognition of Yugoslav aspirations arose in July 1918 when Balfour was invited to address a meeting of the Serbian (Yugo-Slav) National War Aims Committee in Great Britain.[139] Drummond and Hardinge were somewhat nervous because of the danger that by his attendance Balfour might be associated with extremist remarks, but, as Harold Nicolson pointed out, the invitation could not be refused without seriously offending the already sensitive Yugoslavs: 'Abstention in the circumstances would assuredly not be attributed to simple considerations of tact and caution, but would be taken as implying some mysterious reorientation of policy.'[140] Following Nicolson's advice, Balfour attended the meeting at Mansion House on 25 July 1918, and associated himself with its declared aim of 'independence and unity of all Serbs, Croats and Slovenes in a single State'.[141]

Although no one could have realized it at the time, this was the government's last act of recognition of Yugoslav aspirations during the war. Following the Inter-Allied Conference on Propaganda in Enemy Countries in August 1918, Crewe House requested another Allied declaration recognizing 'the establishment of a free and united Yugoslav State, embracing the Serbs, Croats and Slovenes, as one of the conditions of a just and lasting peace and of the rule of right in Europe.[142] The foreign office readily accepted this suggestion on condition that it could be negotiated with the other Allied governments.[143] Although it anticipated Italian opposition to this proposal, on 25 September 1918, the Italian government, aware of the importance of Yugoslav propaganda in its forthcoming offensive against the Austrian army at Vittorio Veneto, issued a declaration in similar terms recognizing the justice of Yugoslav aspirations for an independent state.[144] Even in September 1918 offensive propaganda against Austria-Hungary was still an important aspect of Allied strategy because the Allies did not realize how close the Central powers were to a complete collapse. The Italian declaration gave the British government the opportunity to adopt a more forward policy on the Yugoslav question, but a new obstacle arose from the growing conflict between the Serbian government and the Yugoslav Committee.

In September 1918 the Yugoslav Committee began to request recognition similar to that accorded to the Czechoslovak and Polish committees.[145] Unlike the others, however, the Yugoslavs could not bargain from a position of strength because there was no Yugoslav army. Yugoslav recruits had not been formed into a national army but had been placed in the Serbian army.[146] The émigrés could request recognition, but they could not demand it. Close relations had been established between the Serbian government and the Yugoslav Committee by the pact of Corfu in June 1917 which both parties had signed as equals, agreeing to work for a South Slav state under the Karageorgević dynasty. These good relations were in the process of breaking down throughout 1918 as each party accused the other of violating the pact.[147] In essence the conflict developed because the Yugoslav Committee wanted an independent position so that it could negotiate with the Serbian government on behalf of the Austrian South Slavs, while Pašić and his government, tolerating no rivals, claimed sole leadership of the South Slavs.[148] By October 1918 the British government was willing to recognize a South Slav authority and to give greater endorsement to South Slav aspirations, but it insisted on the maintenance of the pact of Corfu in which the Serbian government and the Yugoslav Committee were equals.[149] In interviews with Trumbić and Pašić Balfour made it quite clear that the government would not recognize either claim to sole leadership of the cause and would only recognize an authority which could speak for all South Slavs.[150] In fact, the foreign office wanted Pašić to establish a coalition government including members of the Yugoslav Committee.[151] The inability of the Yugoslavs and Serbians to agree, despite the efforts of the foreign office to negotiate a compromise, created a stalemate and prevented the British government from recognizing any South Slav authority. On 23 October 1918, as Austria-Hungary was already beginning to collapse, the foreign office attempted to induce Pašić to compromise by threatening to recognize the Yugoslav Committee, but, before any further action could be taken, the war had ended.[152]

The knowledge that Beneš was also dissatisfied with the Versailles declaration led the British and French governments to use the occasion of the presentation of colours to the Czechoslovak army in France to give further recognition to Czechoslovak aspirations.[153] On 1 July 1918, the president of France declared that:

> Le Gouvernement de la République, fidèle aux principes du respect des nationalités et de la libération des peuples opprimés pour lesquels il combat avec ses Alliés, . . . et, s'inspirant des sentiments de haut idéal exprimés par M. le Président Wilson considère comme justes et fondées les revendications du peuple Tchèco-Slovaque et déclare qu'il appuiera de toute sa sollicitude les aspirations à l'indépendance pour lesquelles ses soldats combattent dans les rangs Alliés.

At the same time the foreign office published a statement that: 'His Majesty's Government desire fully to associate themselves with the sentiments so admirably expressed in the speech of the President of the Republic.'[154] In the past, the Allies had expressed sympathy for Czechoslovak aspirations, but this was the first statement with which the British government associated itself which expressed support for these aspirations. The statement was subject to interpretation because there was no indication to what degree the British government would support Czechoslovak aims, but, nevertheless, it was the strongest statement yet made in reference to the Czechoslovak cause.

Once the British government realized that a separate peace was impossible and that the war would have to continue until the enemy was defeated, it quickly abandoned the caution that had marked its previous relations with the nationalities and undertook, without opposition or even hesitation, measures which it had previously avoided. Compared to its hesitation over the preceding three years, it agreed with almost surprising alacrity to the recognition of the Czechoslovak army, to the Versailles declaration and to the supplementary declarations on the Yugoslavs and Czechoslovaks. In July 1918, however, when Masaryk, acting through Beneš and Steed, requested British recognition of a Czechoslovak provisional government, caution reasserted itself.[155]

Initially the foreign office, including those officials favourable to the Czechoslovak cause, opposed this unorthodox and far-reaching proposal and was disposed, despite its desire to guarantee Czechoslovak support for the Entente, to show that there were still limits beyond which it would not go. Harold Nicolson had difficulty in conceiving of a provisional government lacking territory over which it exercised at least *de facto* control and pointed out that recognition of a Czechoslovak provisional government would only offend the Poles and Yugoslavs.[156] Tyrrell and Namier agreed with Nicolson and, while sympathetic to the Czech cause, thought the proposal premature and unnecessary.[157] Hardinge speculated that if such recognition led to a revolution in Bohemia it might be worth consideration, but Balfour ruled that the precedent established in Anglo-Polish relations of not recognizing a provisional government had to be followed in the case of the Czechoslovaks.[158] But, when Cecil pointed out to Balfour that recognition of a Czechoslovak government might prevent the Austrians from executing captured Czechoslovak soldiers, a practice they had hitherto followed, Balfour reconsidered:

> If recognition would really save Bohemian lives we might well throw logic to the winds and acknowledge the Czecho-Slovaks. But the course will almost certainly be inconvenient from a diplomatic point of view; and *unless* it is necessary on grounds of humanity I do not recommend it. I shall be a great deal influenced by what Dr. B. [Beneš] tells you tomorrow. *But of course he is a prejudiced witness.*[159]

In fact the reluctance shown by the foreign office when presented with this proposal was a luxury the government could no longer afford. When he first suggested the proposal to Steed, Beneš commented: 'The position in Siberia gives us the right to do it.'[160] Irrespective of rights, the situation in Siberia gave the Czechoslovaks the power to make such demands. The outbreak of hostilities between the Czechoslovak army in Russia and the Bolsheviks in May 1918 forced the Allies to abandon temporarily the plan, which the British government had only reluctantly accepted, to transfer this army from Siberia to France. The ultimate destination of this army ceased to be a question of immediate importance because Bolshevik hostility cast doubt on its very survival. Since the British government wanted to use the Czechs as the spearhead of Allied intervention in Siberia, these developments fitted perfectly into its military planning.[161] The previous refusal of the French government to use Czechoslovak troops in Russia had been a nuisance, but the real obstacle to British plans for intervention in Siberia had been the complete refusal of the American government to co-operate. Prior to the outbreak of Czech–Bolshevik hostilities the American government had refused to sanction or participate in any form of intervention, despite the strenuous efforts of the British and French governments to convince Wilson that intervention was a military necessity in order to deny the Central powers control of Siberia and in order to re-establish an eastern front.[162] These arguments failed to move President Wilson, but the outbreak of Czech–Bolshevik hostilities now enabled the British government to argue that intervention was necessary in order to save the Czechoslovaks from destruction. On 21 June 1918, Balfour wrote to Lord Reading, the new ambassador in Washington: 'The Czechs are our Allies, and we must save them if we can. Their position seems to me to render immediate Allied action on their behalf a matter of urgent necessity.'[163] On 6 July 1918, responding to this argument, Wilson agreed to intervene in Siberia with limited forces for the specific purpose of assisting the Czechoslovaks to disengage from the Bolsheviks and evacuate their troops.[164] But, unlike the Americans, the British were not interested in assisting the Czechs to evacuate Siberia. On 28 June 1918, Balfour had written Bruce Lockhart, the British representative in Russia:

> I trust you will take every possible step to encourage the Czechs. In no circumstances should they give up their arms. Nor should they abandon control of Western Siberia which is the key to the Russian position. We have great hopes that intervention will shortly take place with a view to re-establish an Eastern front against the Germans. Czech co-operation should be of the utmost importance to the success of this policy and the Czechs cannot serve the allied cause better than by standing firm.[165]

Although the British government found the scope of American plans unsatisfactory, it now hoped that limited involvement, once begun, would lead eventually to unlimited intervention.[166] If the Czechoslovaks continued to fight the Russians, intervention might be prolonged and the Americans might be successfully drawn into committing more troops in Siberia, but if the Czechoslovaks evacuated their forces to eastern Siberia as quickly as possible, the whole policy of intervention might collapse. For that reason, as Lloyd George wrote to Reading: 'The Czecho-Slovaks are the key to the position.'[167] But at the beginning of July 1918 there was no reason to assume that the Czechoslovaks would stay in Siberia. Until hostilities had broken out with the Bolsheviks, the Czechoslovaks had refused to fight on Russian soil and had consistently expressed their desire to leave Russia.[168] In his letter to Steed in which he proposed the recognition of a provisional government, and which Steed passed on to the foreign office, Beneš mentioned the possibility of the evacuation of these forces and insisted that at least some, possibly 5,000, had to be transferred to France.[169] In this situation the British government had every reason to give the most serious consideration to Czech demands, and the Czechs found themselves in the unprecedented position of being able to make demands on the government. The strategic importance of their troops in Russia gave the Czechoslovaks power unparalleled among the subject nationalities.

On 26 July 1917, Beneš, having come to London for negotiations with the foreign office, submitted a memorandum explaining his case for the recognition of a provisional government. He argued that the National Council could only exercise real authority over the Czechoslovak armies and could only maintain the morale and effectiveness of these forces if it was recognized as a provisional government. The army in Russia would be more obedient and more willing to accept orders from its own provisional government than from any of the Allied governments. Taking advantage of the Siberian situation, Beneš pointed out that the Czechoslovak National Council still adhered to the original Allied agreement to transfer the Czechoslovak army to France but was prepared to accept the temporary retention of this army in Siberia until it could be replaced by other Allied forces. The success of these arrangements, however, necessitated in the view of the National Council its recognition as a government with sovereign authority. Beneš also argued that recognition would weaken Austria-Hungary and might lead to a revolution in Bohemia. He ended by reviewing Czechoslovak services to the Entente and stated that recognition would lead to even greater efforts.[170] Although couched in diplomatic language, the message was clear; the price for Czechoslovak services, particularly in Siberia, was the recognition of a provisional government.

Instead of explaining the primary reason for his request, that recognition would be of immeasurable value to the Czechoslovaks in their attempts to establish an independent state, Beneš had concentrated exclusively on those arguments which he knew from experience would carry weight with British officials.

Following the submission of this memorandum, Beneš was interviewed by Cecil and was requested to submit the exact formula of recognition desired by the National Council.[171] In the meantime, Drummond, to whom Beneš had admitted that recognition would do nothing to save the lives of captured Czech soldiers, suggested that the Czechoslovaks might be satisfied if given all the powers of a government without recognition as such.[172] No one in the foreign office opposed extending greater powers to the National Council, and since it would avoid the legal and diplomatic problems of recognizing a provisional government, Balfour found this compromise perfectly acceptable.[173]

On 30 July 1918, Beneš submitted the exact formula of recognition desired by the National Council, the last sentence of which read: 'His Majesty's Government therefore recognize the sovereignty of the Czecho-Slovak National Council who at present exercise the rights of a Provisional Czecho-Slovak Government.'[174] This sentence was obviously unacceptable to the foreign office, and Balfour only agreed to accept the declaration as a whole after he had replaced it with the statement that: 'Great Britain also recognizes the right of the Czecho-Slovak National Council to exercise supreme authority over this Allied and belligerent Army.'[175] When Cecil gave the revised text to Beneš on 2 August 1918, the latter was obviously disappointed that the most significant sentence had been eliminated, but, according to Cecil, he seemed to accept this decision.[176] After consulting Wickham Steed, however, Beneš rejected the text as altered by Balfour because, as he explained, it said even less than Balfour's letter of 3 June 1918. He also submitted documents relating to Czechoslovak relations with Italy and France showing that these countries had already extended more recognition to the National Council than was embodied in the revised declaration.[177] Uninformed of these agreements, Cecil minuted on the letter: 'It seems to me in view of the action of France and Italy – of which I knew nothing till now – that we might well accept the declaration as originally drafted by M. Beneš.'[178] Had Beneš insisted upon his original text it might have been accepted, but instead he suggested an alternative. Following Steed's advice to avoid the word 'sovereignty' and use the word 'trustee', Beneš now suggested that the final sentence should read: 'Great Britain also recognises the right of the Czecho-Slovak National Council, as the supreme organ of the Czecho-Slovak national interests, and as the trustee of the future Czecho-Slovak Government, to exercise supreme authority over this Allied and belligerent Army.'[179]

At a meeting of the war cabinet on 7 August 1918, Sir Henry Wilson, echoing a constant preoccupation of British officials during these negotiations, expressed great concern that the Czechoslovak desire to leave Russia might destroy the plans for intervention.[180] The cabinet considered the danger serious enough to rule that every effort should be made to keep these forces in Russia, but this concern was, for the moment, unnecessary. Drummond informed Hankey on 8 August 1918, that Masaryk had ordered the Czechoslovak army to remain in Siberia and fight.[181] On 9 August 1918, Cecil informed Beneš that the government accepted the declaration as revised by him on 2 August 1918, so that in its final form it read:

> Since the beginning of the war the Czecho-Slovak nation has resisted the common enemy by every means in its power. The Czecho-Slovaks have constituted a considerable Army, fighting on three different battle-fields and attempting, in Russia and Siberia, to arrest the Germanic invasion. In consideration of its efforts to achieve independence, Great Britain regards the Czecho-Slovaks as an Allied Nation, and recognises the unity of the three Czech-Slovak Armies as an Allied and belligerent Army waging regular warfare against Austria-Hungary and Germany. Great Britain also recognises the right of the Czecho-Slovak National Council, as the supreme organ of the Czecho-Slovak national interests, and as the present trustee of the future Czecho-Slovak Government, to exercise supreme authority over this Allied and belligerent Army.[182]

The government also approved in principle a supplementary convention with the Czechoslovaks which in specific terms gave them the prerogatives of a provisional government. Beneš had submitted a draft of this convention on 2 August 1918, a few days after the foreign office had agreed to grant the Czechs at least the powers of a government.[183] The foreign office did not seriously dispute the clauses of this convention but only approved it in principle because the war office, home office and treasury had to be consulted on those terms which affected them.[184] After extensive revision necessitated by the fact that in some clauses Beneš overreached himself, the convention was signed on 3 September 1918.[185] The British government recognized the National Council's authority over the Czechoslovak army and its right to be represented at Allied conferences which dealt with Czechoslovak affairs. It agreed to extend full consular and diplomatic privileges to the council, such as the issuing of passports and the appointment of diplomatic representatives, and to treat Czechs in Britain as friendly aliens and the members of an Allied nation. Finally the government agreed to participate in future Allied loans to the council and to appoint a representative to a financial commission which would supervise the council's budget.[186]

Through the declaration and convention which Beneš had negotiated with the government, the Czechoslovak National Council achieved greater success and greater recognition than the Yugoslav Committee or the Polish National Committee were able to achieve at any time during the war. When an official of the home office questioned the Czechoslovak's special status, Cecil replied: 'that it was intended that this should be so as the Czecho-Slovaks were a more homogeneous body and had done more for the Allied Cause than any of the others'.[187] When the Serbian ambassador, on behalf of the Yugoslavs, queried this special treatment of the Czechoslovaks, Cecil informed him: 'that there were considerable differences between the two cases. The Czecho-Slovaks had a large army in the field, and a National Council, which was recognised by all the Czech forces, and received obedience from them. No such body existed in the case of the Yugo-Slavs.'[188]

The British government was aware that its Czechoslovak policy, as embodied in the declaration and convention, might lead to the dismemberment of Austria-Hungary. But, in almost recognizing a Czechoslovak provisional government, the British government had not become a champion of national self-determination or of Czechoslovak independence. The government had accepted certain obligations to the Czechs but had avoided any form of commitment to an independent Czechoslovakia. As Cecil explained: 'Our recognition of the Czechs was very carefully worded and though it would undoubtedly be consistent with the dismemberment of Austria it does not in fact bind us to that solution.'[189] The agreements between the British government and the Czechoslovak National Council in the summer of 1918 were perfectly consistent with the previous relations between the government and the subject nationalities and can be explained in similar terms. In their negotiations Beneš and Cecil avoided discussion of any crude bargain, but Beneš made it clear enough that recognition was the price of Czechoslovak co-operation in Siberia. The British acceptance of his demands was not based on a belief in national self-determination or in the ultimate political advantages of Czechoslovak independence but rather on a calculation of the immediate strategic advantages of satisfying the Czechoslovak National Council so that it would continue to co-operate in Siberia. As Cecil admitted: 'we have felt compelled to endorse their claims to independence, and . . . we have unquestionably received full value for our endorsement'.[190]

These agreements mark the end of the Czechoslovak struggle in Britain during the war for recognition and support of their right to self-determination. When a Czechoslovak provisional government was formed in Paris in October 1918, the British government did not recognize it.[191] Before 11 November 1918, it gave no further recognition to the Czechoslovaks and undertook no further commitments to their cause. At the time of the armistice it was not committed to Czechoslovak independence or to the territorial claims of the Czechoslovak provisional government.

As late as August 1918 the British government expected that the war would continue for another year.[192] For that reason it continued almost until the end of the war to base its relations with the émigrés on strategic considerations. There seemed to be no urgent need to solve the problem of Serbian–Yugoslav rivalry, and in the case of the Poles the government, despite considerations of political expediency, would not abandon that faction which was making the greatest contribution to the Entente's war effort. When the Central powers collapsed, events moved so quickly that the government did not have time to alter its relations with the subject nationalities to suit those aims it wished to pursue at the peace conference. In fact, on the subject of national self-determination, the government had not decided exactly what aims it wished to pursue.

The collapse of the enemy cut short the war-time relations between the government and the émigrés before they could be developed to their logical conclusion. Throughout the war, even while it sought a separate peace, the government gradually increased its use of the subject nationalities. Had the war continued into 1919 it is almost certain that this pattern would have reached its ultimate conclusion with the British government using the émigrés to promote revolution in Austria-Hungary. Sobanski had suggested such action in November 1917, but at that time a separate peace still seemed possible. Disintegration and revolution were the logical results of the propaganda campaign devised by Crewe House and supported by the British military representatives in Italy.[193] By April 1918 Beneš was already discussing with British military representatives the Czech preparations for revolution in Bohemia.[194] In June 1918 Horodyski informed Drummond that there was considerable unrest in Galicia and suggested that plans be initiated for a joint Polish–Czechoslovak revolution in August.[195] The war cabinet, which discussed the proposal on 11 June 1918, was interested but distrusted Horodyski and thought a revolution within Austria-Hungary premature. It did not want a revolution crushed and would only support the plan if it had a reasonable chance of success. As Balfour explained to Derby:

> Clearly an insurrection in Poland or in Bohemia, if an isolated event in the war, would be easily suppressed by force and the spirit of the people cowed; we should thus have wasted a valuable potential asset; but if such outbreaks formed part of a larger scheme the Central Powers might be placed in a serious position.[196]

Although it withheld immediate approval, the war cabinet authorized the foreign office to begin preparations so that it could take advantage of the opportune moment when it arose.[197] Because of the natural secrecy surrounding such plans it is impossible to determine what preparations were made and to what extent the government was involved. But such involvement cannot be doubted because on 23 August 1918, Balfour authorized a payment of £4,000 to Horodyski to be used in connection with this work.[198] On 27 August 1918, Beneš informed Cecil that preparations for a revolution were almost complete and that it would take place either in December 1918 or April 1919 depending on the strategic situation.[199] Had the war continued into 1919 and had it been a strategic necessity, there can be little doubt that the Allies would have used revolution as the ultimate weapon against Austria-Hungary. This course of action would have necessitated complete recognition of the subject nationalities and at least limited support for their aspirations. In this situation the government might have been forced to make a formal decision on the fate of Austria-Hungary by giving a general endorsement to the idea of national self-determination. Such developments would have carried the pattern of British relations with the subject nationalities during the war to its ultimate, logical and extreme conclusion. But the collapse of the Central powers, premature in terms of British military planning, cut short this development and left the government in a position which was, to say the least, confused. By 11 November 1918, it had not formally endorsed the general application of the idea of national self-determination and had not decided, or accepted a commitment, to destroy Austria-Hungary. But it was obvious that British policy, by implication if not by design, was directed towards that end. The government's relations with the nationality organizations were equally confused. It had endorsed the creation of Polish and Yugoslav states but in neither case could it find a satisfactory authority to represent their national interests. It had almost recognized a Czechoslovak provisional government but had never endorsed the creation of an independent Czechoslovak state. It had not even decided, and had seldom considered, what territories should be allotted to these states should they be created. In November 1918 the government faced the prospect of peace negotiations from a position not based on calculations of its long-term political interests in eastern Europe but determined by its military strategy.

By 11 November 1918, British approval of independence for Poland, Czechoslovakia and Yugoslavia had become irrelevant. On 28 October 1918, Masaryk's followers began to seize power in Bohemia using the revolutionary organization that the British government had sought to promote. On 29 October 1918, the same process began in the Austrian South Slav areas when Yugoslav leaders in Zagreb declared the severance of constitutional ties with Austria-Hungary and the incorporation of Croatia, Slavonia and Dalmatia in a Serbian, Croat and Slovene state. On 10 November 1918, Pilsudski was released from prison and began to assume power in Poland. Austria-Hungary had ceased to exist making British decisions on its fate now irrelevant. During the peace conference the Allies could determine the territorial settlement in eastern Europe but they had as much power to deny independence to these nationalities as they had to deny existence to the Bolsheviks.

CONCLUSION

In August 1914 the British government knew little and cared less about the subject nationalities of eastern Europe. Everyone interested in European affairs knew of the Poles and probably possessed a rudimentary understanding of the Polish problem, but there is no evidence that the foreign office knew anything about the complexities of Polish politics. Serbian politics were better understood, because of the previous Balkan crises, but officials were not well informed about the Austrian South Slavs who were more often referred to as Bosnians, Serbo-Croatians, Croats, Slovenes and Serbs than as South Slavs; the term 'Yugoslav' was a novelty. The Bohemians or Czechs were known but very few had heard of the Slovaks; Czechoslovakia was not yet even a geographical expression. The government knew little of these nationalities because it was not interested in them and because it had no reason to be interested in them.

The British government entered the conflict in 1914 in order to maintain the existing balance of power in western Europe which would be upset either by the violation of Belgian neutrality or by the destruction of France as a great power. The Polish and Czechoslovak problems were totally irrelevant to the July crisis and to the actions of the British government. Although the crisis which precipitated the war stemmed originally from the South Slav problem, this was not a factor in the British decision to enter the conflict. It cannot be said that Britain declared war for Serbia, the cause of national self-determination or the purpose of changing the existing structure of eastern Europe.

Once hostilities began, the British government assumed no specific aims, and showed no interest in a general territorial redistribution in eastern Europe. It could not be indifferent to territorial changes, such as the aggrandizement of one of the great powers, since these changes would affect the balance of power in western Europe. But it was reasonably satisfied with the status quo in eastern Europe and showed no desire to change it. When the leading members of the government – Asquith, Grey and

Lloyd George – set out to explain their reasons for declaring war on Germany, they spoke of the 'public law of Europe' but not of national self-determination. The cause they espoused was that of a European system in which problems would be solved by negotiation, not by force. The enemy of that system, which they vowed to destroy, was Prussian militarism not because it suppressed subject nationalities but because, unwilling to compromise in negotiating European problems, it resorted to the use of force. Having declared war to maintain the balance of power in western Europe and fighting the war to crush Prussian militarism, the government was not interested in plans presented by émigrés for a fundamental reorganization of eastern Europe. The government was, however, interested in promoting any group which might assist it in the conduct of the war. For that reason it began to promote relations with the émigrés as soon as they made themselves known.

The home office found the émigrés useful in dealing with enemy aliens; the war office saw them as one way to ease the problem of manpower shortages. Wellington House, with the assistance of Namier, found the Poles useful in propaganda. The foreign office saw the Yugoslav programme as a solution to the nationality problems in the Balkans which would facilitate the negotiation of a Balkan league. Naval intelligence, working through Gaunt, found the Czechs in the United States useful in espionage and counterespionage. These branches of the government all acted as if they were following a directive from the cabinet to use and encourage all forces opposed to the Central powers. But the cabinet had not considered the question and had not issued such a directive. In most cases the co-operation between the government and the émigrés was well established before the cabinet was informed. The initiation of co-operation between the government and the émigrés was often the work of minor officials who consulted neither the cabinet nor their counterparts in other departments. Officials like Namier, Clerk, Trevelyan, Drummond, Gregory, Spring Rice, Macdonogh and Gaunt acted instinctively to take advantage of the opportunities presented to them. Although they were not acting on any central directive, the similarity of their instincts gave a measure of uniformity to the action of the British government. The non-existent decision to use and encourage all forces opposed to the Central powers was carried out as thoroughly as any formal cabinet decision.

The Yugoslavs were the first subject nationality to play a role in British foreign policy. From its first contact with the Yugoslavs the foreign office realized that their programme might facilitate the negotiations for a Balkan league. If Serbia could be tempted by the idea of a Yugoslav state to make concessions to Bulgaria in Macedonia, it might end the Serbo-Bulgarian hostility which was the major obstacle to a Balkan league. For that reason the foreign office promoted the Yugoslav programme during the negotiations and even after the failure of this policy continued to be attracted to the idea of a Yugoslav state.

The Czechoslovaks and Poles achieved their initial importance in foreign policy because of the apparent threat to British interests in the United States posed by the German and Irish-Americans. Although the seriousness of this threat was exaggerated, the fear of the German and Irish-Americans was an important factor in British policy towards the United States. At first the government attempted to counter this threat by propaganda designed to damage the reputations of Germany and Austria-Hungary by dealing with their treatment of the subject nationalities. This was followed by propaganda aimed at the Slav minorities in the United States and designed to win their support and promote political organization for the purpose of counteracting the effect of the German-American vote. This task was not left solely to the propaganda authorities for there is every indication that Spring Rice, Gaunt, Trevelyan and Horodyski also played a direct part in encouraging the various American Slavic leaders to organize against the German-Americans. This propaganda implicitly promoted the cause of national self-determination and there can be little doubt that the emerging American interest in eastern Europe was promoted, if not caused, by the competition among the belligerents, particularly on the Polish issue, for American support. The seriousness of the German-American threat, the importance of the Slavic minorities and the success of British propaganda may have been exaggerated by the government, but there can be no doubt that, acting on these considerations, it included references to the Poles, Czechoslovaks and Yugoslavs in the reply to President Wilson's peace note because it believed that such references would appeal to Wilson and to the American public. Possibly such references were unnecessary or ineffectual, but their inclusion in the note was consistent with previous British policy in the conduct of Anglo-American relations. The reply to President Wilson in January 1917 was the most advanced statement by the Allies on the subject of national self-determination prior to the declaration of the supreme war council on 3 June 1918. It did not represent British policy but rather what the Allies believed the Americans wanted to hear. If they were right the explanation can be found, to some extent, in previous British propaganda.

Had the émigrés been incapable of contributing to the war effort it is unlikely that relations between them and the government would have developed. But once the process began it was always easier, and more profitable, for the officials to expand the areas of co-operation than to withdraw from it entirely. Although the government adopted no commitments to national self-determination, the co-operation did promote close relations between the officials and the émigrés with the result that the officials were educated on the problems of eastern Europe and often converted to the cause of national self-determination. The co-operation helped the émigrés to establish relations with the government through which they were then able to inform the government of their political programmes and of the problems of eastern Europe. The initial co-operation in espionage and propaganda, which was of infinitesimal significance if compared to the total war effort of the British government, provided the necessary basis upon which more significant co-operation could be based in 1917.

Since eastern Europe was an area of secondary importance, the British government gave very little thought to its post-war settlement. British aims were considered only in the most general terms and, in essence, they would be satisfied by a settlement which would be conducive to peace and stability and which would not increase the military potential of one of the great powers. National self-determination was not the only solution which would fulfil these criteria – an equally good case could be put forward for the *status quo ante bellum* – and there was no reason to assume that it would be the best solution. Lacking any simple solution to the problems of eastern Europe, which in any case were of secondary importance, the government followed a general policy of using these problems to increase the military potential of the Entente.

Between 1914 and 1916 this general policy involved the use and encouragement of the subject nationalities. It also involved the acceptance in the treaty of London, in exchange for Italian support, of terms which were generally recognized as politically reprehensible. The Entente could achieve the greatest strategic advantage from the problem of eastern Europe, however, not through encouragement of the subject nationalities but by the elimination of Austria from the war through negotiation. When the government believed that a separate peace with Austria-Hungary could be negotiated, it pursued this policy just as it had previously encouraged the nationalities. Even while seeking a separate peace it continued to use the émigrés. The apparent military position of the Entente in 1917 and 1918 was not so strong that it could afford to abstain from the use of the nationalities against Austria-Hungary and particularly from the use of their armed forces. For that reason, when a separate peace proved impossible, the Entente was left with no other alternative than to give maximum support to the nationalities and, in return, to use them in every conceivable way against Austria-Hungary. In May 1918 the government decided to give all possible support to the subject nationalities on the assumption that it would either force the Austrians to make a separate peace or would destroy Austria-Hungary. Either alternative was perfectly acceptable to the government and remained so until the armistice.

The Entente could not use the nationalities without becoming somewhat dependent upon them. By 1918 the Poles and Czechoslovaks were in a position, because of the formation of national armies, to make demands on the government which could not be brushed aside. Indeed the government felt compelled to recognize the Czechoslovaks and Poles and to give at least some measure of informal recognition to the Yugoslavs. But despite pressure from the nationalities, it was able to avoid commitments to them which would have the legal force of the terms of the treaty of London and, above all, was able to avoid specific territorial commitments in eastern Europe. It was committed to national self-determination in eastern Europe only by implication.

The development of British relations with the nationalities during the war is an example of the government's handling of an issue of secondary importance. There is no reason to assume that any other issue was handled in a similar fashion but nevertheless the process is itself intrinsically interesting. These relations did not develop according to any clearly defined comprehensive policy for the treatment of the subject nationalities but evolved because of innumerable minor and often unrelated decisions made by lesser officials often without consultation with one another. To solve immediate problems these officials made decisions which established the initial contacts between the government and the émigrés. For example, the home office decision not to intern Poles, Czechoslovaks and Yugoslavs was taken regardless of considerations of foreign policy because of the immediate problems in the internment of enemy aliens. Although this decision appeared trivial in 1914, the émigrés could not have campaigned for national self-determination from an internment camp. The fabric of British relations with the subject nationalities was gradually built up by a series of minor decisions each bringing the government and the émigrés closer together. One decision facilitated the next, and even before the émigrés were brought to the attention of the cabinet, their relations with the government had evolved into a rudimentary but still discernible pattern. As further relations developed they tended to follow this initial pattern so that the government's position in relation to the nationalities in November 1918 was not one which had been planned but one which had evolved as the officials turned to the émigrés for assistance in solving immediate problems arising from the conduct of the war.

NOTES

CHAPTER 1

1 *The Times*, 19 Sept. 1914.
2 *The Times*, 5 Sept. 1914.
3 Crewe to Bryce, 5 Nov. 1914, MSS. E29.
4 Nicolson to Hardinge, 1 Dec. 1914, F.O. 800–276.
5 Grey to Buchanan, 15 Nov. 1914, F.O. 371–2174–71776.
6 Bertie, 18 Dec. 1914, F.O. 800–166–Fr.14–123. F. R. Bridge, 'The British Declaration of War on Austria-Hungary in 1914', *The Slavonic and East European Review*, vol. XLVIII, no. 109, July 1969, pp. 401–23.
7 E. T. S. Dugdale, *Maurice de Bunsen. Diplomat and Friend*, London, 1934, p. 283.
8 W. S. Churchill, *The World Crisis, 1911–1914*, London, 1923, p. 487.
9 Grant Duff to Grey, 1 Feb. 1915, F.O. 371–2241–41098.
10 *The Times*, 26 Sept. 1914.
11 *The Times*, 10 Nov. 1914.
12 D. Lloyd George, *The Truth About the Treaties*, London, 1938, vol. II, p. 752. Harry Hanak; in *Great Britain and Austria-Hungary During the First World War*, London, 1962, pp. 57–8; in regard to Asquith's statements claims that the 'doctrine of nationality' was accepted as an official war aim by the government – whatever that means. In 'The Government, the Foreign Office and Austria-Hungary 1914–1918', *The Slavonic and East European Review*, vol. XLVII, No. 108, Jan. 1969, p. 161, referring to the same statements, he implies that they meant something but refrains from elaborating. C. A. Macartney and A. W. Palmer; in *Independent Eastern Europe*, London, 1966, p. 39; in referring to these statements with overpowering common sense, write that: 'he was thinking in terms, not of self-determination, but of collective security; a speaker of a few years later, to express the same thought, would certainly have used the word "states" in place of "nationalities". No different meaning can be read into other official British pronouncements, couched in similar language.'
13 *The Times*, 31 Aug. 1914.
14 Grey to Bertie, 19 June 1915, F.O. 371–2268–79008.
15 J. S. Mill, *Utilitarianism, Liberty, Representative Government*, London, 1968, pp. 360–1.
16 R. Jenkins, *Asquith*, London, 1964, pp. 18–19.
17 A. E. Zimmern, 'Introductory', *The War and Democracy*, London, 1914, pp. 8–9.
18 R. W. Seton-Watson, 'The Issues of the War', *The War and Democracy*, London, 1914, pp. 240, 296.
19 See H.O. 45–10740–262173 for the initial relations between the Poles and the home office.

20 Law to H.O., 9 Oct. 1914, H.O. 45–10740–262173.
21 Memo. on Polish Information Committee, 22 Dec. 1915, Mepol. 2–1635. H. W. Steed, *Through Thirty Years*, London, 1924, vol. II, p. 41.
22 Henry memo., 30 Oct. 1914, H.O. 45–10760–269116.
23 Troup to Henry, 3 Nov. 1915, H.O. 45–10760–269116. Yugoslav refers to Habsburg subjects who supported the creation of a Yugoslav state. Citizens of the Kingdom of Serbia are referred to as Serbians.
24 Thomson to Hardinge, 27 Feb. 1917, F.O. 371–2862–52214.
25 'Home Office Circular to Chief Constables', 15 Dec. 1914, H.O. 45–10761–269578.
26 Cubitt to Polish Information Committee, 24 Jan. 1915, Mepol. 2–1635.
27 Law to H.O., 9 Oct. 1914, H.O. 45–10740–262173.
28 Grey to Spring Rice, 17 Nov. 1914, F.O. 115–1776–400. H.O. to Nicolson, 14 Jan. 1915, H.O. 45–10761–269578.
29 Crowe minute, 14 Aug. 1914, F.O. 371–2095–39209.
30 Healy to Grey, 16 Aug. 1914, F.O. 371–2095–39631.
31 J. Pomian (ed.), *Joseph Retinger: Memoirs of an Eminence Grise*, Sussex University Press, 1972.
32 Clerk minute, 31 Aug., 1914, F.O. 371–2095–46074.
33 Clerk to Retinger, 4 Sept. 1914, F.O. 371–2095–46074. Clerk to Retinger, 11 Sept. 1914, F.O. 371–2095–47287.
34 Reichel to H.O., 27 Aug. 1914, H.O. 45–10740–262173. Spring Rice to Grey, 4 Nov. 1914, F.O. 115–1960–15.
35 Rosco-Bogdanowicz memo., 19 Sept. 1914, F.O. 371–2095–50881.
36 Alma-Tadema to A. Nicolson, 8 Sept. 1914, F.O. 371–2095–47911.
37 Nicolson minute, 12 Nov. 1914, F.O. 371–1900–69905.
38 R. W. Seton-Watson, *Masaryk in England*, Cambridge, 1943, p. 39.
39 Nicolson minute, 20 Oct. 1914, F.O. 371–1905–55136.
40 Seton-Watson memo., 1 Oct. 1914, F.O. 371–1905–55136.
41 Rodd to Grey, 29 Sept. 1914, F.O. 371–1900–56371.
42 Thomson to Hardinge, 27 Feb. 1917, F.O. 371–2862–52214.
43 P. D. Ostović, *The Truth About Yugoslavia*, New York, 1952, p. 56, says that Supilo met Asquith. There is no evidence of what transpired during the interview. Clerk minute, 31 Dec. 1914, F.O. 371–1900–88470. Steed, *Thirty Years*, p. 53.
44 Supilo, 'Memorandum Respecting the Southern Slavs', 7 Jan. 1915, F.O. 371–2241–4404.
45 Nicolson minute, 4 Oct. 1914, F.O. 371–1905–55136.
46 Seton-Watson memo., 5 Nov. 1914, F.O. 371–1900–67456.
47 Masaryk was influential among the South Slavs and had assisted Supilo in the Friedjung trial. Connections between the Czechs, Yugoslavs, and some of their English allies had been established before 1914 which explains the speed of development of the movement in Britain after the outbreak of war. V. Dedijer, *The Road to Sarajevo*, London, 1966, p. 179; Seton-Watson, *Masaryk*, p. 17. The Serbian Relief Fund, established in September 1914, brought together many who favoured national self-determination and gave them some form of organization. Wickham Steed also held weekly meetings, every Saturday afternoon, in which strategy was co-ordinated. These meetings were attended by in 1915 the Czech National Committee and the Yugoslav Committee the representatives of a number of eastern European nationalities. Early were formed and assumed the leadership of their respective nationalities while co-operating with each other. The details of these organiza-

tions and their activities can be found in Harry Hanak's thorough study, *Great Britain and Austria-Hungary during the First World War.*

CHAPTER 2

1 E. Percy, *Some Memories*, London, 1958, p. 42.
2 Bertie diary, 19 Dec. 1914, F.O. 800–163–FO 14–1.
3 Chirol to Hardinge, 28 April 1915, Hardinge MSS, 93–388.
4 H. Nicolson, *A Study in Old Diplomacy*, London, 1930, p. 427.
5 Runciman to Chalmers, 7 Feb. 1915, Runciman MSS.
6 Bertie diary, 24 Oct. 1915, F.O. 800–167. The best study of the foreign office during this period and particularly of Grey's reaction to the war is M. G. Ekstein-Frankel, 'The Development of British War Aims, August 1914–March 1915', London Ph.D. 1969.
7 Asquith to George V, 11 Aug. 1914, Cab. 41–35–27. Grey to Bax-Ironside, 13 Aug. 1914, F.O. 371–1900–38875. Asquith to Grey, 17 Jan. 1915, F.O. 800–100.
8 Churchill, *Crisis*, pp. 486–7.
9 Bax-Ironside to Grey, 24 Aug. 1914, F.O. 371–1900–42748.
10 Grey to Des Graz, 5 Feb. 1915, F.O. 371–2242–15388.
11 Nicolson minute, 4 Sept. 1914, F.O. 371–1901–46469.
12 Grey to Bax-Ironside, 13 Feb. 1915, F.O. 371–2242–17234.
13 Clerk minute, 7 Jan. 1915, F.O. 371–2247–4404.
14 T. J. Lederer, *Yugoslavia at the Paris Peace Conference*, London, 1963, pp. 4–5. Ostović, *Yugoslavia*, p. 58.
15 Grey to Bertie, 11 Mar. 1915, F.O. 800–177.
16 Grey to Buchanan, 13 Feb. 1915, F.O. 800–75.
17 Nicolson minute, 7 Oct. 1914, F.O. 371–2008–57095.
18 Rodd to Grey, 9 Dec. 1914, F.O. 800–65.
19 Clerk minute, 6 Mar. 1915, F.O. 371–2507–28275.
20 Nicolson to Grey, 9 Mar. 1915, F.O. 371–2507–29374. Nicolson to Grey, 22 Mar. 1915, F.O. 371–2507–34055. H. Nicolson, *Peacemaking 1919*, London, 1933, p. 160.
21 Clerk minute, 13 Mar. 1915, F.O. 371–2507–29374.
22 Grey to Rodd, 8 Mar. 1915, F.O. 371–2507–30446. Grey to Buchanan, 17 Mar. 1915, F.O. 371–2507–30931.
23 Grey to Buchanan, 20 Mar. 1915, F.O. 371–2507–32897.
24 Grey to Buchanan, 25 Mar. 1915, Cab. 37–126–30.
25 Grey to Bertie, 1 Oct. 1914, F.O. 800–71. Barclay to Grey, 18 Mar. 1915, F.O. 371–2243–31886.
26 Grey to Bertie, 4 Mar. 1915, F.O. 371–2375–25017. Grey to Buchanan, 19 April 1915, F.O. 371–2508–46726.
27 Grey to Buchanan, 22 Mar. 1915, F.O. 371–2507–34053.
28 Asquith to George V, 29 Mar. 1915, Cab. 37–126–21.
29 Grey to Buchanan, 27 Mar. 1915, F.O. 371–2507–35979.
30 Grey to Rodd, 1 April 1915, Cab. 37–127–4.
31 Lederer, *Yugoslavia*, p. 11.
32 Steed to McClure, 14 April 1915, Steed to Robinson, 29 April 1915, Steed MSS.
33 *The Times*, 23 April 1915.
34 Interview with Hugh Seton-Watson. A. J. May, 'Seton-Watson and the Treaty of London', *Journal of Modern History*, vol. XXIX, no. 1, pp.

42–8. May supplies the information on Nicolson but does not distinguish between Arthur and Harold.
35 Steed to McClure, 24 April 1915, Steed MSS.
36 Steed to Robinson, 29 April 1915, Steed MSS.
37 Clerk minute, 31 Mar. 1915, F.O. 371–2241–41098.
38 David Davies to Seton-Watson, 3 May 1915, Seton-Watson MSS. IV. Evans to Grey, 27 April 1915, F.O. 371–2376–51706. Steed to Benckendorff, 25 April 1915, Steed MSS.
39 Rodd to Grey, 28 April 1915, F.O. 371–2376–51340.
40 Percy minute, 2 May 1915, F.O. 800–95.
41 Grey to Seton-Watson, 3 May 1915, F.O. 800–112.
42 Nicolson to Rodd, 9 June 1915, F.O. 371–2377–72816.
43 Trevelyan to Montgomery, 22 July 1915, F.O. 371–2568–88450.
44 Nicolson to Seton-Watson, 28 July 1915, Seton-Watson MSS. VIII. Waller to Bigham, 10 April 1917, H.O. 45–10831–326555.
45 Des Graz to Grey, 30 April 1915, F.O. 371–2257–52833.
46 Grey to Des Graz, 4 May 1915, F.O. 371–2257–53757. Des Graz to Grey, 7 May 1971, F.O. 371–2257–56420.
47 Nicolson minute, 24 April 1915, F.O. 371–2244–49484.
48 Grey to Buchanan, 10 May 1915, F.O. 371–2258–57127. Grey to Buchanan, 20 May 1915, F.O. 371–2258–63946.
49 Grey to Buchanan, 19 June 1915, F.O. 371–2259–80322.
50 Clerk minute, 28 June 1915, F.O. 371–2245–85777.
51 Crewe to Bertie, 7 July 1915, F.O. 371–2259–92014.
52 Rodd to Grey, 3 July 1915, F.O. 371–2259–88943. Buchanan to Grey, 9 July 1915, F.O. 371–2259–92586.
53 Grey to Rodd, 31 July 1915, F.O. 371–2263–105071.
54 Percy minute, 2 Aug. 1915, F.O. 371–2263–105450.
55 Grey to Rodd, 5 Aug. 1915, F.O. 371–2263–106337. Buchanan to Grey, 9 Aug. 1915, F.O. 371–2265–109489. Grey to Des Graz, 10 Aug. 1915, F.O. 371–2265–109491. Rodd to Grey, 11 Aug. 1915. Grey to Bertie, 12 Aug. 1915, F.O. 371–2265–111103.
56 Des Graz to Grey, 15 Aug. 1915, F.O. 371–2265–112986.
57 Drummond to Grey, 14 Aug. 1915, F.O. 371–2268–112839.
58 Spring Rice to Grey, 30 Aug. 1915, F.O. 115–1856–39. Percy minute, 16 Aug. 1915, F.O. 371–2264–113137. Percy minute, 26 Aug. 1915, F.O. 371–2241–115057.
59 Seton-Watson to Clerk, 26 Aug. 1915, F.O. 371–2591–121585. See below, p. 49.
60 Clerk minute, 30 Aug. 1915, F.O. 371–2258–123158.
61 Des Graz to Grey, 5 Sept. 1915, F.O. 371–2258–125871.
62 Des Graz to Grey, 1 Sept. 1915, F.O. 371–2265–123653.
63 Grey to Des Graz, 7 Aug. 1915, F.O. 371–2263–107472.
64 Burrows to Bonar Law, 29 Oct. 1915, Bonar Law MS. 51–4–33.
65 R. W. Seton-Watson, 'The Failure of Sir Edward Grey', *English Review*, Feb. 1916, p. 135.
66 Drummond to Lord Grey, 29 Nov. 1915, F.O. 800–95.
67 Grey to Bertie, 30 Dec. 1915, F.O. 371–2281–200194.
68 Percy minute, 30 Dec. 1915, F.O. 371–2281–200194.
69 Grey to Buchanan, 29 Dec. 1915, F.O. 371–1904–86748. Grey to Bertie, 19 Jan. 1915, F.O. 371–2505–7101.
70 Drummond to Bertie, 30 Mar. 1915, F.O. 800–181.
71 Nicolson to Hardinge, 21 July 1915, Hardinge MSS. 95–65a.

CHAPTER 3

1 Inf. 4–1a. This file contains correspondence on the disposal of the records on propaganda.
2 E. Beneš, *My War Memoirs*, London, 1928, p. 74. Steed, *Thirty Years*, p. 129.
3 Clerk minute, 1 July 1915, F.O. 371–2510–87436. Masaryk to F.O., 20 July 1915, F.O. 371–2241–98084.
4 Grey to Callwell and Hall, 19 Aug. 1915, F.O. 371–2241–115057. Seton-Watson, *Masaryk*, p. 77.
5 Seton-Watson to F.O., 10 May 1916, Cab. 37–147–22. Forman to F.O., 10 Jan. 1917, F.O. 395–138–8297. Namier to Butler, 9 March 1917, F.O. 395–108–51960. Stanmore to Seton-Watson, 22 July 1916, Seton-Watson MSS. IV.
6 Seton-Watson to Clerk, 26 August 1915, Clerk to Seton-Watson, 6 Sept. 1915, F.O. 371–2591–121585.
7 Clerk to Seton-Watson, 24 Sept. 1915, F.O. 371–2241–134164.
8 Drummond minute, 12 June 1916, F.O. 800–96.
9 Beneš, *Memoirs*, p. 98.
10 T. Čapek, *The Čechs in America*, New York 1920, p. 270.
11 E. Voska, *Spy and Counter-Spy*, London 1941, p. 29. V. Dedijer, *Sarajevo*, p. 275.
12 Voska, *Spy*, p. 20.
13 T. Masaryk, *The Making of a State, 1914–1918*, London, 1927, p. 241. G. Gaunt, *The Yield of the Years*, London, 1940, p. 167. Voska, *Spy*, p. 29. Beneš, *Memoirs*, p. 74. Seton-Watson, *Masaryk*, p. 96. B. Thomson, *The Scene Changes*, Garden City, N.Y., 1937, p. 323. G. J. Viereck, *Spreading Germs of Hate*, London, 1931, p. 72. W. James, *The Eyes of the Navy: A Biographical Study of Admiral Sir Reginald Hall*, London, 1955. These sources agree on the essentials of Voska's connection with Gaunt and his work for naval intelligence. Where these accounts are consistent with one another or when backed by documentary evidence the information has been considered reliable. The most detailed account of Voska's work can be found in his own autobiography. There is ample reason to suppose that he was prone to exaggeration and since many of his claims cannot be substantiated by documentary evidence they must be viewed with some suspicion.
14 Agent 45 to embassy, 26 Feb. 1917, F.O. 115–2183.
15 Voska, *Spy*, p. 36.
16 Čapek, *Čechs*, p. 268.
17 Gaunt to Spring Rice, 20 Dec. 1915, F.O. 115–1971–141. New York and Chicago had the largest concentrations of the relevant ethnic minorities.
18 Spring Rice to Nicolson, 21 Dec. 1915, Nicolson to Spring Rice, 22 Dec. 1915, F.O. 115–1977–141. Nicolson to Spring Rice, 7 Dec. 1915, F.O. 115–1809–1090. Nicolson to Bertie, 4 Feb. 1916, F.O. 800–190.
19 Gaunt, *The Yield*, pp. 167–8. Voska, *Spy*, p. 38.
20 Gaselee minute, 23 Jan. 1917, F.O. 371–2862–12976.
21 Gaunt to Spring Rice, 29 Nov. 1915, F.O. 115–1955. Voska, *Spy*, pp. 47–8. According to Voska the British and French authorities gave visas which would permit travel within Allied countries to those agents of Austrian nationality who could not travel on Austrian passports.
22 Beneš, *Memoirs*, p. 74.

23 *Ibid.*, p 132. Voska, *Spy*, p. 48. Voska claims that this was a regular procedure for arranging contact between Masaryk and the couriers.
24 Wiseman to Masaryk, 31 July 1918, Wiseman MSS. 91–80. The basic structure of British intelligence is outlined in R. Deacon, *A History of the British Secret Service*, London, 1969. M.I.1c under Captain Mansfield Cumming received its funds from the foreign office and was responsible for espionage and, in neutral countries, counter-espionage. M.I.5 under Colonel Vernon Kell received its funds from the war office and was responsible for counter-espionage in British territory. C. MacKenzie, *My Life and Times*, vol. IV, London, 1965, p. 29.
25 A. Willert, *Road to Safety: A Study in Anglo-American Relations*, London, 1962, p. 24. Willert does not seem to be aware that Voska was already working for Gaunt before Wiseman arrived in America. A great deal of jealousy existed between Wiseman and Gaunt and there is very little evidence on the degree to which the work of their separate organizations was co-ordinated, if at all. Gaunt worked under the director of naval intelligence, Admiral Sir Reginald Hall.
26 *Ibid.*, p. 23.
27 Mounsey to Drummond, 16 July 1915, Drummond to Rodd, 6 July 1916, F.O. 800–66. J. D. Gregory, *On the Edge of Diplomacy*, London, 1929, p. 103.
28 Priestly report, 23 Aug. 1916, W.O. 106–1511–26.
29 Drummond to Rodd, 16 June 1916, Drummond to Rodd, 6 July 1916, F.O. 800–66. See below, p. 60.
30 Report on Wellington House, 2 Dec. 1914, F.O. 371–2207–88913. News department memorandum, 2 Feb. 1915, Report on Wellington House, 7 June 1915, F.O. 371–2555–12467. Report on Wellington House, 1 Feb. 1916, Inf. 4–5.
31 Report on Wellington House, 7 June 1915, F.O. 371–2555–12467. By December 1917 the list had expanded to 170,000. R. Donald, 'Report on the Purchase and Publication of Books', 7 Dec. 1917, Bonar Law MS. 82–7–7.
32 E. Barker, *The Submerged Nationalities of the German Empire*, Oxford, 1915. Also see: J. B. Bury, *Germany and Slavonic Civilization*, London, 1914. A. J. Toynbee, *The Destruction of Poland*, London, 1916; and H. Rosendal, *The Problem of Danish Schleswig*, London, 1916. All of the pamphlets attributed to Wellington House are taken from an official list in T. 102–20.
33 E. Barker, *Great Britain's Reason for Going to War*, London, 1915, p. 10.
34 G. M. Trevelyan, *The Serbians and Austria*, London, 1915, p. 10.
35 L. Namier, *Germany and Eastern Europe*, London, 1915, p. 126.
36 Also see: Anon, *Hungary and the War*, London, 1915. C. Brereton, *Who is Responsible*, London, 1914. J. W. Headlam, *The Issue*, London, 1916. T. Jonescu, *The Policy of National Instinct*, London, 1916. T. Masaryk, *The Slavs Among Nations*, London, 1916; and Anon., *The European War: Reply to the Appeal of German Theologians*, London, 1915.
37 Interview with Lady Namier, 25 Aug. 1969. I. Berlin, 'Lewis Namier: A Personal Impression', *A Century of Conflict, 1850–1950: Essays for A. J. P. Taylor*, London, 1966. A. J. Toynbee, 'Sir Lewis Namier', *Acquaintances*, London, 1967.
38 Namier to Gowers, 15 Dec. 1916, F.O. 395–26–255781.
39 Namier to Gowers, 14 Dec. 1916, F.O. 395–26–255781.

40 Polish Information Committee, *Germany's Economic Policy in Poland*, London, 1915; *Poland Under the Germans*, London, 1916.
41 Parker minute, 8 Dec. 1916, F.O. 395–5–247999. Montgomery to Gowers, 23 Dec. 1916, F.O. 395–26–261032.
42 T. Masaryk, *The Slavs Among Nations*, London, 1916; *Austrian Terrorism in Bohemia*, London, 1916. London Czech Committee, *Memorial to the International From the Bohemian Branch of the Socialist Party in America*, London, 1915.
43 Namier to Gowers, 15 Dec. 1916, F.O. 395–26–255781. Drummond to Miss Stevenson, 2 Nov. 1916, F.O. 800–102.
44 Namier, 'Observations on Polish Activities in America', 31 May 1916, F.O. 395–10–106874.
45 Seton-Watson, *Masaryk*, p. 100. Namier to Koppel, 31 Mar. 1917, F.O. 395–75–68868.
46 Namier to Butler, 9 Mar. 1917, F.O. 395–108–51960.
47 Percy to Seton-Watson, 2 Aug. 1915, F.O. 371–2264–103085. Trumbić to W.O., 20 Oct. 1915, H.O. 45–10795–303789.
48 Sargeant to H.O., 17 Mar. 1916, H.O. 45–10818–317810.
49 Grey to Bertie, 11 May 1916, F.O. 371–2615–83401. W.O. to F.O., 5 Sept. 1916, Grey to Cambon, 12 Sept. 1916, F.O. 371–2615–176290. Pribićević memorandum, 2 Oct. 1916, F.O. 371–2615–195118. Col. Milan Pribićević, an Austrian South Slav, was responsible for recruiting in the United States. F.O. to Reading, 8 May 1918, F.O. 371–3135–83181.
50 F.O. to treasury, 16 Nov. 1916, F.O. 371–2615–222822. War committee, 20 Nov. 1916, Cab. 42–24–13. Bonar Law to Devonshire, 21 Nov. 1916, F.O. 371–2615–236571.
51 Grey to Tower, 11 Dec. 1916, F.O. 371–2615–24489.
52 Army Council Instruction 1156, 8 June 1916, W.O. 32–4773. White (W.O.) to Nolan (H.O.), 22 Aug. 1916, Wainwright to Smith, 16 Nov. 1916, Huggins to Nolan, 9 Dec. 1916, H.O. 45–10818–317810.
53 Army Council Instruction 2120, 10 Nov. 1916, H.O. 45–10818–317810.
54 Hanak, *Great Britain*, pp. 117–18. By July 1917 an estimated 200 Czechs had been recruited for the British army. Seton-Watson, 'Memorandum on the Bohemian Army', 6 July 1917, F.O. 371–2804–137257. Steed, *Thirty Years*, p. 48. Steed claims that he convinced the war office to recruit Czechs.
55 Drummond memorandum, 17 Oct. 1916, Drummond to Grey, 19 Sept. 1916, F.O. 800–96. Drummond minute, 23 Aug. 1916, F.O. 800–102. S. R. Pliska, 'The Polish American Army, 1917–1921', *The Polish Review*, vol. x, no. 3, 1965, p. 50.
56 Healy to Grey, 16 Aug. 1914, F.O. 371–2095–39631.
57 Parker, 'Memorandum on the Attitude of the American Press', 29 Sept. 1914, Lloyd George MS. C/25/21/1.
58 Paćak to Spring Rice, 3 Oct. 1914, F.O. 115–1775–295. Spring Rice to Grey, 2 Nov. 1914, F.O. 371–1900–69905.
59 Spring Rice to Grey, 16 Feb. 1915, F.O. 371–2445–27311. Spring Rice to Grey, 14 Nov. 1914, F.O. 115–1776–398. Grey to Spring Rice, 17 Nov. 1914, F.O. 115–1776–400. Voska to Spring Rice, 8 Jan. 1915, F.O. 115–1856–1. Spring Rice to Pupin, 12 April 1915, F.O. 115–1856–23.
60 Spring Rice to Voska, 27 Jan. 1915, F.O. 115–1856–3. Spring Rice to Grey, 10 Feb. 1915, F.O. 115–1856–7.

61 Spring Rice to Grey, 25 Aug. 1914, F.O. 800–84–2. Spring Rice to Grey, 11 Dec. 1914, F.O. 115–1776–461. Spring Rice to Grey, 15 Jan. 1915, F.O. 115–1898–8. Spring Rice to Cecil, 2 Feb. 1915, F.O. 800–241. Some Irish-American leaders were in contact with the German embassy. D. R. Esslinger, 'American-German and Irish Attitudes Towards Neutrality, 1914–1917: A Study of Catholic Minorities', *Catholic Historical Review*, vol. 53, p. 208.

62 Spring Rice to Grey, 5 Jan. 1915, F.O. 115–1879–38.

63 L. L. Gerson, *The Hyphenate in Recent American Politics and Diplomacy*, Lawrence, Kansas, 1964, p. 50. C. Seymour, *Woodrow Wilson and the World War*, New Haven, Conn., 1947, pp. 75–8. R. Lansing, *War Memoirs*, New York, 1935, pp. 54–72. Additional information on the German-Americans can be found in C. Wittke, *German-Americans and the World War*, Columbus, Ohio, 1936 and C. J. Child, *The German-Americans in Politics, 1914–1917*, Madison, Wisconsin, 1939.

64 Spring Rice to Grey, 12 Feb. 1915, F.O. 800–241.

65 L. L. Gerson, *Woodrow Wilson and the Rebirth of Poland*, New Haven, Conn., 1953, p. 46.

66 Namier, 'Preliminary Report from L. B. Namier based on some Polish-American Newspapers', 12 Mar. 1915, F.O. 371–2450–29614. The date on this memorandum signifies, not when it was written but, when it was submitted to the foreign office. Percy submitted it after writing his own memorandum but it appears, from the contents of each memorandum that Namier's preceded Percy's.

67 Percy, 'Poles in America', 3 Mar. 1915, F.O. 371–2450–29614.

68 Grey to Spring Rice, 19 Mar. 1915, F.O. 371–2450–29614.

69 Grey to Buchanan, 13 Mar. 1915, F.O. 371–2450–29614.

70 Spring Rice to Grey, 1 April 1915, F.O. 115–1960–4.

71 Namier, 'Analysis of the Signatures in the Manifesto', 13 April 1915, F.O. 371–2450–43258. Hammerling came from the same part of Galicia as Namier and was closely connected to Namier's family. Before the war Namier worked for Hammerling in the United States and was, therefore, able to supply the foreign office with information about Hammerling's activities. Interview with Lady Namier, 25 Aug. 1969. Toynbee, *Acquaintances*, pp. 71–2. Berlin, 'Namier', pp. 223–4. Viereck, *Germs of Hate*, pp. 100–1. Pupin to Spring Rice, 31 Mar. 1915, F.O. 371–2450–43258. Martin Egan to Smith, 15 Mar. 1915, F.O. 371–2450–41805. Spring Rice to Grey, 9 April 1915, F.O. 115–1962–179.

72 Grey to Buchanan, 23 April 1915, F.O. 371–2449–46628.

73 Grey to Buchanan, 4 May 1915, F.O. 371–2450–43258. Buchanan to Grey, 30 May 1915, F.O. 371–2450–68990. Buchanan to Grey, 22 April 1915, F.O. 371–2450–55258. Grey to Buchanan, 1 June 1915, F.O. 371–2450–68990. Buchanan to Grey, 8 June 1915, F.O. 371–2450–73841. Spring Rice to Grey, 29 May 1915, F.O. 115–1960–7.

74 Trevelyan, 'Report on Observations, Made on Tour in the United States', April 12–May 22, 1915, 4 June 1915, Cab. 37–129–13.

75 Grey to Spring Rice, 31 Mar. 1915, F.O. 115–1962–156.

76 Trevelyan to Runciman, 9 Mar. 1915, Runciman MSS.

77 Trevelyan to Runciman, 14 Mar. 1915, Runciman MSS.

78 Report on Wellington House, 7 June 1915, Cab. 37–130–35. Grey to Spring Rice, 11 Mar. 1915, F.O. 115–1961–127.

79 Spring Rice to Drummond, 23 Jan. 1916, F.O. 800–86.

80 Spring Rice to Grey, 1 April 1915, F.O. 115–1960–4.

81 Percy minute, 14 April 1915, F.O. 371–2450–43258.
82 Trevelyan, 'Report', 4 June 1915, Cab. 37–129–13.
83 Stepina to Seton-Watson, 11 May 1915, F.O. 115–1960–11.
84 Spring Rice to Grey, 30 April 1915, F.O. 800–85.
85 Spring Rice to F.O., 20 Mar. 1915, F.O. 371–2559–32960.
86 Pupin to Spring Rice, 6 April 1915, F.O. 371–2450–52170. Pupin to Spring Rice, 12 April 1915, Spring Rice to Pupin, 16 April 1915, F.O. 115–1962–184. Spring Rice to Grey, 1 April 1915, F.O. 371–2450–43258. Spring Rice to Grey, 6 June 1915, F.O. 371–2450–81776.
87 Spring Rice to Primrose, 17 April 1915, F.O. 115–1962–189.
88 Voska to Masaryk, 14 March 1914, F.O. 371–2241–58359. Voska, *Spy*, p. 32.
89 Percy minute, 31 May 1915, F.O. 371–2450–68990.
90 Percy to T. Spring Rice, 10 June 1915, F.O. 115–1960–11.
91 Spring Rice to Pupin, 7 April 1915, F.O. 115–1962–176.
92 Spring Rice to Primrose, 7 April 1915, F.O. 371–2560–41690.
93 Stepina to Seton-Watson, 11 May 1915, F.O. 115–1960–11. Seton-Watson, *Masaryk*, p. 98. Voska, *Spy*, pp. 94–110.
94 Seymour, *Wilson*, pp. 78–9. Lansing, *Memoirs*, pp. 64–71. C. C. Tansill, *America Goes to War*, Boston, 1938, p. 385. E. R. May, *The World War and American Isolation, 1914–1917*, Cambridge, 1959, p. 164. C. J. Child, 'German-American Attempts to Prevent the Exportation of Munitions of War, 1914–1915', *Mississippi Valley Historical Review*, vol. xxv, 1938–9, pp. 351–68.
95 Spring Rice to Grey, 10 June 1915, F.O. 800–85.
96 Nicolson to Spring Rice, 15 June 1915, F.O. 115–1957–45. Gaunt to Spring Rice, 16 June 1915, F.O. 115–1960–12.
97 Seton-Watson, *Masaryk*, p. 98. Voska, *Spy*, p. 130.
98 Unsigned note, 28 June 1915, F.O. 115–1957–41. Voska, *Spy*, p. 132.
99 Fisher to Spring Rice, 11 Sept. 1915, F.O. 115–1856–40. Colville Barclay to Grey, 27 Sept. 1915, F.O. 371–2241–149001. Gaunt to Spring Rice, 20 Dec. 1915, F.O. 115–1977–141. Spring Rice to Grey, 30 Aug. 1915, F.O. 115–1856–39.
100 There were about four million Polish-Americans, one million Yugoslavs, 500,000 Czechs (not Slovaks) and about eight million German-Americans. J. Rouček, *Poles in the United States of America*, Gdynia, 1937, p. 11. Wittke, *German-Americans*, p. 3. Čapek, *Čechs*, p. 59. R. J. Kerner, *Yugoslavia*, Berkeley, Calif., 1949, p. 59. These statistics are not entirely reliable particularly in the case of the Yugoslavs and Czechs who, in any pre-war census, were listed as Austrians. But there can be no doubt that the Poles were the largest Slavic minority and that they did not equal the German-Americans.
101 Grey to Buchanan, 14 June 1915, F.O. 371–2447–76757.
102 Gerson, *Woodrow Wilson*, pp. 50–2.
103 Grey to Spring Rice, 19 Mar. 1915, F.O. 115–1960–3. Grey to Buchanan, 23 April 1915, F.O. 371–2449–46628. Grey to Buchanan, 23 July 1915, Grey to Buchanan, 29 July 1915, F.O. 371–2449–96430. Crewe, 'Memorandum on Polish Relief', 24 Dec. 1915, Cab. 37–139–52.
104 Gerson, *Woodrow Wilson*, pp. 55–66. According to Gerson, Wilson's interest in Poland was based on the size of the Polish-American vote.
105 'Correspondence Respecting the Relief of Allied Territories in the Occupation of the Enemy', 31 Aug. 1916, F.O. 395–26. This collection of correspondence was published as part of the propaganda following

the negotiations. It contains the more important letters and gives an outline of the negotiations. It has been cited in preference to citing all the correspondence as separate items.

106 Spring Rice to Drummond, 30 Jan. 1916, Spring Rice to Drummond, 23 Mar. 1916, F.O. 800–86. Spring Rice to F.O., 24 Mar. 1916, F.O. 115–2124–9. Spring Rice to F.O., 6 April 1916, F.O. 115–2124–17. Gaunt to Spring Rice, 12 April 1916, F.O. 115–2124–20. Spring Rice to Grey, 18 April 1916, F.O. 371–2818–83773. Nugent to Spring Rice, 24 April 1916, F.O. 115–2124–28. Spring Rice to Grey, 3 July 1916, F.O. 371–2818–12867.

107 Papers relating to propaganda on Poland can be found in abundance in F.O. 395, volumes: 5, 10, 26, 41, 69, 75, 96, 108, 139.

108 R. Machray, *Poland, 1914–1931*, London, 1932, p. 59. H. H. Fisher, *America and the New Poland*, New York, 1928, pp. 75–91.

109 Smulski to Spring Rice, 26 Jan. 1916, F.O. 115–2124–2. Spring Rice to F.O., 24 Mar. 1916, F.O. 115–2124–9. Paderewski to Spring Rice, 2 April 1916, F.O. 115–2124–17. Gerson, *Woodrow Wilson*, p. 48.

110 Paderewski to Spring Rice, 20 May 1916, F.O. 115–2124–42.

111 Grey to Buchanan, 29 April 1916, Cab. 37–146–28.

112 Spring Rice to F.O., 24 Mar. 1916, F.O. 115–2124–9.

113 Spring Rice to F.O., 17 April 1916, F.O. 115–2124–20. Spring Rice to Grey, 18 April 1916, F.O. 371–2818–83773.

114 Spring Rice to Montgomery, 7 July 1916, F.O. 395–6–139917.

115 Spring Rice to Grey, 21 July 1916, F.O. 115–2126–21.

116 Cecil to cabinet, 17 Oct. 1916, F.O. 395–7–208730. 'Memorandum on American Election', 5 Oct. 1916, H.O. 139–39.

117 Gaunt to Spring Rice, 2 June 1916, F.O. 115–2125–7.

118 Spring Rice to Grey, 3 May 1916, F.O. 115–2125–10.

119 Spring Rice to F.O., 1 Feb. 1916, F.O. 115–2125–3. Spring Rice to Grey, 12 Feb. 1916, Cab. 37–142–35.

120 Spring Rice to Cecil, 12 Feb. 1916, F.O. 800–195.

121 Spring Rice to Grey, 1 May 1916, F.O. 115–2125–5. Spring Rice to Grey, 19 May 1916, F.O. 800–242. Spring Rice to F.O., 30 May 1916, F.O. 800–86. Spring Rice to Grey, 2 June 1916, F.O. 115–2125–9. Spring Rice to F.O., 16 June 1916, F.O. 800–86.

122 Spring Rice to Grey, 31 Mar. 1916, F.O. 899–10–146.

123 Spring Rice to Hardinge, 14 July 1916, Hardinge MSS. 23.

124 Drummond to Rodd, 6 July 1916, F.O. 800–66.

125 Drummond to Grey, 7 July 1916, F.O. 371–2818–128677.

126 Drummond to Spring Rice, 23 Aug. 1916, F.O. 800–86.

127 Spring Rice to Drummond, 6 Sept. 1916, F.O. 800–86.

128 Drummond to Grey, 19 Sept. 1916, F.O. 800–96.

129 Horodyski to Drummond, 14 Nov. 1916. Drummond to Horodyski, 24 Nov. 1916, F.O. 800–108.

130 Montgomery to Gowers, 23 Dec. 1916, F.O. 395–26–261032. Drummond minute, 18 Jan. 1918, F.O. 800–384.

131 Gerson, *Woodrow Wilson*, pp. 65–6. Gerson claims that Wilson, facing a very difficult election, also wanted the Poles to organize the Polish vote into a solid bloc. He also shows in this study that the Polish vote was an important contributing factor to Wilson's victory. There seems to be little doubt that Wilson's interest in Poland was based on the internal political situation.

CHAPTER 4

1 See above, pp. 47–9. Percy minute, 8 Feb. 1916, F.O. 371–2804–28967. Drummond to Grey, 3 Mar. 1916, F.O. 800–96. Clerk minute, 20 June 1916, F.O. 371–2804–117933.
2 Grey to Buchanan, 15 May 1916, F.O. 371–2818–93751.
3 Gregory to Drummond, 24 Feb. 1916, F.O. 371–2602–47196. Rodd to Grey, 29 April 1916, F.O. 800–66. Rodd to Grey, 10 Nov. 1916, Cab. 37–159–49–231670. Drummond to Rodd, 20 Nov. 1916, F.O. 800–66.
4 Drummond minute, 14 May 1915, F.O. 800–67.
5 'Independent Bohemia', 3 May 1915, F.O. 371–2241–53297. De Bunsen minute, 10 April 1915, F.O. 371–2241–58359. 'Independent Bohemia' was distributed to: Robertson, Hankey, Esher, Wilson, Fisher, Hall, Chamberlain, Balfour, Samuel, Bonar Law, Lansdowne, McKenna, Runciman, Crewe, Kerr, Nicolson, Clerk, Percy, Drummond, Paget, Cecil, Hardinge and Spring Rice. Seton-Watson MSS. IV.
6 Clerk minute, 3 May 1915, Nicolson minute, 6 May 1915, F.O. 371–2241–53297.
7 Grey to Masaryk, 10 Aug. 1916, F.O. 800–109.
8 Clerk to Drummond, 10 Aug. 1916, F.O. 800–96.
9 A. Bromke, *Poland's Politics: Idealism v.s. Realism*, Cambridge, 1967, p. 14. W. F. Reddaway (ed.), *The Cambridge History of Poland*, Cambridge, 1951, vol. II, pp. 462–70. T. Komarnicki, *Rebirth of the Polish Republic*, London, 1957, pp. 30–141. Machray, *Poland*, pp. 39–94. O. S. Pidhaini, *The Ukrainian-Polish Problem in the Dissolution of the Russian Empire, 1914–1917*, Toronto, 1962, pp. 26–51.
10 See above, pp. 19–25, 75–7.
11 See above, pp. 63–5, 71–4. H. H. Fisher, *America and the New Poland*, New York, 1928, pp. 58–9.
12 Interview with August Zaleski, 13 Aug. 1969.
13 Sienkiewicz to Repphan, 2 Aug. 1915, H.O. 45–10836–330094. H. Sienkiewicz, the famous Polish novelist and president of the *Comité Général du Secours pour les Victimes de la Guerre en Pologne*, seems to have initiated the move to replace the Polish Information Committee. The negotiations between the home office and Alma-Tadema between Sept. 1915 and May 1916 are covered in the home office files (H.O. 45): 10740–262173, 10836–330094, 10836–330095, 10818–317810, and Mepol 2–1635–839801.
14 Alma-Tadema to Steel-Maitland, 4 May 1915, Steel-Maitland MS GD 193–165–2. Buchan to Seton-Watson, 28 Aug. 1916, Seton-Watson MSS. IV.
15 Waller minutes, 2 Sept. 1915, H.O. 45–10837–330095, 12 Nov. 1915, H.O. 45–10836–330094.
16 Waller to Henry, 8 Oct. 1915, Henry minute, 26 Oct. 1915, Waller to Thomson, 25 Feb. 1916, Henry minute, 17 April 1916, Mepol 2–1635–839801. Waller to Henry, 12 April 1916, H.O. 45–10836–330094.
17 Curry report (C.I.D.), 7 April 1916, Kell (M.I.5) to Thomson, 9 Jan. 1916, Mepol 2–1635–839801.
18 Montgomery to Gowers, 6 Dec. 1916, F.O. 395–26–231987.
19 Namier to Gowers, 14 Dec. 1916, Namier to Gowers, 15 Dec. 1916, F.O. 395–26–255781. See above, pp. 56–7.
20 Wallesley to Buchanan, 30 Dec. 1916, F.O. 395–26–261032.
21 Grey minute. 2 Mar. 1915, F.O. 371–2445–27478.

22 *Parliamentary Debates, Commons*, vol. 85, col. 2671, 23 Aug. 1916.
23 F.O. to Buchanan, 23 Mar. 1916, F.O. 371–2747–53114.
24 Lindley to Grey, 19 April 1916, F.O. 800–75. Buchanan to F.O., 26 April 1916, F.O. 371–2747–79517.
25 Bertie diary, 17 Aug. 1916, F.O. 800–178. Grey to Bertie, 24 Aug. 1916, F.O. 371–2804–170012. Hardinge to Howard, 27 Oct. 1916, Hardinge MSS. 26.
26 Grey minute, 21 Nov. 1916, F.O. 371–2747–238962.
27 Grey to Buchanan, 15 May 1916, F.O. 371–2818–93751.
28 War committee, 7 Nov. 1916, Cab. 42–23–9. Bertie to F.O., 4 May 1916, F.O. 371–2747–86893. F.O. to Buchanan, 10 July 1916, F.O. 800–75. F. Fischer, *Germany's Aims in the First World War*, London, 1967, pp. 120–41, 245.
29 Hardinge to Bertie, 15 Sept. 1916, F.O. 800–178.
30 Grant Duff to F.O., 20 Dec. 1914, F.O. 371–2095–84889. Staniszewski to F.O., 8 April 1915, F.O. 371–2445–40846. Lipkowski to F.O., 5 July 1915, F.O. 371–2445–89634. See above, p. 24.
31 Interview with August Zaleski, 13 Aug. 1969. Interview with Lady Namier, 25 Aug. 1969. During the war Zaleski taught Polish at King's College, The Strand, and contributed to Seton-Watson's periodical, *The New Europe*.
32 Drummond minute, 23 Mar. 1915, F.O. 371–2445–34420.
33 Drummond minute, 27 Mar. 1915, F.O. 371–2445– 35952.
34 Percy minute, 31 Mar., 1915, F.O. 371–2445–35952.
35 Komarnicki, *Rebirth*, pp. 48–9. Gregory, 'Notes Obtained From a Reliable Source with Regard to the Polish Conference at Lausanne', 20 Mar. 1916, 'The Polish Case for Internationalisation of the Polish Question', 23 Mar. 1916, F.O. 371–2747–63471. The reliable sources were almost certainly National Democrats or other conservatives allied to Dmowski with whom Gregory had contact.
36 Percy minute, 7 Dec. 1915, F.O. 371–2510–187184.
37 See above, pp. 63–5.
38 Nicolson minute, 10 Dec. 1915, F.O. 371–2510–187184.
39 Percy minute, Nicolson minute, 17 Dec. 1915, F.O. 371–2449–193104.
40 Dmowski seems to have been cautious about mentioning independence to British officials. In his written submissions to the foreign office the plans for the future structure of Poland are vague although he seems to have spoken on occasion to some officials about independence. It is significant that Nicolson, who always supported Dmowski, did not support the idea of independence but only autonomy. O'Beirne minute, 22 March, 1916, F.O. 371–2747–53414.
41 Dmowski memo., 21 Mar. 1916, Dmowski to Cecil, 11 Mar. 1916, Lansdowne to Cecil, 18 Mar. 1916, F.O. 371–2747–53414. A. Dallin, 'The Future of Poland', *Russian Diplomacy and Eastern Europe, 1914–1917*, New York, 1963, p. 37.
42 F.O. to Buchanan, 23 Mar. 1916, Grey minute, 22 Mar. 1916, Nicolson minute, 24 Mar. 1916, F.O. 371–2747–53414.
43 A copy of the press summary cannot be located. The leak might have come from Gregory who was the most pro-Polish.
44 Nicolson to Grey, 6 May 1916, F.O. 395–25–95630.
45 Namier, 'Observations on Polish Activities in America', 31 May 1916, F.O. 395–10–106874.
46 Montgomery minute, 19 May 1915, F.O. 395–25–95630.

47 Clerk memo. on Retinger, 25 May 1916, F.O. 371–2747–98112,
48 Nicolson minute, 3 June 1916, F.O. 371–2747–119621.
49 Clerk minute, 1 June 1916, F.O. 371–2747–119621. Retinger to F.O., 17 July 1916, F.O. 371–2747–138666.
50 Drummond minute, 12 June 1916, F.O. 800–96. See above, pp. 75–7.
51 See above, pp. 83–5. Bray, 'Report on August Zaleski', 20 Sept. 1917, F.O. 371–3016–216797. Drummond to Cecil, Cecil minute, 15 June 1916, F.O. 800–96.
52 Grey to Buchanan, 22 July 1916, F.O. 371–2747–138666.
53 Drummond to Rumbold, 23 Dec. 1916, F.O. 800–197.
54 Percy to Clerk, 5 July 1916, F.O. 395–26–131839.
55 F.O. to Buchanan, 23 Aug. 1916, F.O. 800–75.
56 F.O. (Drummond) to Buchanan, 23 Aug. 1916, F.O. 800–75.
57 Drummond minute, Buchanan to Drummond, 29 Aug. 1916, F.O. 800–75.
58 Gregory to Drummond, 11 May 1915, F.O. 371–2445–61430.
59 Seton-Watson to Allison Phillips, 30 Nov. 1916, Seton-Watson MSS. III.
60 War committee, 21 Mar. 1916, Cab. 42–11–6. P. Guinn, *British Strategy and Politics, 1914 to 1918*, Oxford, 1965, pp. 121–91.
61 Hardinge to Chirol, 9 Aug. 1916, Hardinge MSS. 24. Paget to Findlay, 2 Oct. 1916, Paget MSS. 51256.
62 Paget and Tyrrell, 'Suggested Basis for a Territorial Settlement in Europe', 7 Aug. 1916, Cab. 24–2–78.
63 See above, p. 41. There can be no doubt that the foreign office in general shared the opinion that Montenegro should cease to exist. King Nikita of Montenegro was suspected of treachery during the Balkan campaign in 1915 and considered by the foreign office unworthy of consideration. In September 1916 Grey wrote: 'There is no occasion for our authorities to put themselves out to please the King of Montenegro who tried to sell the allied cause as far as Montenegro was concerned to the Austrians.' (Bertie to Hardinge, 7 Sept. 1916, Hardinge MSS. 25.) The Montenegrin government was still recognized and, to some extent, financially supported by the British government but only because the French and Italian governments were doing likewise. In contrast to their attitude towards the Yugoslavs the British were unlikely, should an opportunity arise, to give assistance to the Montenegrins. Grey to Bertie, 13 Sept. 1915, F.O. 371–2268–127443. Hardinge to Rodd, 4 Oct. 1916, Hardinge MSS. 26.
64 A. J. P. Taylor, *The Habsburg Monarchy, 1809–1918*, New York, 1965, pp. 203–4.
65 R. Cecil, *All the Way*, London, 1949, p. 141.
66 See above, p. 231, n. 35.
67 Hardinge minute, 11 Sept. 1916, F.O. 371–2804–180510.
68 Paget to Findlay, 2 Oct. 1916, Paget MSS. 51256. Seton-Watson conversation with Hardinge, 25 July 1916, Seton-Watson MSS. VI.
69 Grey minute, 11 Sept. 1916, F.O. 371–2804–180510. See above, pp. 37–8, 42–3, 80. Grey seems to have accepted the idea that Austria-Hungary was no longer an independent great power. Grey to Laughlin, 7 Aug. 1916, F.O. 115–2130–230.
70 Bertie diary, 11 Aug. 1916, F.O. 800–171. Grey to Lloyd George, 29 Sept. 1916, Lloyd George MS. 62–13–5. Bertie to Hardinge, 24 Aug.

1916, Hardinge MSS. 24. Hardinge to Bertie, 4 Oct. 1916, F.O. 800–172. Bertie to Hardinge, 16 Oct. 1916, F.O. 800–178. Bertie and Hardinge may have exaggerated Grey's interest in a negotiated peace but it was a possibility which certainly disturbed them.

71 Cecil minute, 23 Dec. 1916, F.O. 371–2634–260531. Cecil, 'Principles of Foreign Policy', undated, Cecil MSS. 51195.

72 War committee, 10 Aug. 1916, Cab. 42–17–5.

73 Robertson to Lloyd George, 17 Aug. 1916, W.O. 106–1510.

74 Robertson, 'General Staff Memorandum Submitted in Accordance With the Prime Minister's Instructions', 31 Aug. 1916, Cab. 29–1–4.

75 War committee, 30 Aug. 1916, Cab. 42–18.

76 Balfour, 'Irresponsible Reflections on the Part which the Pacific Nations Might Play in Discouraging Future Wars', 19 Jan. 1916, Cab. 37–141–11.

77 In discussions of nationalism in eastern Europe Ireland was seldom mentioned. The similarities may have been too obvious to merit comment but they were undoubtedly apparent to those who considered the problem of national self-determination. The problem of Ireland obviously made it difficult for the government to approach the Russians on the Polish issue. When action on behalf of Finland was suggested Crewe wrote, 'We might get in return some good advice how to deal with Sein Fein.' Clerk to Nicolson, 27 April 1916, F.O. 371–2825–80250.

78 D. Judd, *Balfour and the British Empire*, London 1968, p. 165, Cab. 37–49–29. A. J. Balfour, *Opinions and Argument*, London, 1927, pp. 88–9. A J. Balfour, 'Race and Nationality', *The Transactions of the Honourable Society of Cymmrodorion*, Session 1908–1909, London, 1910, p. 240.

79 Balfour, 'The Peace Settlement in Europe', 4 Oct. 1916, Cab. 37–157–7.

80 See above, pp. 17, 36. Delmé-Radcliffe to Bonham Carter, 27 April 1916, F.O. 371–2602–86039.

81 Fisher, 'Notes on conversation with Lloyd George', 27 Aug. 1916, Fisher MSS. 24.

82 Hankey, 'The General Review of the War', 31 Oct. 1916, Cab. 24–2–92.

83 Robertson memo., 14 Dec. 1916, Cab. 29–1–11. War committee, 21 Mar. 1916, Cab. 42–11–6. War committee, 10 Aug. 1916, Cab. 42–17–5. Scott diary, 20–22 Nov. 1916, Scott MSS. 50903.

84 Spring Rice to Grey, 17 July 1916, F.O. 115–2090–20. Bertie diary, 15 Aug. 1916, F.O. 800–175.

85 Grey to Lloyd George, 29 Sept. 1916, Lloyd George MS. E2–13–5. Scott diary, 2–3 Oct. 1916, Scott MSS. 50903. Northcliffe to Lloyd George, 27 Sept. 1916, Lloyd George MS. E2–21–3.

86 Grey to Runciman, 30 Sept. 1916, Runciman MSS. Bertie diary, 11 Aug. 1916, F.O. 800–171.

87 Cecil, 'Proposed Action in Regard to American Note', 22 Dec. 1916, Cab. 37–162–12.

88 The Entente was preparing a reply to the German peace note and much of the advice given for the first seems to have been used for the second. Buchanan to Grey, 13 Dec. 1916, F.O. 371–2805–25212. Spring Rice to F.O., 14 Dec. 1916, F.O. 115–2090–54. Cecil minute, 15 Dec. 1916, F.O. 800–197. Spring Rice to F.O., 17 Dec. 1916, F.O. 115–2090–60. Spring Rice to F.O., 20 Dec. 1916, F.O. 115–2090–65.

89 War cabinet 15, 23 Dec. 1916, Cab. 37–162–12. Balfour to Spring Rice, 26 Dec. 1916, F.O. 371–2806–260988. Balfour minute, 29 Dec. 1916, F.O. 371–2806–264041.
90 War cabinet 18, 26 Dec. 1916, Cab. 37–162–17. Cecil minute, Scott to Balfour, 24 Dec. 1916, Balfour MSS. 49865.
91 Drummond to Cecil, 21 Dec. 1916, F.O. 800–197. Cecil, cabinet minute, 21 Dec. 1916, Lloyd George MS. F160–1–4. L. Woodward, *Great Britain and the War of 1914–1918*, London, 1967, pp. 217–23. The government had contact with House through Gaunt, W. B. Fowler, *British–American Relations, 1917–1918*, Princeton, 1969, pp. 14–15.
92 War cabinet 18, 26 Dec. 1916, Cab. 37–162–17.
93 Anglo-French conference, 26–28 Dec. 1916, Cab. 28–2.
94 Balfour to Sanderson, 4 Jan. 1917, Balfour MSS. 49739.
95 Cecil, 'Proposed Action in Regard to American Note', 22 Dec. 1916, Cab. 37–162–12. Cecil draft, 24 Dec. 1916, F.O. 371–2805–260746. Balfour draft, 30 Dec. 1916, Cab. 37–162–31. Draft reply, 29 Dec. 1916, F.O. 371–2806–264233.
96 *The Times*, 12 Jan. 1917. The Russian proclamation referred to in the note was the tsar's Order of the Day for 25 Dec. 1916. It stated that one of the tasks of the war was to create a free Poland consisting of all of its three parts. In this context 'free' undoubtedly meant autonomous. Komarnicki, *Rebirth*, pp. 46–7.
97 Cecil minute, 26 Dec. 1916, F.O. 371–2806–262697.
98 *Parliamentary Debates, Commons*, vol. 96, col. 1202, 24 July 1917.
99 A. Ribot, *Letters to a Friend, Recollections of My Political Life*. London, 1926, pp. 224–8.
100 Z. A. B. Zeman, *The Break-up of the Habsburg Empire, 1914–1918*, London, 1961, pp. 113–18. A. J. May, *The Passing of the Habsburg Monarchy, 1914–1918*, Philadelphia, 1966, pp. 471–4.
101 J. W. Headlam, *The Peace Terms of the Allies*, London, 1917. L. B. Namier, *The Case of Bohemia*, London, 1917 and *The Czecho-Slovaks*, London, 1917.
102 Balfour draft, 30 Dec. 1916, Cab. 37–162–31. Cecil draft, 24 Dec. 1916, F.O. 371–2805–260746.
103 Spring Rice to Balfour, 29 Dec. 1916, Balfour MSS. 49740.
104 Balfour to Buchanan, 3 Jan. 1917, F.O. 371–3075–2031. Buchanan to F.O., 1 Jan. 1917, F.O. 371–3075–1290. Buchanan to Hardinge, 2 Jan. 1917, Hardinge MSS. 29. F.O. to Buchanan, 6 Jan. 1917, F.O. 371–3075–4588. Buchanan to F.O., 5 Jan. 1917, F.O. 371–3075–5269. Buchanan to F.O., 8 Jan. 1917, F.O. 371–3075–6675.
105 Macartney, *Eastern Europe*, p. 67. Hanak, *Great Britain*, p. 216. The theory seems to have originated with Seton-Watson. Cecil's original wording probably referred to Slavs in general. The reference to Czechoslovaks was added later and the Italians may have prevented the addition of a more specific reference to the Yugoslavs.
106 Cecil, 'Proposed Action in Regard to American Note', 22 Dec. 1916, Cab. 37–162–12.
107 Beneš, *Memoirs*, pp. 153–7.
108 Cecil to Dugdale, 14 May 1934, Cecil MSS. 51157.
109 Wiseman tel., 13 Dec. 1916, Wiseman MSS. 90–38.

CHAPTER 5

1 See above, p. 98.
2 Findlay to F.O., 10 Jan. 1917, F.O. 371–3079–7661. The best and most thorough study of negotiations for a separate peace is W. B. Fest, 'The Habsburg Monarchy in British Policy, 1914–1918', Oxford D.Phil., 1970. Fest has outlined the negotiations in exhaustive detail but exaggerates the British desire to maintain the Habsburg monarchy.
3 Balfour minute, 11 Jan. 1917, F.O. 371–3079–7661.
4 Hankey, 'Proceedings in Regard to a Separate Peace with Austria', Cab. 1–27. War cabinet 37a, 18 Jan. 1917, Cab. 23–13. Hardinge to Findlay, 19 Jan. 1917, F.O. 371–3079–7661. Hardinge to Paget, 2 Feb. 1917, Paget to Hardinge, 9 Feb. 1917, Paget MSS. 51253. Balfour to Paget, 17 Feb. 1917, Paget MSS. 51252. Lloyd George to Balfour, 17 Feb. 1917, Lloyd George MS. F3–3–13. Hopwood memo., 17 Mar. 1917, Cab. 1–24–9.
5 War cabinet 37a, 18 Jan. 1917, Cab. 23–13.
6 War cabinet 121, 17 April 1917, Cab. 23–2. War cabinet 200, 13 July 1917, Cab. 23–13. Robertson to Lloyd George, 29 Sept. 1917, W.O. 106–1515.
7 Robertson memo., 29 Dec. 1917, W.O. 106–1517.
8 Smuts to Lloyd George, 21 Jan. 1918, Lloyd George MS. F45–9–9.
9 Robertson memo., 29 Mar. 1917, W.O. 106–1512–13. Robertson, 9 May 1917, Cecil MSS. 51093. General staff memo., 7 July 1917, W.O. 106–1516. War cabinet 200, 13 July 1917, Cab. 23–13. Robertson, 29 July 1917, Cecil MSS. 51093.
10 Intelligence bureau, 'Office Orders', 1 June 1917, F.O. 395–148–117714. Gleichen memo. 15 May 1917, Cab. 24–14. Headlam to Drummond, 29 July 1917, F.O. 800–197. Hanak, *Great Britain*, p. 176.
11 See above, pp. 34–6.
12 Namier memo., 11 May 1917, F.O. 371–2862–97435. Seton-Watson memo., 15 May 1917, F.O. 371–2862–94508. Intelligence bureau memo., 24 May 1917, F.O. 371–2862–103995. Weekly report, 18 June 1917, F.O. 371–2862–129141. Weekly report, 9 July 1917, Milner MSS. 108–1.
13 Hardinge minute, 18 Jan. 1917, F.O. 371–3079–13580. Hardinge to Beaumont, 1 Feb. 1917, Hardinge MSS. 29. Hardinge to Paget, 7 Feb. 1917, F.O. 371–3079–25651.
14 Drummond memo. GT 43, 12 Feb. 1917, Cab. 24–6.
15 S. Roskill, *Hankey: Man of Secrets*, vol. I, 1877–1918, London, 1970, pp. 401, 507.
16 Tyrrell to Drummond, 26 Feb. 1917, F.O. 800–384. Paget to Hardinge, 1 Feb. 1917, F.O. 371–3079–25651. Oliphant minute, Graham minute, 15 Jan. 1917, F.O. 371–3079–11312. Gregory memo., 18 Nov. 1917, F.O. 371–3002–218943. Clerk minute, 31 Mar. 1917, F.O. 371–2863–68110. Clerk minute, 13 April 1917, F.O. 371–2864–157767.
17 Oliphant minute, 2 Feb. 1917, F.O. 371–3079–25651. Oliphant minute, Graham minute, 12 Mar. 1917, F.O. 371–3133–45538.
18 Cecil minute GT 43, 19 Feb. 1917, Cab. 24–6.
19 Cecil to St Loe Strachey, 13 Nov. 1917, F.O. 800–196.
20 Balfour minute, 11 Jan. 1917, F.O. 371–3079–7661. Thornton diary, 28 Mar. 1917, Milner MSS. 299. Imperial war cabinet minutes, printed

in *Papers Relating to the Foreign Relations of the United States: The Lansing Papers, 1914–1920*, vol. II, p. 19. Roskill, *Hankey*, p. 401.
21 Hardinge minute GT43, 17 Feb. 1917, Cab. 24–6.
22 Ribot, *Letters*, pp. 246–58. D. Lloyd George, *The War Memoirs of David Lloyd George*, London, 1938, vol. II, pp. 1182–4.
23 Minutes of the conference of Saint-Jean de Maurienne, 19 April 1917, F.O. 371–3082–85598. Roskill, *Hankey*, p. 378.
24 Ribot to Lloyd George, 12 May 1917, Lloyd George MS. F50–1–5. Lloyd George to Ribot, 15 May 1917, Lloyd George MS. F50–1–6. Ribot to Lloyd George, 20 May 1917, Lloyd George MS. F50–1–7. Lloyd George to Ribot, 23 May 1917, F.O. 371–3134–88265.
25 War cabinet 135a, 9 May 1917, Cab. 23–13.
26 See above, pp. 100–1. V. S. Mamatey, *The United States and East Central Europe, 1914–1918: A Study in Wilsonian Diplomacy and Propaganda*, Princeton, 1957, p. 59.
27 War cabinet, 8 June 1917, Cab. 23–16.
28 See above, pp. 38–9.
29 Lloyd George, speech at Queen's Hall, *The Times*, 21 Sept. 1914.
30 Scott diary, 26–30 Jan. 1917, Scott MSS. 50903. Lloyd George to Ribot, 15 May 1917, Lloyd George MS. F50–1–6. Lloyd George to Ribot, 23 May 1917, F.O. 371–3134–88265.
31 Cabinet committee on war policy, 21 June 1917, Cab. 1–27–1.
32 Thornton diary, 24 Mar. 1917. Milner MSS. 299. War cabinet 121, 17 April 1917, Cab. 23–2.
33 Imperial war cabinet, committee on territorial desiderata of peace, 23 April 1917, Cab. 29–1–17.
34 D. Chapman-Huston, *The Lost Historian: A Memoir of Sir Sidney Low*, London, 1936, pp. 267–8, 28 Mar. 1917.
35 Amery, 'Possible Terms of Peace', 11 April 1917, Cab. 29–1.
36 Amery, 'The Russian Situation and Its Consequences', 20 May 1917, Cab. 24–14.
37 Amery memo., 10 July 1917, Milner MSS. 108–1.
38 Imperial war cabinet, 28 April 1917, Cab. 29–1–17.
39 Scott diary, 24 August 1917, Scott MSS. 50904.
40 Cabinet committee on war policy, 21 June 1917, Cab. 1–27–1. Cabinet committee on war policy, 10 Aug. 1917, Lloyd George MS. F161–2. Lloyd George to Robertson, 26 Aug. 1917, Lloyd George MS. F30–2–24. Robertson, 20 June 1917, Lloyd MS. F161–2.
41 Allied conference, 26 July 1917, Cab. 28–2–24.
42 Allied conference, 8 Aug. 1917, Cab. 28–2–25. War cabinet, 24 Sept. 1917, Cab. 23–16.
43 Hall memo. GT1324, 7 July 1917, Cab. 24–19. War cabinet committee on war policy, 10 Aug. 1917, Lloyd George MS. F161–2. Rumbold to Bertie, 12 Sept. 1917, F.O. 800–161.
44 War cabinet, 16 July 1917, Cab. 23–3. War cabinet, 27 Sept. 1917, Cab. 23–16.
45 Clerk to Hardinge, 26 Oct. 1917, F.O. 371–2864–207244.
46 War cabinet, 14 Aug. 1917, Cab. 23–16. Roskill, *Hankey*, pp. 635–6.
47 War cabinet, 24 Sept. 1917, Cab. 23–16.
48 Nicolson memo., 22 Aug. 1917, F.O. 371–2864–164751.
49 Oliphant, Graham, Hardinge minutes, 23 Aug. 1917, F.O. 371–2864–164751. Clerk minute, 27 Aug. 1917, F.O. 371–2864–155578. Hardinge to Townley, 30 Nov. 1917, Hardinge MSS. 35.

50 General staff memo., 7 July 1917, W.O. 106–1516.
51 Roskill, *Hankey*, pp. 467–70. F.O. to Rumbold, 26 Nov. 1917, F.O. 371–2864–224082.
52 Nicolson memo., 5 Dec. 1917, F.O. 371–3086–230895. Oliphant, Graham, Hardinge and Clerk minutes, 10 Dec. 1917, F.O. 371–3086–230895. Gregory minute, 18 Dec. 1917, F.O. 371–3002–238348.
53 Balfour memo., 15 Dec. 1917, F.O. 800–241. Balfour to Landsdowne, 22 Nov. 1917, Cab. 24–34.
54 Balfour to Cecil, 29 Dec. 1917, Balfour MSS. 49783.
55 Balfour to Lloyd George, 10 Dec. 1917, F.O. 800–199.
56 Rumbold to F.O., 3 Jan. 1918, F.O. 371–3133–2002. Rumbold to F.O., 20 Jan. 1918, F.O. 371–3133–12697.
57 Balfour to House, 27 Feb. 1918, F.O. 800–222.
58 Milner to Paget, 16 Oct. 1917, Paget MSS. 51257. Thornton Diary, 28 Oct. 1917, Milner MSS. 301. Roskill, *Hankey*, p. 467.
59 Cecil to Lloyd George, 5 Dec. 1917, Lloyd George MS. F6–5–10. Cecil to Balfour, 28 Dec. 1917, F.O. 800–207.
60 Drummond memo. GT 2976, 10 Dec. 1917, Cab. 24–35.
61 Hardinge minute GT 2976, 10 Dec. 1917, Cab. 24–35. Hardinge minute, 23 Jan. 1918, F.O. 371–3133–14351. Gregory minute, 26 Jan. 1918, F.O. 371–3277–16767.
62 Clerk minute, 23 Jan. 1917, F.O. 371–3133–14351.
63 Scott diary, 28 Dec. 1917, Scott MSS. 50904.
64 Smuts, 'Peace Conversations', 13 Dec. 1917, F.O. 800–214.
65 Smuts memo., 18–19 Dec. 1917, F.O. 371–2864–246162. Lloyd George, *War Memoirs*, p. 2461.
66 Rumbold to F.O., 20 Dec. 1917, F.O. 800–200. Smuts, 'Peace Preparations', 26 Dec. 1917, Cab. 1–25–27. War cabinet, 2 Jan. 1918, Cab. 23–16. Balfour to Wilson (draft), 28 Dec. 1917, F.O. 371–3133–3465.
67 War cabinet 313, 3 Jan. 1918, Cab. 23–5. Ormesby Gore to Hankey, 1 Jan. 1918, Lloyd George MS. F23–2–1. Henderson to Lloyd George, 20 Dec. 1917, Lloyd George MS. F27–3–22. Guest to Lloyd George, 13 Dec. 1917, Lloyd George MS. F21–2–10.
68 Lord Hankey, *The Supreme Command, 1914–1918*, London, 1961, pp. 734–8. Roskill, *Hankey*, p. 479. Malcolm to Balfour, 5 Jan. 1918, Balfour MSS. 49748.
69 Smuts, 'War Aims', GT 3180, 3 Jan. 1918, Cab. 24–37. War cabinet 308, 31 Dec. 1917, Cab. 23–13.
70 Cecil memo., 3 Jan. 1918, Cab. 24–37.
71 Kerr memo., 29 Dec. 1917, Lloyd George MS. F89–1–12.
72 'The Prime Minister's Speech', 5 Jan. 1918, F.O. 800–199.
73 War cabinet 314, 4 Jan. 1918, Cab. 23–5.
74 War cabinet 312, 3 Jan. 1918, Cab. 23–5.
75 Cecil to Des Graz, 9 Jan. 1918, F.O. 371–3149–6573. Horodyski to Keynes, 10 Jan. 1918, F.O. 800–385. Milner to Cecil, 11 Jan. 1918, F.O. 371–3149–8527.
76 Roskill, *Hankey*, pp. 503–7. War cabinet, 4 Feb. 1918, Cab. 23–16. Milner to Lloyd George, 27 Feb. 1918, Lloyd George MS. F38–3–16.
77 Cecil to Findlay, 15 Feb. 1918, Cecil MSS. 51091.
78 Rumbold to F.O., 11 Mar. 1918, F.O. 371–3133–45538. Rumbold to F.O., 14 Mar. 1918, F.O. 371–3133–47443. Kerr report, 19 Mar. 1918, Cab. 1–26–10.
79 F.O. to Rumbold, 28 Mar. 1918, F.O. 371–3133–55733.

80 War cabinet, 15 April 1918, Cab. 23–16.
81 Cecil minute, 2 Jan. 1918, F.O. 371–3133–3465.
82 Drummond minute, 18 Jan. 1917, F.O. 800–384.
83 Namier to Koppel, 31 Mar. 1917, F.O. 395–75–68868. Roxborough to Namier, 26 June 1917, F.O. 395–67–124735.
84 Bayley to F.O., 22 June 1917, F.O. 395–67–124735. Wiseman memo., 30 June 1917, Wiseman MSS. 91–112. Voska, *Spy*, p. 103. Čapek, *Čechs*, p. 272.
85 Montgomery to Bayley, 26 June 1917, F.O. 395–67–124735. Ashcroft to Roxborough, 4 July 1917, F.O. 395–78–133102. Thwaites to Butler, 30 Nov. 1917, F.O. 395–85–223899.
86 Zelenka to Sykora, 30 Mar. 1917, F.O. 395–75–68868. Namier to Butler, 8 Feb. 1917, F.O. 395–108–51960.
87 War cabinet 25, 2 Jan. 1917, Cab. 23–1.
88 Sloss (*Chicago Daily News*) to Montgomery, 12 Jan. 1917, F.O. 395–5–247960. Montgomery minute, 6 Jan. 1917, F.O. 395–65–5642. Butler to Montgomery, 22 Mar. 1917, F.O. 395–76–65520. Butler to Dmowski, 3 April 1917, F.O. 395–76–67726.
89 G. W. Prothero, *A Lasting Peace*, London, 1917, p. 33.
90 L. B. Namier, *The Case of Bohemia*, London, 1917, *The Czecho-Slovaks*, London, 1917.
91 Rumbold to Campbell, 6 Dec. 1919, F.O. 800–329.
92 Drummond minute, 15 Jan. 1917, F.O. 800–384.
93 Drummond to Howard, 11 Feb. 1918, F.O. 800–385.
94 Roskill, *Hankey*, p. 465. Drummond memo., 13 June 1918, F.O. 371–3282–106670.
95 Agent 45 to embassy, 26 Feb. 1917, F.O. 115–2183, B.N.A. to Lansing, 20 April 1917, Wiseman MSS. 91–112. Agent 45, 'Bohemian and Slovak Question', 23 April 1917, Wiseman MSS. 90–7.
96 Wiseman memo., 18 May 1918, Wiseman MSS. 91–112. Wiseman to Osborne, 24 May 1917, F.O. 115–2322. Wiseman to Drummond, 16 June 1917, F.O. 800–205. Fowler, *British-American Relations*, pp. 111–18.
97 F.O. to Wiseman, 19 June 1917, F.O. 800–205.
98 F.O. to Wiseman, 25 June 1917, F.O. 800–205.
99 Wiseman to Drummond, 20 June 1917, F.O. 800–205.
100 Maugham to Wiseman, 7 July 1917, Voska to Lansing, 13 July 1917, Voska memo., 30 June 1917, Wiseman MSS. 91–112.
101 Wiseman to Drummond, 22 Aug. 1917, Wiseman MSS. 90–42. Voska receipt, 16 July 1917, Voska receipt, 21 July 1917, Maugham receipt, 18 July 1917, Wiseman memo., 12 July 1917, Maugham to Wiseman, 14 July 1917, Wiseman MSS. 91–112.
102 Hardinge to Hall, 15 May 1917, F.O. 371–3008–96719. S (Maugham) report, 3–16 Sept. 1917, Wiseman MSS. 91–112.
103 Wiseman memo., 11 Sept. 1917, House MSS. 20–45.
104 Wiseman memo., 21 Oct. 1917, House MSS. 20–46. Voska memo., 6 Nov. 1917, Wiseman MSS. 91–112. Wiseman memo., 19 Jan. 1918, Wiseman MSS. 91–113. Koukol to B.N.A., 20 Mar. 1918, Wiseman MSS. 91–114.
105 Maugham memo., 18 Nov. 1917, Lloyd George MS. F60–2–36. Maugham described his work for the secret service in a novel entitled *Ashenden, or the British Agent*, London, 1927. It contains six stories one of which deals with his work in Russia. Originally there were

twenty Ashenden stories but fourteen were never published, on the insistence of Churchill, and were eventually destroyed. R. A. Cordell, *Somerset Maugham*, Bloomington, Indiana, 1969, p. 283.

106 Wiseman to Murray, 8 June 1918, Wiseman MSS. 91–85. Thwaites memo., 4 Nov. 1917, Wiseman MSS. 91–106. Czech agents also appeared in novels, other than *Ashenden*, about the First World War. In *A Prince of the Captivity*, London, 1933, Buchan, who was in a position to know, wrote (p. 71): 'He is a Czech, and the Czechs having no fatherland at present, are the greatest secret agents in this war.'
107 F.O. to Fleurian, 11 Jan. 1917, F.O. 371–2870–4989. Nicolson minute, 14 April 1917, F.O. 371–2870–80515.
108 Nicolson minute, 2 Sept. 1917, Cab. 24–25. Balfour to Spring Rice, 5 Sept. 1917, F.O. 115–2321.
109 Spring Rice to Balfour, 6 Sept. 1917, Balfour to Spring Rice, 19 Sept. 1917, Spring Rice to Balfour, 21 Sept. 1917, Spring Rice to Balfour, 26 Oct. 1917, F.O. 115–2322.
110 Balfour to Spring Rice, 14 Nov. 1917, Spring Rice to F.O., 20 Nov. 1917, F.O. 115–2322. F.O. to Spring Rice, 5 Jan. 1918, F.O. 371–3144–1245.
111 Balfour to Spring Rice, 5 Sept. 1917, F.O. 115–2321.
112 F.O. to Erskine, 29 Sept. 1917, F.O. 371–2885–185876. Erskine to F.O., 3 Oct. 1917, F.O. 371–2885–190147.
113 War cabinet 294, 7 Dec. 1917, Cab. 23–4. Rodd to F.O., 8 Dec. 1917, F.O. 371–2885–233317. Rodd to Balfour, 24 Dec. 1917, F.O. 371–2885–244599.
114 Cecil minute, 29 Dec. 1917, F.O. 371–2885–244599.
115 Waller to Bigham, 26 Feb. 1917, Waller to Sykora, 13 Mar. 1917, Sykora to Waller, 11 April 1917, H.O. 45–10831–326555.
116 Waller to Sykora, 9 May 1917, H.O. 45–10831–326555.
117 Metropolitan Police to H.O., 23 May 1917, Waller minute, 29 May 1917, H.O. 45–10831–326555.
118 Western and General Report 24, 11 July 1917, Cab. 24–146.
119 Beneš, *Memoirs*, pp. 101, 182.
120 D. Perman, *The Shaping of the Czechoslovak State*, Leiden, 1962, p. 33. J. Bradley, *Allied Intervention in Russia*, London, 1968, p. 66. C. MacKenzie, *Dr. Beneš*, London, 1946, p. 89. Beneš memo., 13 May 1918, F.O. 371–3135–84727.
121 War office, *Statistics of the Military Effort of the British During the Great War, 1914–1920*, London, 1922, pp. 634–5. One hundred Austro-Hungarian prisoners were released for military service but it is probable that not all of them were Czechoslovaks.
122 'Western and General Report', 12 Sept. 1917, Cab. 24–146. Rodd to Balfour, 24 Dec. 1917, F.O. 371–2885–244599.
123 Rodd to Balfour, 10 Mar. 1918, F.O. 371–3149–49674. Spiers memo., 13 Mar. 1918, F.O. 371–3149–49226. Cubitt to F.O., 2 April 1918, F.O. 371–3149–58584. Spiers memo., 30 Mar. 1918, F.O. 371–3149–58590.
124 R. H. Ullman, *Anglo-Soviet Relations, 1917–1921: Intervention and the War*, Princeton, 1961, p. 151.
125 Steed to Buchanan, 12 May 1917, F.O. 395–109–97534. Hardinge to Hall, 15 May 1917, F.O. 371–3008–96719.
126 Bradley, *Intervention*, p. 65.
127 Seton-Watson, *Masaryk*, pp. 100–1.

128 Ullman, *Anglo-Soviet*, pp. 40–57. Memo., 26 Oct. 1917, F.O. 371–2895–216380.
129 Clerk minute, 4 Nov. 1917, F.O. 371–2895–216380.
130 Abraham, 'Policy of the War Cabinet Relative to Revolutionary Governments at Petrograd', 23 Feb. 1918, Milner MSS. 109.
131 Graham to treasury, 26 Jan. 1918, F.O. 371–3283–14389.
132 Wardrop to F.O., 18 Mar. 1918, F.O. 371–3323–50420.
133 D.M.I. to F.O., 30 Mar. 1918, F.O. 371–3323–57780.
134 Beneš, *Memoirs*, p. 189.
135 Gaselee minute, 23 Jan. 1917, F.O. 371–2862–12976. Hardinge to Hall, 15 May 1917, F.O. 371–3008–96719.
136 Thomson to F.O., 8 Feb. 1917, F.O. 371–2863–38799.
137 Thomson to F.O., 27 Feb. 1917, H.O. to F.O., 9 Mar. 1917, Graham to H.O., 15 Mar. 1917, F.O. 371–2863–52214. Clerk to Supilo, 9 April 1917, F.O. 371–2863–70830.
138 Nicolson minute, 13 Mar. 1917, F.O. 371–2863–52214.
139 Clerk minute, 14 Mar. 1917, F.O. 371–2863–52214.
140 Müller minute, 23 Jan. 1917, Gaselee minute, 30 Jan. 1917, F.O. 395–139–14565.
141 H. N. Fieldhouse, 'Noel Buxton and A. J. P. Taylor's *The Trouble Maker's*', in *A Century of Conflict, 1850–1950, Essays for A. J. P. Taylor*, M. Gilbert (ed.), London 1966, p. 188.
142 War cabinet 119, 16 April 1917, Cab. 23–2.
143 Hutton to Montgomery, 31 May 1917, Nicolson minute, F.O. 395–98–108461.
144 Hardinge to Cockerill, 13 Feb. 1917, F.O. 395–141–30311.
145 Crowe to Rennie, 31 Aug. 1917, F.O. 371–2870–166836.
146 Seton-Watson to Vesnić, 10 Jan. 1917, Seton-Watson MSS. VIII. Clerk minute, 29 Mar. 1917, F.O. 371–2870–64572. See above, p. 80.
147 Ostović, *Yugoslavia*, p. 83. Seton-Watson memo., 15 Sept. 1917, F.O. 371–2889–180815. Seton-Watson memo., 6 July 1917, F.O. 371–3081–133073.
148 Hoare to Balfour, 1 Nov. 1917, Clerk minute, F.O. 371–2864–207239.
149 Clerk to Hardinge, 26 Oct. 1917, F.O. 371–2864–207244.
150 War cabinet 279, 21 Nov. 1917, Cab. 23–4.
151 Cecil minute, 19 Mar. 1918, F.O. 371–3280–49989.
152 W. S. Maugham, *A Writer's Notebook*, London, 1949, p. 142.
153 Cecil to Des Graz, 9 Jan. 1918, F.O. 371–3149–6573.
154 Jovanović to Balfour, 26 Jan. 1918, F.O. 371–3149–16711. Jovanović to Balfour, 25 Jan. 1918, F.O. 371–3149–16712. Des Graz to F.O., 7 Mar. 1918, F.O. 371–3154–44197.
155 Balfour to Page, 20 Mar. 1918, F.O. 371–3154–48660. Troubridge to Milner, 30 Mar. 1918, W.O. 32–5130.
156 Hardinge minute, 26 Jan. 1918, F.O. 371–3149–167212.

CHAPTER 6

1 Drummond memo., 16 Aug. 1916, F.O. 800–96.
2 Clerk minute, 16 Aug. 1916, F.O. 371–2747–161698.
3 Bertie diary, 17 Aug. 1916, F.O. 800–178. Buchanan to Hardinge, 18 Aug. 1916, Hardinge MSS. 24. Pares memo., 16 Sept. 1916, Lloyd George MS. E5–1–8.
4 Grey to Bertie, 24 Aug. 1916, F.O. 371–2804–170012.

5 Grey minute, Howard to Hardinge, 14 Oct. 1916, Hardinge MSS. 26.
6 Hardinge to Bertie, 14 Nov. 1916, Hardinge MSS. 27.
7 Fischer, *Germany's Aims*, p. 245.
8 War committee, 7 Nov. 1916, Cab. 42–23–9.
9 Hardinge to Grey, 12 Nov. 1916, F.O. 371–2747–227662. F.O., 'Official Communique', 10 Nov. 1916, F.O. 395–26–233257.
10 *The Times*, 18 Nov. 1918. Hankey, 'Note on Paris Conference', 15 Nov. 1916, Cab. 28–1–12.
11 Clerk minute, 6 Nov. 1916, F.O. 371–2747–225639.
12 Clerk and Grey minutes, 21 Nov. 1916, F.O. 371–2747–238962.
13 Buchanan to Hardinge, 19 Jan. 1917, Hardinge MSS. 29.
14 Buchanan to F.O., 1 Jan. 1917, F.O. 371–3075–1290.
15 Buchanan to Hardinge, 2 Jan. 1917, Hardinge MSS. 29.
16 Balfour to Buchanan, 3 Jan. 1917, F.O. 371–3075–2031. Buchanan to F.O., 5 Jan. 1917, F.O. 371–3075–5269.
17 Buchanan to F.O., 8 Jan. 1917, F.O. 371–3075–6675.
18 War cabinet 37, 18 Jan. 1917, Cab. 23–1.
19 Komarnicki, *Rebirth*, pp. 115–16. Howard to F.O., 22 Jan. 1917, F.O. 371–3000–18454. Rumbold to F.O., 5 Feb. 1917, F.O. 371–3000–28868.
20 Buchanan to Balfour, 5 Feb. 1917, F.O. 371–3000–47422. Lindley, 'Summary of Events', 5 Mar. 1917, F.O. 371–2998–48291.
21 Clerk to Milner, 1 Mar. 1917, Cab. 28–2.
22 See above, pp. 85–7. Hardinge to Beaumont, 1 Feb. 1917, Hardinge MSS. 29.
23 Drummond memo., 12 Feb. 1917, Cab. 24–6.
24 Dmowski memo., 22 Mar. 1917, F.O. 371–3000–62097.
25 Balfour to Buchanan, 22 Mar. 1917, F.O. 371–3000–62097.
26 Buchanan to F.O., 25 Mar. 1917, F.O. 371–3000–63340.
27 Clerk minute, 26 Mar. 1917, F.O. 371–3000–63340.
28 Hardinge minute, 26 Mar. 1917, F.O. 371–3000–63340.
29 Balfour to Buchanan, 28 Mar. 1917, F.O. 371–3000–63340.
30 Buchanan to F.O., 29 Mar. 1917, F.O. 371–3000–66637.
31 Buchanan to F.O., 29 Mar. 1917, F.O. 371–3000–66637.
32 Drummond to House, 28 April 1917, F.O. 800–208.
33 Clerk and Hardinge minutes, 30 Mar. 1917, F.O. 371–3000–66637. Clerk minute, 31 Mar. 1917, F.O. 371–3000–66640.
34 Buchanan to F.O., 29 Mar. 1917, F.O. 371–3000–66640.
35 Rumbold to F.O., 1 April 1917, Lloyd George MS. F59–9–2. Clerk minute, 31 Mar. 1917, F.O. 371–3000–67338.
36 F.O. to Buchanan, 5 April 1917, F.O. 371–3000–68947.
37 Clerk minute, 3 April 1917, F.O. 371–3000–68947.
38 War cabinet, 23 April 1917, Cab. 23–2. Bonar Law, 26 April 1917, F.O. 371–3000–86957.
39 Clerk minute, 31 Mar. 1917, F.O. 371–3000–67338. Clerk to Cecil, 16 April 1917, F.O. 800–384.
40 Buchanan to F.O., 19 April 1917, F.O. 800–205.
41 Rumbold to Balfour, 16 Mar. 1917, F.O. 395–108–62108. Waller minute, 12 April 1917, H.O. 45–10836–330095. Alma-Tadema to Dmowski, 27 April 1917, F.O. 371–3012–88528.
42 Buchan to Davidson, 29 May 1917, F.O. 395–108–104074.
43 Rumbold to Balfour, 4 July 1917, F.O. 371–3003–138638.
44 Howard to Hardinge, 10 May 1917, Hardinge MSS. 32. E. Howard,

Theatre of Life: Life Seen from the Stalls, 1905–1936, London, 1936, p. 263.
45 Rumbold to Spring Rice, 29 April 1917, F.O. 115–2302.
46 Drummond memo., 13 June 1918, F.O. 371–3282–106670. See above, pp. 89–91.
47 Dmowski memo., 26 Mar. 1917, F.O. 371–3000–63741. Dmowski to Balfour, 1 April 1917, F.O. 371–3016–194676.
48 See above, pp. 87–93. Namier, memo., 3 May 1917, F.O. 371–3001–92381, memo., 24 May 1917, F.O. 371–3001–104735.
49 Drummond to Kerr, 6 April 1917, F.O. 800–384. The historian C. W. C. Oman, who was advising the foreign office on Polish affairs, wrote of Namier: 'I know Mr. Namier well, having examined him when he was an Oxford undergraduate, and seen him a good many times in later years. He is quite sincere, but very self-centred and disputatious: he used to consider himself as the only authority in England on the Ruthenian question, and to resent any one having independent views upon it.' Oman memo., 26 Sept. 1917, F.O. 371–3016–194676.
50 Namier to Kerr, 2 April 1917, F.O. 800–384.
51 Intelligence bureau, 'Office Orders', 1 June 1917, F.O. 395–148–117714. Oliphant to Montgomery, 28 May 1917, F.O. 371–3010–105964.
52 Graham to W.O., 23 Jan. 1917, F.O. 371–3003–11832. Drummond memo., 16 Jan. 1917, F.O. 800–384. Drummond to Campbell, 17 May 1917, F.O. 115–2302. There is also a receipt for £2,300 for September 1917, F.O. 115–2322. S. R. Pliska, 'The Polish American Army, 1917–1921', *The Polish Review*, vol. x, no. 3, 1965, p. 50.
53 Horodyski memo., 7 Mar. 1917, F.O. 371–3118–50659.
54 Drummond to Hardinge, 26 Mar. 1917, F.O. 371–3118–50659.
55 Fowler, *British–American Relations*, pp. 25–31.
56 'General Military Report', 11 June 1917, W.O. 32–5403.
57 Memo., 9 May 1917, Wiseman MSS. 91–105. Drummond to Cecil, 20 May 1917, F.O. 115–2302.
58 Balfour mission report, 21 May 1917, W.O. 32–5403.
59 Balfour to F.O. (draft), 23 May 1917, F.O. 115–2302. F.O. to Buchanan, 31 May 1917, F.O. 371–3003–106300.
60 Langley to W.O., 4 June 1917, F.O. 371–3003–108187.
61 Horodyski to Drummond, 20 June 1917, F.O. 371–3082–123459.
62 Drummond to Horodyski, 21 June 1917, F.O. 371–3082–123459.
63 Rumbold to F.O., 4 July 1917, F.O. 371–3003–132679. Spring Rice to F.O., 23 July 1917, F.O. 115–2302. Drummond to Balfour, 7 Aug., 1917, F.O. 800–204. Paderewski to Horodyski, 28 Aug. 1917, F.O. 371–3001–169054.
64 Graham to H.O., 24 July 1917, H.O. 45–10740–262173. Langley to Bertie, 6 Aug. 1917, F.O. 371–3012–152470. War Office, *Statistics*, pp. 634–5.
65 F.O. to D.M.I., 25 Aug. 1917, F.O. 371–3003–163638. Drummond to Cecil, 29 Aug. 1917, F.O. 800–197.
66 Spring Rice to Balfour, 6 Sept. 1917, F.O. 115–2321. Spring Rice to Devonshire, 15 Sept. 1917, F.O. 115–2302.
67 Spring Rice to F.O., 27 Sept. 1917, F.O. 371–3003–187302. Spring Rice to F.O., 7 Oct. 1917, F.O. 115–2302.
68 W. B. Makowski, *History and Integration of Poles in Canada*, Niagara, Ontario, 1967, p. 182.

69 Spring Rice to Devonshire, 10 Oct. 1917, F.O. 115–2302.
70 Langley to Cambon, 16 June 1917, F.O. 371–3003–115713.
71 F.O. to Buchanan, 31 May 1917, F.O. 371–3003–106300.
72 Wiseman to Drummond, 24 Sept. 1917, Wiseman MSS. 91–105. F.O. to Wiseman, 4 Oct. 1917, F.O. 800–204.
73 Dmowski to Clerk, 30 April 1917, F.O. 371–3012–88528. H.O. to F.O., 5 July 1917, H.O. 45–10740–262173.
74 Spring Rice to F.O., 15 June 1917, F.O. 371–3001–119346. Komarnicki, *Rebirth*, p. 170.
75 Drummond to Horodyski, 21 June 1917, F.O. 371–3082–123459.
76 Clerk minute, 8 July 1917, F.O. 371–3012–133576.
77 F.O. to Buchanan, 21 July 1917, F.O. 371–3012–133576.
78 Spring Rice to F.O., 23 July 1917, F.O. 115–2302. Buchanan to F.O., 24 July 1917, F.O. 371–3001–146480. Bertie to F.O., 1 Aug. 1917, F.O. 371–3001–151514.
79 F.O. to Spring Rice, 22 Aug. 1917, F.O. 371–3001–163770. Mackray, *Poland*, p. 82.
80 Horodyski to Paderewski, 21 Aug. 1917, F.O. 371–3001–164526. Cecil memo., 3 Sept. 1917, F.O. 800–205.
81 Namier memo., 3 May 1917, F.O. 371–3001–92381.
82 Pidhaini, *Ukrainian–Polish Problem*, p. 31.
83 Zaleski memo., 16 July 1917, F.O. 371–3012–141126. Howard to Hardinge, 16 May 1917, F.O. 371–3001–99577.
84 Komarnicki, *Rebirth*, pp. 116–17. Namier memo., 3 May 1917, F.O. 371–3001–92381. Fischer, *Germany's Aims*, p. 453. Namier memo., 4 June 1917, Cab. 24–15. Howard to Hardinge, 10 May 1917, Hardinge MSS. 32.
85 Zaleski memo., 16 July 1917, F.O. 371–3012–141126.
86 Clerk minute, 18 July 1917, F.O. 371–3012–133576.
87 Hardinge minute, 4 July 1917, Drummond minute, 4 Aug. 1917, F.O. 371–3001–147721.
88 Nicolson, Clerk and Drummond minutes, 8 Aug. 1917, F.O. 371–3015–162614.
89 Drummond to Kerr, 20 Aug. 1917, F.O. 800–199.
90 Kell to Nicolson, 17 Aug. 1917, F.O. 371–3015–162614.
91 Macdonogh to F.O., 10 Oct. 1917, Bray, 'Report on August Zaleski', 20 Sept. 1917, M.I.7d memo., 14 Sept. 1917, F.O. 371–3016–195993.
92 Clerk minute, 12 Oct. 1917, F.O. 371–3016–195993.
93 F.O. to Macdonogh, 17 Oct. 1917, F.O. 371–3016–195993.
94 Howard to Hardinge, 4 Sept. 1917, Hardinge MSS. 34. Namier memo., 4 Sept. 1917, Cab. 24–25.
95 R. P. Browder and A. F. Kerensky (eds.), *The Russian Provisional Government 1917*, vol. I, Stanford, Calif., 1961, p. 327.
96 *Ibid.*, p. 330.
97 Buchanan to F.O., 24 July 1917, F.O. 371–3001–146480.
98 Howard to Hardinge, 8 Sept. 1917, F.O. 371–3001–175905. Howard to Hardinge, 4 Sept. 1917, Hardinge MSS. 34.
99 Clerk minute, 10 Sept. 1917, F.O. 371–3001–175906.
100 F.O. to Howard, 14 Sept. 1917, F.O. 371–3001–175906.
101 Polish National Committee to Balfour, 28 Aug. 1917, F.O. 371–3001–169539.
102 Cecil to Page, 30 Aug. 1917, F.O. 371–3001–170618.
103 F.O. to Spring Rice, 2 Sept. 1917, F.O. 371–3001–169539.

104 Buchanan to F.O., 1 Oct. 1917, F.O. 371–3001–189230.
105 Graham to Sobanski, 15 Oct. 1917, F.O. 371–3001–193915.
106 Spring Rice to F.O., 25 Oct. 1917, F.O. 115–2302.
107 Graham to Sobanski, 15 Oct. 1917, F.O. 371–3001–193915.
108 Clerk minute, 8 Oct. 1917, F.O. 371–3001–193261. Clerk minute, 7 Nov. 1917, F.O. 371–3002–209774.
109 Balfour to Weardale, 22 Nov. 1917, F.O. 800–210.
110 Drummond minute, 13 Oct. 1917, F.O. 371–3016–193872.
111 Balfour to Sobanski, 22 Feb. 1918, F.O. 371–3280–33950. Moylan memo., 8 Jan. 1918, F.O. 371–3280–7341.
112 Gregory minute, 24 Oct. 1917, F.O. 371–3017–209310.
113 Home office circular, 12 Mar. 1918, H.O. 45–10890–355329.
114 Sobanski to Kell, 31 Dec. 1917, F.O. 371–3280–5738.
115 Moylan memo., 8 Jan. 1918, F.O. 371–3280–7341.
116 Moylan memo., 8 Jan. 1918, F.O. 371–3280–7341.
117 Clerk to Moylan, 8 Jan. 1918, H.O. 45–10889–352661.
118 See above, pp. 83–5. F.O. to Howard, 15 Jan. 1918, F.O. 371–3277–6702.
119 Graham to treasury, 22 Dec. 1917, F.O. 371–3002–236697. Thwaites memo., 4 Nov. 1917, Wiseman MSS. 91–106
120 Chalmers to F.O., 28 Dec. 1917, T 12–38. Chalmers to F.O., 22 Feb. 1918, T 12–39.
121 F.O. to Derby, 11 June 1918, F.O. 371–3277–102644.
122 M.I.2e, memo., 27 April 1918, F.O. 371–3286–78150.
123 Macdonogh to Drummond, 4 July 1917, F.O. 800–204. W.O. to Knox, August 1917, F.O. 800–384. Knox, memo., 15 Nov. 1917, F.O. 371–3012–218506.
124 F.O. to Bertie, 26 Nov. 1917, F.O. 371–3018–225397.
125 Spring Rice to F.O., 31 Oct. 1917, F.O. 371–3017–209501.
126 Buchanan to Balfour, 14 Dec. 1917, F.O. 115–2318.
127 J. W. Wheeler-Bennett, *Brest-Litovsk: The Forgotten Peace*, London, 1938, pp. 75–99.
128 War cabinet, 306, 26 Dec. 1917, Cab. 23–4. Bertie to F.O., 4 Jan. 1918, F.O. 371–3277–3658.
129 Langley to treasury, 9 Jan. 1918, F.O. 371–3277–2658. War cabinet 341, 8 Feb. 1918, Cab. 23–5.
130 War cabinet 262, 1 Nov. 1917, Cab. 23–4. War cabinet 316, 7 Jan. 1918, Cab. 23–5.
131 Dmowski memo., 26 Mar. 1917, F.O. 371–3000–63741.
132 Namier memo., 24 Aug. 1917, Cab. 24–24, memo., 9 Sept. 1917, F.O. 371–3016–194676.
133 Oman, memo., 3 April 1917, F.O. 371–3016–194676.
134 Drummond minute, 9 Oct. 1917, F.O. 371–3016–193872. Balfour to Lansdowne, 22 Nov. 1917, Cab. 24–34. Clerk Minute, 25 Jan. 1918, F.O. 371–3277–16767.
135 Cecil to Strachey, 13 Nov. 1917, F.O. 800–196.
136 Amery, 'Possible Terms of Peace', 11 April 1917, Cab. 24–10. Cecil to Balfour, 10 July 1917, Cab. 1–25–4.
137 Amery, 'The Russian Situation and its Consequences', 20 May 1917, Cab. 24–14.
138 Cecil minute, 9 Oct. 1917, F.O. 371–3016–193872.
139 Scott diary, 26–28 Sept. 1917, Scott MSS. 50904.
140 War cabinet, 24 Sept. 1917, Cab. 23–16.

141 Fischer, *Germany's Aims*, p. 455.
142 Howard to F.O., 26 Oct. 1917, F.O. 371–3002–206047. Howard to Hardinge, 4 Sept. 1917, Hardinge MSS. 34.
143 Gregory minute, 3 Oct. 1917, F.O. 371–3001–189230.
144 Clerk and Hardinge minutes, 3 Oct. 1917, F.O. 371–3001–189230.
145 Lindley, 'Summary of Events', 30 Oct. 1917, F.O. 371–2997–218507.
146 Howard to F.O., 29 Oct. 1917, F.O. 371–3002–207473. Howard to F.O., 26 Oct. 1917, F.O. 371–3002–211205.
147 Balfour minute, 14 Nov. 1917, F.O. 371–3002–216593. War cabinet 279, 21 Nov. 1917, Cab. 23–4.
148 Drummond memo., 12 Feb. 1917, Cab. 24–6.
149 Beak to Langley, 21 July 1917, F.O. 371–2864–155578.
150 Balfour to Rumbold, 30 Nov. 1917, F.O. 371–2861–227704.
151 Supreme war council, 2 Dec. 1917, Cab. 28–3.
152 Conference of foreign ministers, 3 Dec. 1917, Cab. 23–3.
153 Clerk minutes, 12 Dec. 1917, F.O. 371–3002–236697, F.O. 371–3002–234811.
154 Rumbold to F.O., 6 Dec. 1917, F.O. 371–3002–34811. Howard to Hardinge, 27 Dec. 1917, Hardinge MSS. 35.
155 Hardinge to Howard, 7 Dec. 1917, Hardinge MSS. 35.
156 Drummond memo., 10 Dec. 1917, F.O. 800–200.
157 Smuts, 'Peace Conversations', 13 Dec. 1917, F.O. 800–214.

CHAPTER 7

1 Sobanski to Balfour, 13 Nov. 1917, F.O. 371–3002–218943.
2 Gregory minute, 18 Nov. 1917, F.O. 371–3002–218943.
3 Nicolson memo., 5 Dec. 1917, F.O. 371–3086–230895.
4 War cabinet, 1 Mar. 1918, Cab. 23–16.
5 Addison to Lloyd George, 13 Dec. 1917, Lloyd George MS. F1–4–4.
6 H. W. Steed, *The Fifth Arm*, London, 1940, p. 14.
7 Hanak, *Great Britain*, pp. 276–9. R. Pound and G. Harmsworth, *Northcliffe*, London, 1959, p. 613. Also see C. Stuart, *Secrets of Crewe House*, London, 1920.
8 File on activities of Crewe House, Seton-Watson MSS. IV.
9 Steed to Northcliffe, 7 Mar. 1918, Steed MSS. H. W. Steed, *Thirty Years*, vol. II, pp. 185–220, Stuart, *Crewe House*, p. 11.
10 Mitchell, 'Propaganda', Inf. 4–4a, p. 12.
11 Steed, *Thirty Years*, pp. 191–205, *Fifth Arm*, pp. 15–31.
12 Northcliffe to Balfour, 24 Feb. 1918, Cab. 24–43–GT 3762.
13 Drummond to Balfour, 25 Feb. 1918, F.O. 800–213.
14 Cecil minute, 25 Feb. 1918, F.O. 800–213.
15 Balfour to Northcliffe, 26 Feb. 1918, Cab. 24–43–GT 3762.
16 Northcliffe to Balfour, 27 Feb. 1918, Cab. 24–43–GT 3762.
17 War cabinet 359, 5 Mar. 1918, Cab. 23–5.
18 Steed, *Thirty Years*, pp. 168–85.
19 Hanak, *Great Britain*, pp. 198–200.
20 Cecil to Balfour, 9 Mar. 1918, Cecil MSS. 51093.
21 Zeman, *Habsburg Monarchy*, p. 191.
22 Hanak, *Great Britain*, pp. 260–1. May, *Habsburg Monarchy*, pp. 596–604. Cecil to Rodd, 18 Mar. 1918, Cecil MSS. 51093. Steed to Cecil, 19 Mar. 1918, F.O. 371–3135–75021. Steed to Northcliffe, 13 April

1918, F.O. 371–3135–66616. Rodd to Balfour, 10 April 1918, F.O. 371–3135–66462.

23 *Parliamentary Debates, Commons,* vol. 105, col. 188, 16 April 1918.

24 *Parliamentary Debates, Commons,* vol. 105, col. 1270, 29 April 1918.

25 Zeman, *Habsburg Monarchy,* p. 192.

26 May, *Habsburg Monarchy,* pp. 604–9. Hanak, *Great Britain,* pp. 276–8.

27 Steed, *Thirty Years,* p. 205.

28 Delmé-Radcliffe to D.M.I., 2 April 1918, Northcliffe to Steed, 4 April 1918, F.O. 371–3134–59242. Steed, *Fifth Arm,* p. 29.

29 Northcliffe memo., 14 May 1918, H.O. 139–37. Steed memo., 27 May 1918, Steed MSS. Committee for Propaganda in Enemy Countries, 27 May 1918, F.O. 371–3474–99386.

30 F.O. to Rumbold, 20 May 1918, F.O. 371–3135–90068. F.O. to Rumbold, 27 May 1918, F.O. 371–3474–94400.

31 Northcliffe to Lloyd George, 28 April 1918, Lloyd George MS. F41–8–8. May, *Habsburg Monarchy,* p. 608.

32 May, *Habsburg Monarchy,* p. 718.

33 Wiseman to Drummond, 3 June 1918, F.O. 800–223. May, *Habsburg Monarchy,* p. 631. See above, pp. 127–8.

34 F.O. to Derby, 21 May 1918, F.O. 371–3135–89828.

35 M.I.2e, 'Russian Policy towards Poland in connection with the Polish Army in Russia', 27 April 1918, F.O. 371–3280–78150. Knox to D.M.I., 6 Feb. 1918, F.O. 371–3280–25758. Drummond to Reading, 7 Feb. 1918, F.O. 800–222. P. S. Wandycz, *Soviet-Polish Relations, 1917–1921,* Cambridge, 1969, pp. 54–7.

36 War cabinet 341, 8 Feb. 1918, Cab. 23–5.

37 Wardrop to F.O., 2 Mar. 1918, Namier memo., 22 Feb. 1918, Cab. 24–43.

38 War cabinet 358, 4 Mar. 1918. Cab. 23–5.

39 Howard to Hardinge, 27 Dec. 1917, Hardinge MSS. 35.

40 Rumbold to F.O., 19 April 1918, F.O. 371–3278–69989. Komarnicki, *Rebirth,* p. 117.

41 Namier memo., 21 Mar. 1918, Cab. 24–46–GT–4016.

42 War cabinet 429, 11 June 1918, Cab. 23–14.

43 *New Europe,* vol. IV, no. 47, 6 Sept. 1917.

44 Wolf memo., 9 July 1917, F.O. 371–3001–147721. Wolf to Cecil, 26 Nov. 1917, F.O. 371–3019–226666. H. Frankel, *Poland: The Struggle for Power,* London, 1946, pp. 82–3.

45 Gregory minutes, 29 Nov. 1917, 10 Dec. 1917, F.O. 371–3019–226666.

46 Cecil minute, 29 Nov. 1917, F.O. 371–3019–226666. Cecil minute, 12 Dec. 1917, F.O. 371–3019–226994.

47 Cecil minute, 27 Dec. 1917, F.O. 371–3019–241740. Cecil minute, 5 Jan. 1918, F.O. 371–3277–3361.

48 F.O. to W.O., 24 Dec. 1917, F.O. 371–3019–226994.

49 Balfour to Spring Rice, 26 Dec. 1917, F.O. 115–2303.

50 F.O. to Reading, 23 April 1918, F.O. 371–3277–70004.

51 Beaverbrook to Hall, 4 Mar. 1918, Drummond to Beaverbrook, 7 Mar. 1918, Drummond to Macdonogh, 22 April 1918, Macdonogh to Drummond, 8 May 1918, F.O. 800–385.

52 F.O. to H.O., 13 May 1918, F.O. 371–3280–81294. Majdewicz to H.O., 18 Mar. 1918, H.O. 45–10889–352661.

53 Crowe to H.O., 9 May 1918. Waller minute, 29 Mar. 1918, H.O. 45–10889–352661.

54 D.M.I. to F.O., 11 May 1918, F.O. to D.M.I., 17 May 1918, F.O. 371–3281–84759.
55 Gregory minute, 11 April 1918, F.O. 371–3280–63936.
56 War cabinet 429, 11 June 1918, Cab. 23–14.
57 May, *Habsburg Monarchy*, pp. 547–53. Also see M. Swartz, 'The Union of Democratic Control in British Politics During World War I', Yale Ph.D., 1969.
58 *Parliamentary Debates, Commons*, vol. 105, col. 188, 16 April 1918.
59 Gregory minute, 17 May 1918, F.O. 371–3281–84759. Clerk minute, 26 July 1918, F.O. 371–3281–135129.
60 War cabinet 349, 19 Feb. 1918, Cab. 23–5.
61 Namier memo., 26 April 1918, F.O. 371–4359–PID72. Namier memo., 3 May 1918, F.O. 371–3278–74361. Namier memo., 25 April 1918, Cab. 24–50–GT 4439.
62 Namier, 'Weekly Report on Poland', 21 Mar. 1918, Cab. 24–46–GT 4016.
63 Clerk minute, 18 July 1917, F.O. 371–3012–133576.
64 See above, pp. 89–91.
65 Drummond to Hall, 8 Feb. 1918, Hall to Drummond, 19 Feb. 1918, F.O. 800–204.
66 Cecil minute, Namier memo., 12 April 1918, F.O. 371–4359–PID22.
67 Drummond to Balfour, 4 May 1918, F.O. 371–3278–74361.
68 Namier memo., 15 May 1918, Hardinge to Drummond, 16 May 1918, F.O. 371–4363–PID137. Drummond to Dmowski, 17 May 1918, F.O. 800–329.
69 Sargent to Oliphant, 16 April 1918, Tyrrell to Sargent, 13 May 1918, F.O. 371–3281–74529. Rumbold to Balfour, 17 May 1918, F.O. 371–3278–92307. Rumbold to Balfour, 19 April 1918, F.O. 371–3278–74361.
70 Hardinge to Maurice, 22 April 1918, Maurice to Hardinge, 23 April 1918, F.O. to treasury, 9 May 1918, F.O. 371–3144–79787. Devonshire to Long, 5 July 1918, F.O. 371–3144–13129.
71 Ministry of Shipping to W.O., 8 May 1918, F.O. 371–3323–84358.
72 F.O. to Rodd, 8 Oct. 1918, F.O. 371–3149–168047. Rodd to Balfour, 10 Mar. 1918, F.O. 371–3149–49674. Cubitt to F.O., 2 April 1918, Nicolson minute, 3 April 1918, F.O. 371–3149–58584.
73 F.O. to Rodd, 5 April 1918, F.O. 371–3149–58584. Bertie to F.O., 9 April 1918, F.O. 371–3149–63085.
74 F.O. to Rodd, 22 June 1918, F.O. 371–3135–110595. F.O. to Rodd, 7 July 1918, F.O. 371–3149–116401. Supreme war council, 4 July 1918, Cab. 28–14. F.O. to Rodd, 19 July 1918, F.O. 371–3228–124860.
75 Nicolson minute, 22 July 1918, F.O. 371–3149–127287. F.O. to Rodd, 8 Oct. 1918, F.O. 371–3149–168047.
76 Macdonogh to F.O., 18 July 1918, F.O. 371–3228–124860.
77 Graham minute, Oct. 1918, F.O. 371–3149–174605.
78 Granville Barker memo., 30 April 1918, F.O. 371–3135–82126. Stanhope, 'The Czecho-Slovak Movement', 22 April 1918, F.O. 371–3443–80235–GT 4414.
79 Spiers to W.O., 31 Mar. 1918, F.O. 371–3323–57780. F.O. to Lockhart, 20 April 1918, F.O. 371–3323–68874.
80 Macdonogh to F.O., 30 Mar. 1918, F.O. 371–3323–57780. Ministry of Shipping to F.O., 8 May 1918, F.O. 371–3323–84358.
81 Supreme war council, 2 May 1918, F.O. 371–3323–79525.

82 Smuts–Milner memo., 'Intervention in Russia', 11 May 1918, Cab. 23–6. Amery memo., 14 May 1918, Milner MSS. 118.
83 Spiers memo., 30 Mar. 1918, F.O. 371–3149–58590.
84 Delmé-Radcliffe to C.I.G.S., 24 April 1918, F.O. 371–3135–75654.
85 Rodd to F.O., 8 May 1918, F.O. 371–3135–82446.
86 Macdonogh to Hardinge, 26 April 1918, F.O. 371–3135–75654. Delmé-Radcliffe to Macdonogh, 4 May 1918, F.O. 371–3135–81475. Steed report, 27 May 1918, Steed MSS.
87 Delmé-Radcliffe to C.I.G.S., 4 April 1918, Milner MSS. 118. Delmé-Radcliffe memo., 4 May 1918, F.O. 371–3135–81475.
88 Cecil, Hardinge and Balfour minutes, 26 April 1918, F.O. 371–3135–75645.
89 Steed report, 27 May 1918, Steed MSS. Beneš to Balfour, 11 May 1918, F.O. 371–3135–85869.
90 Beneš, *Memoirs*, pp. 373–4.
91 War cabinet 413, 17 May 1918, Cab. 23–6.
92 Cecil memo., 18 May 1918, F.O. 371–3443–89880.
93 Nicolson, Oliphant and Clerk minutes, 20 May 1918, F.O. 371–3135–89425.
94 Cecil minute, 22 May 1918, F.O. 371–3135–90542.
95 Namier memo., 18 May 1918, F.O. 371–3135–89425.
96 War cabinet 418, 27 May 1918, F.O. 371–3135–89425. Cecil memo., 25 May 1918, Cab. 25–52–GT 4647.
97 Balfour to Beneš, 3 June 1918, F.O. 371–3135–89425. H.O. 45–10761–269578. D.M.I. to F.O., 21 May 1918, F.O. 371–3218–90995.
98 F.O. to Reading, 5 June 1918, F.O. 371–3135–89425.
99 Cecil to Clemenceau, 18 May 1918, F.O. 371–3443–89881. Anglo-French conference, 28 May 1918, F.O. 371–3334–115535.
100 Lockhart to F.O., 23 May 1918, F.O. 371–3323–95495. Bradley, *Intervention*, p. 91.
101 Des Graz to F.O., 7 Mar. 1918, F.O. to Des Graz, 11 Mar. 1918, F.O. 371–3154–44197. Balfour to Page, 20 Mar. 1918, F.O. 371–3154–48660. Troubridge to Milner, 30 Mar. 1918, W.O. 32–5130. Graham memo., 2 April 1918, F.O. 371–3440–60266.
102 Steed to Lloyd George, 30 May 1918, Lloyd George MS. F41–8–15.
103 *The Times*, 9 Jan. 1918.
104 Drummond to Balfour, 7 Mar. 1918, F.O. 371–3277–43908. Drummond to *Tygodnik Polski*, 7 Mar. 1918, F.O. 800–210. F.O. to Barclay, 8 Mar. 1918, F.O. 371–3277–41169.
105 Anglo-French conference, 28 Mar. 1918, Cab. 28–3.
106 Reading to F.O., 30 May 1918, F.O. 371–3135–96610.
107 F.O. to Derby, 21 May 1918, F.O. 371–3135–89828.
108 Supreme war council, 3 June 1918, F.O. 371–3135–101920.
109 Balfour memo., 11 Mar. 1918, F.O. 371–3277–46350. Sobanski to Gregory, 15 Mar. 1918, F.O. 371–3278–49693.
110 Balfour to Rumbold, 2 July 1918, F.O. 371–3278–92307.
111 Tyrrell to Hardinge, 22 July 1918, F.O. 371–3281–135128.
112 Headlam memo., 25 June 1918, F.O. 371–3281–135128. Headlam to Tyrrell, 22 July 1918, F.O. 371–3281–135129.
113 Dickson, 'Present Condition of Political Parties in the Kingdom of Poland', 25 June 1918, F.O. 371–3279–169676.
114 Zaleski to Balfour, 31 May 1918, F.O. 371–3278–98133. Rumbold to Balfour, 12 June 1918, F.O. 371–3278–108501.

115 Gregory and Hardinge minutes, 12 June 1918, F.O. 371–3278–108501.
Clerk and Hardinge minutes, 7 June 1918, F.O. 371–3278–98133.
Tyrrell to Hardinge, 22 July 1918 F.O. 371–3281–135128.
116 Tyrrell to Hardinge, 25 July 1918, Balfour minute, 26 July 1918, F.O.
371–3281–135129.
117 Clerk minutes, 23 July 1918, 26 July 1918, F.O. 371–3281–135129.
118 D.M.I. to F.O., 20 Aug. 1918, F.O. 371–3281–145937. D.M.I. to F.O.,
18 Sept. 1918, F.O. 371–3281–159019.
119 Balfour to Sobanski, 12 Oct. 1918, F.O. 371–3280–167666.
120 Rumbold to F.O., 23 Aug. 1918, F.O. 371–3278–146017. Clerk minutes,
26 Aug. 1918, 4 Sept. 1918, F.O. 371–3278–148264. S. R. Pliska, 'The
Polish-American Army, 1917–1921', *Polish Review*, vol. x, no. 3, p. 56.
121 Clerk minute, 4 Sept. 1918, F.O. 371–3278–148264.
122 Drummond minute, 15 Aug., 1918, F.O. 371–3280–148973. Namier
memo., 9 Sept. 1918, F.O. 371–3278–150054. Rumbold to Balfour, 3
Oct. 1918, F.O. 371–3279–170725.
123 Acton to F.O., 25 Oct. 1918, Drummond minute, 25 Oct. 1918, F.O.
371–3279–177312. Cecil memo., 26 Oct. 1918, Cecil MSS. 51094.
124 Gregory minute, 14 Oct. 1918, F.O. 371–3279–170725.
125 Treasury to F.O., 19 Oct. 1918, T12–41.
126 War cabinet 457, 13 Aug. 1918, Cab. 23–7.
127 Supreme war council, 2 Nov. 1918, Milner MSS. 124–2.
128 Drummond minute, 3 June 1918, F.O. 371–3135–101920. Delmé-
Radcliffe to D.M.I., 10 June 1918, F.O. 371–3474–105849. Reading to
F.O., 12 June 1918, F.O. 371–3135–105559. Hardinge to Rodd, 17
June 1918, Hardinge MSS. 38.
129 Balfour to Northcliffe, 8 June 1918, F.O. 800–212.
130 Northcliffe to Balfour, 6 June 1918, F.O. 800–212.
131 *Parliamentary Debates, Commons*, vol. 106, col. 2022, 11 June 1918,
F.O. 371–3135–107939.
132 Reading to F.O., 10 June 1918, F.O. 371–3135–103493. Balfour to Des
Graz, 13 June 1918, F.O. 371–3135–107108. Jovanović to Balfour, 12
June 1918, F.O. 371–3135–106348. Coleville Barclay to Balfour, 4 June
1918, F.O. 371–3135–111985. Yugoslav Workman's Ass. to Balfour, 27
June 1918, F.O. 371–3135–115053. Hohler to Balfour, 12 June 1918,
F.O. 371–3135–117008.
133 Delmé-Radcliffe to Macdonogh, 21 June 1918, W.O. 106–824.
134 Hardinge minute, 12 June 1918, F.O. 371–3135–105559. Nicolson
minute, 14 June 1918, F.O. 371–3135–106348. Oliphant and Graham
minutes, 29 June 1918, F.O. 371–3135–115053.
135 Balfour to Northcliffe, 8 June 1918, F.O. 800–212.
136 Hardinge to Rodd, 17 June 1918, Hardinge MSS. 38.
137 Temperley (M.I.2e) memo., 28 June 1918, F.O. 371–3135–116831.
138 Tyrrell to Hardinge, 28 June 1918, F.O. 371–3135–116831. P.I.D.
memo., 3 July 1918, Cab. 24–57–GT 5028. Namier memo., 26 June
1918, F.O. 371–3135–111985. Drummond to Rodd, 9 July 1918, F.O.
800–385.
139 Oman to Drummond, 26 June 1918, F.O. 371–3157–114762. Jovanović
to Balfour, 6 July 1918, F.O. 371–3157–120332.
140 Nicolson minute, 10 July 1918, F.O. 371–3157–120332. Drummond
and Hardinge minutes, 26 June 1918, F.O. 371–3157–714762.
141 Balfour minute, 25 July 1918, F.O. 371–3135–130170. Steed, *Thirty
Years*, p. 230. *The Times*, 26 July 1918.

142 'Propaganda in Enemy Countries: Report of the Policy Committee', 24 Aug. 1918, F.O. 371–3475–151047. Northcliffe to Lloyd George, 7 Aug. 1918, Lloyd George MS. F41–8–20.
143 Balfour memo., 13 Sept. 1918, Cab. 24–63–GT 5677. War cabinet 482, 3 Oct. 1918, Cab. 23–8. Balfour to Montagu, 31 Oct. 1918, F.O. 800–207.
144 Erskine to F.O., 14 Sept. 1918, F.O. 371–3137–157243. Borghese to F.O., 20 Sept. 1918, F.O. to Borghese, 20 Sept. 1918, F.O. 371–3137–158233. Rodd to Balfour, 25 Sept. 1918, F.O. 371–3135–166419.
145 Cecil to Des Graz, 26 Aug. 1918, F.O. 371–3135–147786. Cecil to Balfour, 9 Sept. 1918, F.O. 371–3137–154848.
146 Cecil to Balfour, 9 Sept. 1918, F.O. 371–3137–154848.
147 Steed, *Thirty Years*, pp. 233–9. Lederer, *Yugoslavia*, p. 39. Ostović, *Yugoslavia*, pp. 83–9.
148 Trumbić memo., 7 Oct. 1918, Leeper memo., 9 Oct. 1918, F.O. 371–3137–169690.
149 Seton-Watson memo., 4 Oct. 1918, Phillips memo., 5 Oct. 1918, Drummond to Balfour, 5 Oct. 1918, F.O. 371–3154–169142.
150 Balfour to Des Graz, 9 Oct. 1918, F.O. 371–3137–171759.
151 Graham to Balfour, 17 Oct. 1918, F.O. 371–3137–176415.
152 F.O. to Derby, 23 Oct. 1918, F.O. 371–3137–176415.
153 Drummond minute, 3 June 1918, F.O. 371–3135–101920. Pichon to Balfour, 28 June 1918, Hardinge to Balfour, 28 June 1918, Cambon to Hardinge, 29 June 1918, F.O. 371–3135–115851.
154 F.O. to Press Bureau, 1 July 1918, F.O. 371–3135–115851.
155 Masaryk to Beneš, 15 July 1918, F.O. 371–3135–135132. Beneš to Steed, 16 July 1918, F.O. 371–3135–127473. Masaryk, *State*, p. 183.
156 Nicolson minute, 22 July 1918, F.O. 371–3135–127473.
157 Tyrrell minute, 23 July 1918, Namier memo., 23 July 1918, F.O. 371–3135–127473.
158 Hardinge and Balfour minutes, 24 July 1918, F.O. 371–3135–127473.
159 Drummond and Balfour minutes, 24 July 1918, F.O. 371–3135–127473.
160 Beneš to Steed, 16 July 1918, F.O. 371–3135–127473.
161 Lloyd George to Cecil, 7 June 1918, Cecil MSS. 51076. Lockhart to F.O., 2 June 1918, Milner MSS. 110. Ullman, *Anglo-Soviet*, pp. 153–90.
162 Ullman, *Anglo-Soviet*, pp. 105–6, 196–210.
163 Balfour to Reading, 21 June 1918, F.O. 371–3324–110145.
164 Ullman, *Anglo-Soviet*, p. 214.
165 Balfour to Lockhart, 28 June 1918, F.O. 371–3324–113393.
166 Ullman, *Anglo-Soviet*, p. 219.
167 Lloyd George to Reading, 18 July 1918, Balfour MSS. 49692.
168 F.O. to Jordan, 17 June 1918, F.O. 371–3323–106087.
169 Beneš to Steed, 16 July 1918, F.O. 371–3135–127473.
170 Beneš memo., 26 July 1918, F.O. 371–3135–130680.
171 Cecil to Balfour, 27 July 1918, F.O. 371–3135–135132.
172 Drummond to Balfour, 30 July 1918, F.O. 371–3135–135132.
173 Balfour minute, 30 July 1918, F.O. 371–3135–135132.
174 Beneš to Cecil, 30 July 1918, F.O. 371–3135–132422.
175 Graham, Hardinge and Balfour minutes, 31 July 1918, F.O. 371–3135–132422.
176 Cecil minute, 2 Aug. 1918, F.O. 371–3135–135135.
177 Beneš to Cecil, 3 Aug. 1918, F.O. 371–3135–135903.

178 Cecil minute, 3 Aug. 1918, F.O. 371–3135–135903.
179 Beneš, *Memoirs*, pp. 397–410. Steed, *Thirty Years*, pp. 231–3.
180 War cabinet 455, 7 Aug. 1918, Cab. 23–7.
181 Jordan to F.O., 6 Aug. 1918, F.O. 800–200. Drummond to Hankey, 8 Aug. 1918, F.O. 800–200.
182 Declaration, 9 Aug. 1918, F.O. 371–3135–135903. Cecil minute, 9 Aug. 1918, F.O. 371–3135–138537. Beneš to Cecil, 11 Aug. 1918, F.O. 371–3135–139628.
183 Cecil minute, 2 Aug. 1918, F.O. 371–3135–135135.
184 Drummond to Balfour, 7 Aug. 1918, F.O. 371–3135–135135.
185 Graham to H.O., 13 Aug. 1918, F.O. 371–3135–135135. Waller memo., 14–16 Aug. 1918, H.O. 45–10761–269578. F.O. to Beneš, 19 Aug. 1918, F.O. 371–3135–139628. Beneš to Cecil, 28 Aug. 1918, F.O. 371–3136–148362. Inter-department conference, 16 Aug. 1918, F.O. 371–3136–142344. Home office circular to chief constables, 20 Aug. 1918, F.O. 371–3136–145968.
186 'Agreement between His Majesty's Government and the Czecho-Slovak National Council', 3 Sept. 1918, H.O. 45–10761–269578. Graham to Beneš, 31 Aug. 1918, F.O. 371–3136–148362. Cecil minute, 3 Sept. 1918, F.O. 371–3136–152047.
187 Waller memo., 16 Aug. 1918, H.O. 45–10761–269588.
188 Cecil to Des Graz, 26 Aug. 1918, F.O. 371–3137–147786.
189 Cecil minute, 2 Sept. 1918, F.O. 371–3136–152102.
190 Cecil memo., 7 Aug. 1918, Cecil MSS. 51105.
191 Derby to F.O., 15 Oct. 1918, F.O. 371–3136–173025. Derby to F.O., 20 Oct. 1918, F.O. 371–3136–175975. Rodd to F.O., 22 Oct. 1918, F.O. 371–3136–176524.
192 War cabinet 457, 13 Aug. 1918, Cab. 23–7. War cabinet 458, 19 Aug. 1918, Cab. 23–7, Fisher diary, 15 Aug. 1918, Fisher MSS. 8.
193 Delmé-Radcliffe memo., 19 May 1918, F.O. 371–3135–90542.
194 Stanhope memo., 22 April 1918, F.O. 371–3443–80235.
195 Drummond memo., 8 June 1918, F.O. 800–329.
196 Balfour to Derby, 13 June 1918, Balfour MSS. 49743.
197 War cabinet 429, 11 June 1918, Cab. 23–14.
198 'Western and General Report', 3 July 1918, Cab. 24–148–75. Drummond memo., 23 Aug. 1918, F.O. 800–385. Roskill, *Hankey*, p. 562.
199 Cecil memo., 27 Aug. 1918, F.O. 371–3133–148060.

BIBLIOGRAPHY

UNPUBLISHED SOURCES

Official: Public Record Office

Cabinet Office
Treasury
Admiralty
Foreign Office
Home Office
Ministry of Information
Metropolitan Police Office
War Office

Private Papers

Asquith MSS. Bodleian Library.
Balfour MSS. Public Record Office, British Museum.
Bertie MSS. Public Record Office.
Bonar Law MSS. Beaverbrook Library.
Bryce MSS. Public Record Office, Bodleian Library.
Buchan MSS. Queen's University, Kingston, Ontario.
Carnock (Nicolson) MSS. Public Record Office.
Cecil MSS. Public Record Office, British Museum.
Drummond MSS. Public Record Office.
H. A. L. Fisher MSS. Bodleian Library.
Grey MSS. Public Record Office.
Hardinge MSS. Cambridge University Library.
E. M. House MSS. Yale University Library.
Kitchener MSS. Public Record Office.
Lloyd George MSS. Beaverbrook Library.
Milner MSS. Bodleian Library.
G. Murray MSS. Bodleian Library.
Murray-Robertson MSS. British Museum.
Northcliffe MSS. *The Times* Archives, New Printing House Square, London.
R. Paget MSS. British Museum.
Reading MSS. Public Record Office.
Runciman MSS. The University of Newcastle Upon Tyne.
C. P. Scott MSS. British Museum.
Seton-Watson MSS. School of Eastern European and Slavonic Studies.
Spring Rice MSS. Public Record Office.
Steel-Maitland MSS. Scottish Record Office.
Wickham Steed MSS. *The Times* Archives, New Printing House Square, London.
William Wiseman MSS. Yale University Library.

INTERVIEWS

Lady Namier, 25 Aug. 1969.
August Zaleski, 13 Aug. 1969.

PUBLISHED SOURCES

PRIMARY

Amery, L. S., *My Political Life*, vol. II, London, 1953.
Anon., *Hungary and the War*, London, 1915.
    The European War: Reply to the Appeal of German Theologians, London, 1915.
Asquith, Earl of Oxford and, *The Genesis of the War*, London, 1923.
    Memoirs and Reflections, 1852–1927, London, 1928.
Baker, R. S. and Dodd, W. F. (eds.), *The Public Papers of Woodrow Wilson*, 6 vols, New York, 1925–7.
Balfour, A. J., *Opinions and Argument: From Speeches and Addresses of the Earl of Balfour*, London, 1927.
    'Race and Nationality', *The Transactions of the Honourable Society of Cymmrodorion*, Session 1908–1909, London, 1910.
Barker, E., *Great Britain's Reason for Going to War*, London, 1915.
    The Submerged Nationalities of the German Empire, Oxford, 1915.
Beaverbrook, Lord, *Politicians and the War, 1914–1916*, London, 1928.
    Men and Power, 1917–1918, London, 1956.
Beneš, E., *My War Memoirs*, London, 1928.
Bennett, A., *The Journals of Arnold Bennett*, vol. II, London, 1952.
Bernstorff, J. H., *My Three Years in America*, London, 1920.
Bertie of Thame, Lord, *The Diary of Lord Bertie of Thame, 1914–1918*, 2 vols, London, 1924.
Brereton, C., *Who is Responsible*, London, 1914.
Browder, R. P. and Kerensky, A. F. (eds.), *The Russian Provisional Government 1917*, vol. I, Stanford, Calif., 1961.
Buchan, J., *A Prince of the Captivity*, London, 1933.
Buchanan, G., *My Mission to Russia and Other Diplomatic Memories*, 2 vols, London, 1923.
Bunyan, J. and Fischer, H. H. (eds.), *The Bolshevik Revolution 1917–1918: Documents and Materials*, Stanford, Calif., 1934.
Bury, J. B., *Germany and Slavonic Civilization*, London, 1914.
Cecil of Chelwood, Viscount, *A Great Experiment: An Autobiography*, London, 1941.
    All the Way, London, 1949.
Churchill, W. S., *The World Crisis, 1911–1918*, 4 vols, London, 1923–9.
Cole, M. (ed.), *Beatrice Webb's Diaries, 1912–1924*, London, 1952.
Conwell-Evans, T. P., *Foreign Policy from a Back Bench, 1904–1913*, London, 1932.
Davies, J., *The Prime Minister's Secretariat, 1916–1920*, London, 1951.
Dickinson, G. L. (ed.), *Documents and Statements Relating to Peace Proposals and War Aims*, London, 1919.
Esher, Reginald, Viscount, *Journals and Letters*, 4 vols, London, 1934–8.
Fisher, H. A. L., *An Unfinished Autobiography*, London, 1940.
    The Value of Small States, London, 1914.
Gaunt, G., *The Yield of the Years*, London, 1940.
George, W., *My Brother and I*, London, 1958.

Great Britain, Foreign Office, Historical Section, *Peace Conference Pamphlets*, London, 1920.

Great Britain, *Parliamentary Debates, Commons*, 1914–1918.

Great Britain, War Office, *Statistics of the Military Effort of the British Empire During the Great War, 1914–1920*, London, 1922.

Gregory, J. D., *On the Edge of Diplomacy: Rambles and Reflections, 1902–1928*, London, 1929.

Grey of Falloden, Viscount, *Twenty-Five Years, 1892–1916*, 2 vols, London, 1925.

Gwynn, S. (ed.), *The Letters and Friendships of Sir Cecil Spring Rice*, 2 vols, London, 1929.

Hankey, Lord, *The Supreme Command, 1914–1918*, 2 vols, London, 1961.

Hardinge of Penshurst, Lord, *Old Diplomacy*, London, 1947.

Headlam, J. W., *The Peace Terms of the Allies*, London, 1917.

The Issue, London, 1916.

England, Germany and Europe, London, 1914.

Hoare, S., *The Fourth Seal*, London, 1930.

Howard of Penrith, Lord, *Theatre of Life: Life Seen from the Stalls, 1905–1936*, 2 vols, London, 1936.

Jones, T., *Whitehall Diary*, vol. I, 1916–1925, London, 1969.

Jonescu, T., *The Policy of National Instinct*, London, 1916.

Lansing, R., *War Memoirs*, New York, 1935.

Lloyd George, D., *The War Memoirs of David Lloyd George*, 6 vols, London, 1933–7.

The Truth About the Treaties, 2 vols, London, 1938.

Lloyd George, Earl, *Lloyd George*, London, 1960.

Lloyd George, F., *The Years That Are Past*, London, 1967.

Lockhart, R. H. B., *Memoirs of a British Agent*, London, 1932.

London Czech Committee, *Memorial to the International from the Bohemian Branch of the Socialist Party in America*, London, 1915.

MacKenzie, C., *My Life and Times*, vols IV and V, London, 1965–6.

Masaryk, T. G., *The Making of a State: Memories and Observations, 1914–1918*, London, 1927.

At the Eleventh Hour, London, 1916.

The Slavs Among Nations, London, 1916.

Austrian Terrorism in Bohemia, London, 1916.

Maugham, W. S., *Ashenden, or the British Agent*, New York, 1927.

The Summing Up, London, 1938.

A Writer's Notebook, London, 1949.

Mill, J. S., *Utilitarianism, Liberty and Representative Government*, London, 1910.

Muir, R., *The National Principle and the War*, London, 1914.

Murray, A. C., *At Close Quarters: A Sidelight on Anglo-American Diplomatic Relations*, London, 1946.

Namier, L. B., *Germany and Eastern Europe*, London, 1914.

The Czecho-Slovaks, London, 1917.

The Case of Bohemia, London, 1917.

Nicolson, H., *Peacemaking 1919*, London, 1933.

Oppenheimer, F., *Stranger Within*, London, 1960.

Oxford Historians, *Why We Are At War*, Oxford, 1914.

Paderewski, I. J. and Lawton, M., *The Paderewski Memoirs*, London, 1939.

Pares, B., *My Russian Memoirs*, London, 1931.

Percy E., *Some Memories*, London, 1958.

Polish Information Committee, *Poland Under the Germans*, London, 1916.
Germany's Economic Policy in Poland, London, 1915.
Prothero, G. W., *A Lasting Peace*, London, 1917.
Reading, Marquess of, *Rufus Isaacs, First Marquess of Reading*, 2 vols, London, 1942–5.
Ribot, A., *Letters to a Friend: Recollections of My Political Life*, London, 1926.
Riddell, Lord, *Lord Riddell's War Diary, 1914–1918*, London, 1933.
Robertson, W. R., *Soldiers and Statesmen, 1914–1918*, 2 vols, London, 1926.
From Private to Field Marshal, London, 1921.
Rodd, J. R., *Social and Diplomatic Memoirs, 1902–1919*, London, 1925.
Rolleston, T. W., *Ireland and Poland*, New York, 1917.
Rosendal, H., *The Problem of Danish Schleswig*, London, 1916.
Seton-Watson, R. W., 'The Failure of Sir Edward Grey', *English Review*, Feb. 1916.
German, Slav and Magyar: A Study of the Origins of the Great War, *The Future of Bohemia*, London, 1915.
London, 1916.
The Spirit of the Serb, London, 1916.
Masaryk in England, Cambridge, 1943.
Seton-Watson, R. W., Zimmern, A., Wilson, J. D. and Greenwood, A., *The War and Democracy*, London 1914.
Seymour, C. (ed.), *The Intimate Papers of Colonel House*, 4 vols, London, 1926–8.
Steed, H. W., *The Fifth Arm*, London, 1940.
Through Thirty Years, 1892–1922, 2 vols, London, 1924.
Stuart, C., *Secrets of Crewe House*, London, 1920.
Thomson, B., *Queer People*, London, 1922.
The Scene Changes, Garden City, N.Y., 1937.
Thwaites, N., *Velvet and Vinegar*, London, 1932.
Toynbee, A. J., *Acquaintances*, London, 1967.
The Destruction of Poland, London, 1916.
Trevelyan, G. M., *The Serbians and Austria*, London, n.d.
United States, Department of State, *Papers Relating to the Foreign Relations of the United States: The Lansing Papers, 1914–1920*, 2 vols, Washington, 1940.
Viereck, G. A., *Spreading Germs of Hate*, London, 1931.
The Strangest Friendship in History, London, 1933.
Voska, E. V. and Irwin, W., *Spy and Counterspy*, London, 1941.
Willert, A., *Road to Safety: A Study in Anglo-American Relations*, London, 1952.

SECONDARY

Abrash, M., 'War Aims toward Austria-Hungary; The Czechoslovak Pivot', *Russian Diplomacy and Eastern Europe, 1914–1917*, New York, 1963.
Albrecht-Carrie, R., *Italy at the Peace Conference*, New York, 1938.
Anderson, M., *Noel Buxton: A Life*, London, 1952.
Anon., 'Masaryk and Seine Aktion während des Weltkrieges', *Berliner Monatschefte*, vol. xv, no. 2, 1937.
Arnez, J., *Slovenia in European Affairs: Reflections on Slovenian Political History*, New York, 1958.
Baerlein, H., *The Birth of Yugoslavia*, London, 1922.

Baker, R. S., *Woodrow Wilson and the World Settlement*, London, 1923.
   Woodrow Wilson, Life and Letters, 8 vols, New York, 1927–35.
Bass, H. J. (ed.), *America's Entry into World War I*, New York, 1964.
Becvar, G., *The Lost Legion: A Czechoslovakian Epic*, London, 1939.
Berlin, I., 'Lewis Namier: A personal Impression', *A Century of Conflict, 1850–1950: Essays for A. J. P. Taylor* (ed. M. Gilbert), London, 1966.
Birnbaum, K., *Peace Moves and U-Boat Warfare: A Study of Imperial Germany's Policy Towards the United States, April 18, 1916–January 9, 1917*, Stockholm, 1958.
Blake, R., *The Unknown Prime Minister: The Life and Times of Andrew Bonar Law, 1858–1923*, London, 1955.
Bonham Carter, V., *Soldier True: The Life and Times of Field Marshal Sir William Robertson, 1860–1933*, London, 1963.
Borchard, E. and Lage, W. P., *Neutrality for the United States*, London, 1937.
Bradley, J. F. N., *Allied Intervention in Russia*, London, 1968.
   'Czech Nationalism in the Light of French Diplomatic Report, 1867–1914', *The Slavonic and East European Review*, vol. xlii, no. 98, 1963.
   'The Allies and the Czech Revolt against the Bolsheviks in 1918', *The Slavonic and East European Review*, vol. xliii, no. 101, 1965.
Bridge, F. R., 'The British Declaration of War on Austria-Hungary in 1914', *The Slavonic and East European Review*, vol. xlvii, no. 109, 1969.
Bromke, A., *Poland's Politics: Idealism vs. Realism*, Cambridge, 1967.
Bruntz, G., *Allied Propaganda and the Collapse of the German Empire in 1918*, Stanford, Calif., 1938.
Bryant, F. R., 'Britain and the Polish Settlement, 1919', Oxford D.Phil., 1969.
Bunyan, J., *Intervention, Civil War, and Communism in Russia, April–December, 1918*, Baltimore, Md., 1936.
Butler, J. R. M., *Lord Lothian, 1882–1942*, London, 1960.
Callwell, C. E., *Field Marshal Sir Henry Wilson, His Life and Letters*, 2 vols, London, 1927.
Čapek, K., *President Masaryk Tells His Own Story*, London, 1934.
Čapek, T., *The Čechs in America*, New York, 1926.
   Origins of the Czechoslovak State, London, 1926.
Carless-Davis, H. W., *History of the Blockade*, London, 1921.
Chapman-Houston, D. *The Lost Historian: A Memoir of Sir Sidney Low*, London, 1936.
Child, C. J., *The German-Americans in Politics, 1914–1917*, Maddison, Wisc., 1939.
   'German-American Attempts to prevent the Exportation of Munitions of War, 1914–1915', *Mississippi Valley Historical Review*, vol. xxv, 1938–9.
Cobban, A., *National Self-Determination*, London, 1944.
Cohen, V., *The Life and Times of Masaryk*, London, 1941.
Collier, B., *Brasshat: Field Marshal Sir Henry Wilson, 1864–1922*, London, 1961.
Collins, D., *Aspects of British Politics, 1904–1919*, Oxford, 1965.
Cordell, R. A., *Somerset Maugham*, Bloomington, Indiana, 1969.
Crabites, P., *Beneš: Statesman of Central Europe*, London, 1935.
Cruttwell, C. R. M., *The Role of British Strategy in the Great War*, Cambridge, 1936.
   A History of the Great War, 1914–1918, Oxford, 1934.

Cuddy, E., 'Pro-Germanism and American Catholicism, 1914–1917', *Catholic Historical Review*, vol. LIV, 1968.
Dallin, A., 'The Future of Poland', *Russian Diplomacy and Eastern Europe, 1914–1917*, New York, 1963.
Daniels, J., *The Wilson Era*, 2 vols, Chapel Hill, N. Carolina, 1944–6.
Deacon, R., *A History of the British Secret Service*, London, 1969.
Dedijer, V., *The Road to Sarajevo*, London, 1966.
Doree, S. G., 'Fiume as a Problem in Anglo-Italian Relations, 1915–1920', London Ph.D., 1969.
Dugdale, B. E. C., *Arthur James Balfour*, 2 vols, London, 1936.
Dugdale, E. T. S., *Maurice de Bunsen: Diplomat and Friend*, London, 1934.
Ehrman, J. P. W., *Cabinet Government and War, 1890–1940*, Cambridge, 1958.
'Lloyd George and Churchill as War Ministers', *Transactions of the Royal Historical Society*, vol. XI, 1961.
Ekstein-Frankel, M. G., 'The Development of British War Aims, August 1914–March 1915', London Ph.D., 1969.
Esslinger, D. R., 'American-German and Irish Attitudes Towards Neutrality, 1914–1917: A Study of Catholic Minorities', *Catholic Historical Review*, vol. LIV, 1968.
Fest, W. B., 'The Habsburg Monarchy in British Policy, 1914–1918', Oxford D.Phil., 1970.
Fieldhouse, H. N., 'Noel Buxton and A. J. P. Taylor's 'The Trouble Makers', *A Century of Conflict, 1850–1950: Essays for A. J. P. Taylor* (ed. M. Gilbert), London, 1966.
Fischer, F., *Germany's Aims in the First World War*, London, 1967.
Fischer, L., *The Soviets in World Affairs*, London, 1930.
Fisher, H. H., *America and the New Poland*, New York, 1938.
Forster, K., *The Failures of Peace: The Search for a Negotiated Peace During the First World War*, Washington, 1941.
Fowler, W. B., *British–American Relations, 1917–1918: The Role of Sir William Wiseman*, Princeton, N.J., 1969.
Frankel, H., *Poland: The Struggle for Power*, London, 1946.
Gelfand, L. E., *The Inquiry: American Preparations for Peace, 1917–1919*, New Haven, Conn., 1963.
Gerson, L. L., *Woodrow Wilson and the Rebirth of Poland*, New Haven, Conn., 1953.
The Hyphenate in Recent American Politics and Diplomacy, Lawrence, Kansas, 1964.
Glaise-Horstenau, E., *The Collapse of the Austro-Hungarian Monarchy*, London, 1931.
Gleason, J. H., *The Genesis of Russophobia in Great Britain*, Cambridge, 1950.
Gollin, A. M., *Proconsul in Politics: A Study of Lord Milner in Opposition and in Power*, London, 1964.
Gottlieb, W. W., *Studies in Secret Diplomacy during the First World War*, London, 1957.
Great Britain, War Office, *A History of the Blockade of Germany*, A. C. Bell, London, 1961.
Guinn, P., *British Strategy and Politics, 1914 to 1918*, Oxford, 1965.
Halevy, E., *The World Crisis of 1914–1918*, Oxford, 1930.
Halperin, V., *Lord Milner and the Empire*, London, 1952.

Hamilton, M. A., *Arthur Henderson: A Biography*, London, 1938.

Hammond, J. L., *C. P. Scott of the Manchester Guardian*, London, 1934.

Hanak, H., *Great Britain and Austria-Hungary During the First World War*, London, 1962.

'A Lost Cause: the English Radicals and the Habsburg Empire, 1914–1918', *Journal of Central European Affairs*, vol. 23, no. 2, 1963.

'Government, Foreign Office and Austria-Hungary, 1914–1918', *The Slavonic and East European Review*, vol. XLVIII, no. 108, 1969.

'T. G. Masaryk's Journalistic Activity in England during the First World War', *The Slavonic and East European Review*, vol. XLII, no. 98, 1963.

'The Union of Democratic Control during the First World War', *Bulletin of the Institute of Historical Research*, vol. XXXVI, no. 94, 1963.

Hancock, W. K., *Four Studies of War and Peace in This Century*, Cambridge, 1961.

Smuts: The Sanguine Years, 1870–1919, Cambridge, 1962.

Hazlehurst, C., 'Asquith as Prime Minister, 1908–1917', *The English Historical Review*, vol. LXXXV, no. 336, 1970.

Hennessy, J. P., *Crewe, 1858–1945*, London, 1945.

Heppell, M. and Singleton, F. B., *Yugoslavia*, London, 1961.

Hertz, F., *Nationality in History and Politics: A Study of the Psychology and Sociology of National Sentiment and Character*, London, 1944.

Higgins, T., *Winston Churchill and the Dardanelles: A Dialogue of Ends and Means*, London, 1963.

Hitchcock, E. E., *Beneš: The Man and the Statesman*, London, 1940.

Howard, C., 'The Treaty of London', *History*, vol. XXV, no. 100, 1941.

Huston, J. A., 'The Election of 1916', *Current History*, vol. 47, no. 278, 1964.

James, W., *The Eyes of the Navy: A Biographical Study of Admiral Sir Reginald Hall*, London, 1955.

Jaszi, O., *The Dissolution of the Habsburg Monarchy*, Chicago, 1929.

Jenkins, R., *Asquith*, London, 1964.

Johnson. H. J. T., *Vatican Diplomacy in World War*, Oxford, 1933.

Jones, T., *Lloyd George*, London, 1951.

Judd, D., *Balfour and the British Empire*, London, 1968.

Kann, R. A., *The Multinational Empire*, New York, 1950. 'The Defeat of Austria-Hungary in 1918 and the European Balance of Power', *Central European History*, vol. II, no. 3, 1969.

Kennan, G. F., *Russia Leaves the War*, London, 1956.

Decision to Intervene, London, 1958.

Kernek, S., 'The British Government's Reactions to President Wilson's "Peace" Note of December 1916', *The Historical Journal*, vol. XIII, no. 4, 1970.

Kerner, R. J. (ed.), *Czechoslovakia*, Berkeley, Calif., 1945.

Yugoslavia, Berkeley, Calif., 1949.

Kisch, G., 'Woodrow Wilson and the Independence of Small Nations in Central Europe', *Journal of Modern History*, vol. XIX, no. 3, 1947.

Knoles, G. H., 'American Intellectuals and World War I', *Pacific Northwest Quarterly*, vol. LIX, no. 4, 1968.

Kolarz, W., *Myths and Realities in Eastern Europe*, London, 1946.

Komarnicki, T., *The Rebirth of the Polish Republic*, London, 1957.

Koralka, J., 'The Czech Question in International Relations at the Beginning of the 20th Century', *The Slavonic and East European Review*, vol. XLVIII, no. 3, 1970.

Kurtz, H., 'The Lansdowne Letter', *History Today*, vol. xvIII, no. 2, 1968.
Kuzman, B., 'Austro-Hungarian Diplomacy before the Collapse of the Empire', *Journal of Contemporary History*, vol. 4, no. 2, 1969.
Landau, R., *Ignace Paderewski*, London, 1934.
Lasswell, H. D., *Propaganda Technique in the World War*, London, 1937.
Lederer, I. J., *Yugoslavia at the Paris Peace Conference*, London, 1963.
Levin, N. G., *Woodrow Wilson and World Politics*, New York, 1968.
Lias, G., *Beneš of Czechoslovakia*, London, 1940.
Link, A. S., *Wilson*, 5 vols, Princeton, N.J., 1947–65.
Lockwood, P. A., 'Milner's Entry into the War Cabinet', *Historical Journal*, vol. vII, no. 1, 1964.
Lowe, C. J., 'Britain and Italian Intervention, 1914–1915', *Historical Journal*, vol. xII, no. 3, 1969.
'The Failure of British Diplomacy in the Balkans, 1914–1916', *Canadian Journal of History*, vol. 4, no. 1, 1969.
Lowrie, D. A., *Masaryk of Czechoslovakia*, London, 1937.
Lutz, R. H., 'Studies of World War Propaganda', *Journal of Modern History*, vol. 5, no. 4, 1933.
Macartney, C. A., *National States and National Minorities*, London, 1934.
Macartney, C. A. and Palmer, A. W., *Independent Eastern Europe: A History*, London, 1962.
Machray, R., *Poland 1914–1931*, London, 1932.
MacKenzie, C., *Dr. Beneš*, London, 1946.
Makowski, W. B., *History and Integration of Poles in Canada*, Niagara, Ontario, 1967.
Mamatey, V. S., *The United States and East Central Europe, 1914–1918: A Study in Wilsonian Diplomacy and Propaganda*, Princeton, N.J., 1957.
'The United States Recognition of the Czechoslovak National Council of Paris', *Journal of Central European Affairs*, vol. xIII, no. 1, 1953.
Marcovitch, L., *Serbia and Europe, 1914–1920*, London, 1920.
Marwick, A., *The Deluge: British Society and the First World War*, London, 1965.
Masterman, E., *C. F. G. Masterman*, London, 1939.
Maurice, F., *The Armistice of 1918*, London, 1943.
Intrigues of War, London, 1922.
May, A. J., *The Passing of the Habsburg Monarchy*, 2 vols, Philadelphia, 1966.
'Seton-Watson and the Treaty of London', *Journal of Modern History*, vol. xxIx, no. 1, 1957.
'Woodrow Wilson and Austria-Hungary to the End of 1917', *Festschrift für Heinrich Benedikt*, Wien, 1957.
'R. W. Seton-Watson and British Anti-Habsburg Sentiment', *American Slavic and Eastern European Review*, vol. xx, no. 1, 1961.
May, E. R., *The World War and American Isolation, 1914–1917*, Cambridge, 1959.
Mayer, A. J., *Political Origins of New Diplomacy, 1917–1918*, New Haven, Conn., 1959.
'Internal Causes and Purposes of War in Europe, 1870–1956', *Journal of Modern History*, vol. xLI, no. 3, 1969.
McCallum, R. B., *Public Opinion and the Last Peace*, London, 1944.
McCormick, D., *The Mask of Merlin: A Critical Biography of David Lloyd George*, London, 1963.
McKenna, S., *Reginald McKenna, 1863–1943*, London, 1948.

Millis, W., *Road to War*, London, 1935.

Monticone R. C., 'Nationalities Problems in the Austro-Hungarian Empire', *Polish Review*, vol. 13, no. 4, 1968.

Morgan, K. O., *David Lloyd George: Welsh Radical as World Statesman*, Cardiff, 1963.

'Lloyd George's Premiership a Study in "Prime Ministerial Government" ', *Historical Journal*, vol. 13, no. 1, 1970.

Morison, S., 'Personality and Diplomacy in Anglo-American Relations, 1917', *Essays Presented to Sir Lewis Namier* (eds. R. Pares and A. J. P. Taylor), London, 1956.

Namier, J., *Lewis Namier: A Biography*, London, 1971.

Namier, L., *Vanished Supremacies: Essays on European History, 1812–1918*, London, 1958.

Avenues of History, London, 1952.

Nelson, H. I., *Land and Power: British and Allied Policy on Germany's Frontier, 1916–1919*, London, 1963.

Newman, E. P., *Masaryk*, London, 1960.

Nicholson, I., 'An Aspect of British Official Wartime Propaganda', *Cornhill Magazine*, vol. LXX, 1931.

Nicolson, H., *Sir Arthur Nicolson, Bart: A Study in Old Diplomacy*, London, 1930.

Nosek, V., *Independent Bohemia: An Account of the Czecho-Slovak Struggle for Liberty*, London, 1918.

The Spirit of Bohemia, London, 1926.

Notter, H., *The Origins of the Foreign Policy of Wilson*, Baltimore, Md., 1937.

Nowak, K. F., *The Collapse of Central Europe*, London, 1924.

Ogg, D., *Herbert Fisher, 1865–1940*, London, 1947.

Opocensky, J., *The Collapse of the Austro-Hungarian Monarchy and the Rise of the Czechoslovak State*, Prague, 1928.

Ostović, D., *The Truth About Yugoslavia*, New York, 1952.

Owen, F., *Tempestuous Journey: Lloyd George, His Life and Times*, London, 1954.

Papoušek, L., *The Czechoslovak Nation's Struggle for Independence*, Prague, 1928.

Paxson, F. L., *American Democracy and the World War*, 3 vols, Cambridge, 1936–48.

Perman, D., *The Shaping of the Czechoslovak State: Diplomatic History of the Boundaries of Czechoslovakia, 1914–1920*, Lieden, 1962.

Peterson, H. C., *Propaganda for War: The Campaign Against American Neutrality, 1914–1917*, Norman, Okla., 1939.

Petrovich, M. B., 'The Italo-Yugoslav Boundary Question, 1914–1915', *Russian Diplomacy and Eastern Europe, 1914–1917*, New York, 1963.

Pidhaini, O. S., *The Ukranian–Polish Problem in the Dissolution of the Russian Empire, 1914–1917*, Toronto, 1962.

Pliska, S. R., 'The Polish American Army, 1917–1921', *Polish Review*, vol. x, no. 3, 1965.

Pomian, J. (ed.), *Joseph Retinger: Memoirs of an Eminence Grise*. Sussex University Press, 1972.

Ponsonby, A., *Falsehood in War Time*, London, 1928.

Potts, J. M., 'The Loss of Bulgaria', *Russian Diplomacy and Eastern Europe, 1914–1917*, New York, 1963.

Pound, R. and Harmsworth, G., *Northcliffe*, London, 1959.

Read, J. M., *Atrocity Propaganda, 1914–1919*, New Haven, Conn., 1941.
Reddaway, W. F. (ed.), *The Cambridge History of Poland, 1697–1935*, Cambridge, 1951.
Marshal Pilsudski, London, 1939.
Renzi, W. A., 'Great Britain, Russia and the Straits, 1914–1915', *Journal of Modern History*, vol. XLII, no. 1, 1970.
'The Russian Foreign Office and Italy's Entrance into the Great War, 1914–1915', *Historian*, vol. XXVII, no. 4, 1966.
Rieber, A. J., 'Russian Diplomacy and Rumania', *Russian Diplomacy and Eastern Europe, 1914–1917*, New York, 1963.
Rose, W. J., *The Rise of Polish Democracy*, London, 1944.
Roskill, S., *Hankey: Man of Secrets*, vol. I, London, 1970.
Rothwell, V. H., *British War Aims and Peace Diplomacy*, Oxford 1971.
Rouček, J., *Poles in the United States of America*, Gdynia, 1937.
Rudin, H. R., *Armistice 1918*, New Haven, Conn., 1944.
Schreiber, H., *Teuton and Slav: The Struggle for Central Europe*, London, 1965.
Selver, P., *Masaryk*, London, 1940.
Šepić, D., 'The Question of Yugoslav Union in 1918', *The Journal of Contemporary History*, vol. III, no. 4, 1968.
Seton-Watson, R. W., 'The Origins of the School of Slavonic Studies', *The Slavonic and East European Review*, vol. XVII, no. 50, 1939.
'Italy's Balkan Policy in 1914', *Slavonic Review*, vol. V, no. 13, 1926.
'Italian Intervention and the Secret Treaty of London', *Slavonic Review*, vol. V, no. 14, 1925.
Seymour, C., *Woodrow Wilson and the World War*, New Haven, Conn., 1947.
American Neutrality, 1914–1917, New Haven, Conn., 1935.
Smith, D. M., *Robert Lansing and American Neutrality, 1914–1917*, Berkeley, Calif., 1958.
Spender, J. A. and Asquith, C., *Life of Henry Herbert Asquith*, 2 vols, London, 1932.
Squires, J. D., *British Propaganda at Home and in the United States from 1914 to 1917*, London, 1935.
Stadler, K. R., 'The Disintegration of the Austrian Empire', *Journal of Contemporary History*, vol. III, no. 4, 1968.
Steed, H. W., *The Antecedents of Post-War Europe*, London, 1932.
Stein, L., *The Balfour Declaration*, London, 1961.
Steiner, Z. S., *The Foreign Office and Foreign Policy, 1898–1914*, Cambridge, 1969.
'Grey, Hardinge and the Foreign Office, 1906–1910', *Historical Journal*, vol. X, no. 3, 1967.
Swartz, M., 'The Union of Democratic Control in British Politics During World War I', Yale Ph.D., 1969.
Tansill, C. C., *America Goes to War*, Boston, 1938.
Taylor, A. J. P., *The Habsburg Monarchy*, London, 1948.
The Trouble Makers: Dissent over Foreign Policy, 1792–1939, London, 1957.
Politics in Wartime and other Essays, London, 1957.
Temperley, H. W. V., *A History of the Paris Peace Conference*, 6 vols, London, 1920–24.
Thomson, M., *David Lloyd George: The Official Biography*, London, 1948.
Tilley, J. and Gasalee, S., *The Foreign Office*, London, 1933.

The Times, The History of The Times: *The 150th Anniversary and Beyond, 1912–1948*, London, 1952.

Torrey, C., 'Irredentism and Diplomacy', *Südost-Forschungen*, vol. xxv, 1966.

Trevelyan, G. M., *Grey of Falloden*, London, 1937.

Tuchman, B. W., *The Zimmermann Telegram*, London, 1959.

Ullman, R. H., *Anglo-Soviet Relations, 1917–1921*, vol. i, London, 1961.

Walworth, A. C., *Woodrow Wilson*, 2 vols, London, 1958.

Wandycz, P. S., *Soviet–Polish Relations, 1917–1921*, Cambridge, 1969.

Warth, R. D., *The Allies and the Russian Revolution: From the Fall of the Monarchy to the Peace of Brest-Litovsk*, Durham, N. Carolina, 1954.

Watt, D. C., *Personalities and Policies: Studies in the Formulation of British Foreign Policy in the Twentieth Century*, London, 1965.

Wheeler-Bennett, J. W., *Brest-Litovsk: The Forgotten Peace*, London, 1938.

White, J. A., *The Siberian Intervention*, Princeton, N.J., 1950.

Wittke, C., *German-Americans and the World War*, Columbus, Ohio, 1936.

Woodward, L., *Great Britain and the War of 1914–1918*, London, 1967.

Wrench, J. E., *Alfred Lord Milner: The Man of No Illusions, 1854–1925*, London, 1958.

Wytrwal, J. A., *America's Polish Heritage*, Detroit, Mich., 1961.

Young, K., *Arthur James Balfour*, London, 1963.

Zeman, Z. A. B., *The Breakup of the Habsburg Empire, 1914–1918*, London, 1961.

Zoltowski, A., *Border of Europe: A Study of the Polish Eastern Provinces*, London, 1950.

INDEX